"Knowing God as He is, in all the fullness He will allow us, is the church's highest priority and greatest privilege today. Scott Oliphint's powerful exposition of the majesty of mystery is a much-needed and bracing antidote to the casual, buddy-buddy theology that is so common in our times."

Os Guinness
Author of *The Call*

"At first when we hear that God is mysterious, we think: he's unknowable. What Scott Oliphint argues in this extraordinary book is just the opposite. Divine mystery, as he proves from Scripture, provides the only real hope that we can know God. It is just his greatness that makes him accessible to us. God is indeed way beyond our imagination. But in his love he has 'stooped to conquer.' Indeed, unless mystery pervades all of life we are left with a gray, purposeless existence. This book is far from a cold theological study. It sings! When we put it down, we want to say not 'what a great text,' but 'what a great and worthy God.'"

Dr William Edgar
Professor of Apologetics
Westminster Theological Seminary, Philadelphia

"Nothing is more important about our knowledge of God than recognizing that it begins with his incomprehensibility and remains bounded by that recognition. Reflecting the results of a major area of Oliphint's interest in his lecturing and writing over many years, a key concern of this book is to speak about the mystery surrounding God and his activity in a way that honors the way that God himself speaks to us in Scripture. Its careful, often penetrating handling of this sublime mystery is enhanced by a worshipful tone throughout. An instructive and edifying read for those wanting to grow in their knowledge of God."

Richard B. Gaffin, Jr.
Professor of Biblical and Systematic Theology, Emeritus
Westminster Theological Seminary

T0002255

The word "majesty," when applied to God, is always a declaration of His greatness and an invitation to worship. ... But this is knowledge which Christians today largely lack: and that is one reason why our faith is so feeble and our worship so flabby.

—J. I. Packer

Knowing God

THE MAJESTY
OF MYSTERY

THE MAJESTY
OF MYSTERY

CELEBRATING THE GLORY
OF AN INCOMPREHENSIBLE GOD

K. SCOTT OLIPHINT

LEXHAM PRESS

The Majesty of Mystery: Celebrating the Glory of an Incomprehensible God

Copyright 2016 K. Scott Oliphint

Lexham Press, 1313 Commercial St., Bellingham, WA 98225
LexhamPress.com

Print ISBN 978-1-57-799742-9
Digital ISBN 978-1-57-799743-6

Lexham Editorial: David Bomar, Abigail Stocker, Joel Wilcox, Brannon Ellis, Scott Hausman
Cover Design: Micah Ellis
Back Cover Design: Brittany Schrock
Typesetting: ProjectLuz.com

Contents

Contents

To Steve and Paula Cairns
Friends who stick closer than a brother (Prov 18:24)

Preface

For many years, I have taught a seminary course on "The Doctrine of God." Routinely, as students grapple with God's incomprehensibility and His self-revelation to us in Christ, many begin to recognize the reality of the God we worship. Nothing will motivate worship more than a glimpse of the glory of our incomprehensible God.

My experiences teaching that course have led to this book, which explores the relationship between God's character and our worship. Since God's character is inexhaustible, it is the mysteries of His character and ways that should form the foundation for our worship of Him. I am hoping this discussion will be helpful to anyone in the church who is struggling, or has struggled, with some of these deep and abiding mysteries.

One inevitable source of mystery and paradox for us involves the very reality of knowing God and acting in covenant with Him. Throughout the book, I refer to this relationship in gender-specific terms—that is, as a relationship between God and "man." Although such usage has fallen out of favor in much biblical and theological writing, I continue to find it helpful and appropriate, for three reasons:

(1) Until forty or so years ago, the word "man," when used generically, was understood to represent both genders. This usage is rooted in the biblical narrative of God determining to create "man," male and female (Gen 1:26; the Hebrew word for "man" is *adam*).

(2) The use of the term "man" in this rich biblical sense tacitly acknowledges that Adam *personally* represents each and every human being, covenantally speaking. Regardless of gender, all people are children of Adam; there are no "sons of Adam and daughters of Eve."

(3) "Humanity" is an abstraction by definition, referring only to our common nature. In that sense, ironically, "humanity" is not nearly as inclusive as it seems; it does not represent either gender or any

particular individual. In my opinion, this abstract language, even if used in the interests of inclusion, serves in its own small way to further enable the deep and distressing gender confusion rampant in so many cultures around the world. God did not create humanity in the abstract; He created Adam as the covenant representative of all men (male and female), and he created Eve from Adam.

I am convinced that the church can better serve the cause of the gospel by returning to biblical language (and its underlying rationale) in this matter. The editors of Lexham Press were kind enough to leave this style decision to me.

Thanks to Brannon Ellis, David Bomar, and the Lexham team for their work and encouragement throughout the editorial process. It has been a joy to work with them. Thanks also to my wife, Peggy, for patiently reading through each chapter and offering good suggestions along the way. Thanks finally to the students at Westminster Theological Seminary for their constant encouragement.

K. Scott Oliphint, August 2016
Westminster Theological Seminary
Philadelphia, PA

CHAPTER 1

Mystery:
Our Lifeblood

Mystery is the lifeblood of dogmatics.
… In truth, the knowledge that God
has revealed of himself in nature
and Scripture far surpasses human
imagination and understanding. In that
sense it is all mystery with which the
science of dogmatics is concerned, for
it does not deal with finite creatures,
but from beginning to end looks past
all creatures and focuses on the eternal
and infinite One himself.

—Herman Bavinck

Reformed Dogmatics: God and Creation

Have you ever wondered how God can be Three-in-One? Have you been uneasy trying to explain that the One in whom you've put your trust has two completely different natures? Have you thought about your affirmation that God is eternal in light of His activity in time and in history? Are you tempted to think that if God is in complete control we cannot be responsible for what we do? Does your confession of God's sovereignty conflict with your understanding of prayer? Does it make more sense to you to deny that God is sovereign?

If any of these questions has crossed your mind, you are typical of most Christians. You don't have to be a Christian for too long to begin to see some tensions in what Scripture requires us to affirm. But we also recognize that, even as we affirm certain things, we aren't capable of thinking about them in the way that we think about so many other things in the world. These are matters that create intellectual tension for us; they seem to conflict in some ways. As I hope to show in this book, this is as it should be. In revealing Himself and His ways in the world to us, God is pointing us to our own limits as creatures. He is reminding us that He is God and we are not.

How, then, do we respond to this reminder? In the course of this book, I hope to spell out what some of these mysteries in Scripture are. I also want to show a proper way for us to see them that should enhance the way we live as Christians—including, especially, the way we worship. Specifically, in light of what Scripture calls us to believe, I will highlight the central reason why we should praise and adore God *for the mysteries* He reveals to us.

BEGINNING WITH MYSTERY

Nothing should motivate true Christian worship more than the majestic mystery of God. Things that we understand, that we can wrap our minds around, are rarely objects of our worship. We may seek to control them. We may try to manipulate them. We may want to change them. But we will not worship them, not really. If what we are seeking is true worship, it is the riches of the mystery of God and His ways in the world that will produce and motivate worship *in* us and *to* Him.

Christian worship, as well as Christian theology, *begins* with mystery. Mystery is not something that functions simply as a *conclusion* to our thinking about God. It is not that we learn and think and reason as much as we can and then admit in the end that there is some mystery left over. Instead, we *begin* by acknowledging the mystery of God and His ways. We *begin* with the happy recognition that God and His activities are ultimately incomprehensible to us. When we begin with that recognition, we can begin to understand God properly and so worship Him in light of who He is and what He has done.

In his monumental work of theology, Herman Bavinck says that "mystery is the lifeblood of theology."[1] "Lifeblood" is a particularly apt metaphor here. Whenever certain kinds of illnesses arise in the body, one of the primary ways that doctors begin their diagnosis is through an analysis of the blood. Our blood speaks volumes about what is actually going on with specific organs, muscles, and nerves inside of us. Because all aspects of our bodies need blood to flow through them properly, the effect of blood on our bodies and our bodies on our blood is a central diagnostic tool in medicine. If there is no blood, there is no real life (Lev 17:11). What permeates our bodies, and brings life to them, is the blood.

So also, what gives life to all dimensions of our Christian thinking and living is the "lifeblood" of the mystery of God's character and His working in the world. If we think that mystery is no part, or only a "leftover" part, of our understanding of Christian truth, then what we think is Christian truth can actually be a dry, "bloodless" idea, with no real life remaining in it.

Suppose, to carry the metaphor further, we pick up one of the latest Christian books that deals with the topic of salvation. As we begin to read it, we notice that there is something wrong with the way the author is thinking about his topic. Suppose, for example, that he wants us to believe that the faith that we have is self-generated; we produce it, and God responds to it. How do we begin to diagnose what exactly the problem is with this view?

---

1. Herman Bavinck, *Reformed Dogmatics: God and Creation*, ed. John Bolt, trans. John Vriend, vol. 2 (Grand Rapids: Baker Academic, 2004), 29.

We might begin by looking into what God actually says about salvation, in all of its multifaceted beauty and complexity. As we do that, one of the first things we could ask in this circumstance is whether, and how, the biblical notion of mystery fits into the author's thinking about salvation. Is it possible, we could ask, that the reason he wants to argue that our faith is from ourselves (and not from God) is because if it were not from us it would not be our responsibility to have and exercise it? It has to be only and completely *our* faith, *self*-generated, he maintains, or we could make no sense of the biblical command to have faith, or believe in, Jesus Christ.

But is that how Scripture views our faith (just to cite one example, see Ephesians 2:8)? Could it be that Scripture affirms *both* that the faith that we have is ours and our responsibility to have, and at the same time that we cannot have it unless and until God changes our hearts and gives us that faith? Could it be that the view set forth in our imaginary book has yet to give due credit to the "lifeblood" of biblical thinking? We might then want to explore whether our own view of faith undermines the biblical truth of the mystery of God's salvation to us.

In other words, because—as we shall see—there is mystery at every point of our Christian thinking and living, it is important to give a proper, biblical account of that mystery as we think through the various truths of Scripture. If mystery is absent from our considerations of biblical truth, it may be that we will need to reconsider those truths in light of the "lifeblood" of theology. It might just be that the reason we have come to believe certain things about God, or about Scripture, or about salvation, or about anything else in Scripture, is because we are less than comfortable with a robust, majestic, biblical view of the mystery of God and His ways.

THE RATIONALIST REFLEX

But if mystery is indeed the "lifeblood" of biblical truth, what would make us wary of mystery in our attempt to understand that truth? There are many answers to this question, but chief among them, at least historically, is that we have a natural (i.e., sinful) tendency to ensure that everything that we believe is easily and obviously palatable to anyone at any time.

We can see this clearly in the history of ideas. For example, John Locke, a 17th-century philosopher, wrote a small book titled *The Reasonableness of Christianity*. In that work, Locke set out to discover just exactly which truths in Scripture could be grasped fully by the human mind. He argued that only "reasonable" truths were worthy of belief. He was deeply concerned to cull out all mystery in Scripture, since our usual ways of thinking could not contain such things. Consequently, Locke's view of Christianity was "bloodless"; it had no life left in it. For him, Christianity could teach only what was comprehensible to limited (and sinful) minds like ours. Thus, Locke created a dull, empty, minimalist religion. Locke's "rational" religion was a far cry from the glorious and majestic mysteries of the truth of our Christian faith.

What is ironic about Locke's book is that he was trying to combat the Deism of his day. Deism believed in a god, but it was not a god who was present in the world. Around the same time as Locke published his work, John Toland, a deist, published a work with the long and formidable title *Christianity not Mysterious: Or, a Treatise showing, That there is nothing in the Gospel Contrary to Reason, Nor above it: And that no Christian Doctrine can be properly call'd A Mystery*. Toland's deism was set forth so that we would have no more difficulty in conceiving of God than conceiving of anything else in the world. Toland's view, for example, was that we should view God's character in the same way that we view human characteristics. It must all be reasonable to us; nothing could be left to mystery.

Locke wanted to combat this view, but his own response to Toland was too similar to the view he wanted to reject. For both Locke and Toland, our beliefs were restricted to only those things that could be comprehended by the human mind. For Locke, Toland, and others, Christianity *could not* be mysterious. If it were, it could not be "adequately" understood, and if it could not be adequately understood, they thought, it should not be believed.

These ideas undermine the glories of Christianity at its root; they make the human mind the sole judge of what is true. If the mind is the judge, only what is able to be contained by our typical ways of thinking can be affirmed by us as true. As with Locke, the depths of the riches of God's ways are drained dry, and nothing but a shallow pool of superficial affirmations remains.

This view of things is light-years away from the "lifeblood" of Christianity. We are called to love the Lord with all of our minds, but we are not meant to seek to *contain* Him with our minds. If we approach our Bibles as Locke did, seeking to expunge anything that goes against our natural ways of thinking, then we will, in the process, lose the heart and soul of the Christian faith. This is a price not worth paying; its cost requires that we miss the glorious mystery of God's triune majesty.

MYSTICISM OR MYSTERY?

When it comes to biblical mysteries, the temptation that most Christians face is the one we just discussed—i.e., to favor our own thinking, to trust our own minds. If we do this, however, we exclude the rich mysteries of the Christian faith.

But there is another, though not as pervasive, tendency that also could be a temptation. Trusting our own way of thinking buries the biblical notion of mystery, but so does its opposite. The mystery that is the lifeblood of Christian truth is not compatible with a trust in our own minds, but neither is it compatible with a *denial* of the use of our minds, sometimes called "mysticism." Mysticism, in the way we're using the term here, seeks to promote and praise a *total lack* of understanding and of thinking. It prizes the ineffable above all and sees reason and thinking as obstacles to true faith.

A somewhat obscure example of this can be seen in the medieval mystic Meister Eckhart. As a mystic, Eckhart determined that a *lack* of understanding was the best way to relate to God. For example, in Eckhart's sermon on Matthew 5:3 ("Blessed are the poor in spirit, for theirs is the kingdom of heaven") we see an example of a distorted view of mystery.

Eckhart's sermon had three points. He focused on a poverty of the soul, which he called a "stilling." His first point was that there must be a stilling of the will if we are to be poor in spirit. His second point was that there must be a stilling of the *intellect*, so that our goal would be to have no conceptual knowledge of God at all. In attempting to make that point, he says:

> Why I pray God to rid me of God is because conditionless
> being is above God and above distinction: it was therein

I was myself, therein I willed myself and knew myself to make this man and in this sense I am my own cause, both of my nature which is eternal and of my nature which is temporal. For this am I born, and as to my birth which is eternal I can never die. In my eternal mode of birth I have always been, am now, and shall eternally remain. That which I am in time shall die and come to naught, for it is of the day and passes with the day. In my birth all things were born, and I was the cause of mine own self and all things, and had I willed it I had never been, nor any thing, and if I had not been then God had not been either. To understand this is not necessary.[2]

Any reader or hearer of this sermon would be happy to hear the last sentence—"to understand this is not necessary." Not only is understanding this sermon not *necessary*, it may not even be possible! But what Eckhart has in mind in that last statement is that it is *better* not to understand with the mind what he is attempting to communicate. To the extent that you *do* understand, you miss the real import of who God is. The way to "know" God, in other words, is by *not* knowing him (or it).

This is a view that sees understanding and intellectual effort, particularly with respect to God and His character and ways, as detrimental to a proper relationship to God. The best way to know God, the mystic would say, is to affirm that we cannot in any way really understand who he is. All that is left for us is an "experience" of God.

Are there parallels to this kind of temptation in Christianity today? Perhaps. I remember when the phrase "let go and let God" was a mantra for some Christians. The idea was not simply to cease trying to earn salvation—which would be a good thing. The phrase was meant to emphasize that it is best for Christians to take a docile, experiential attitude toward their faith. The more intensely you try to understand or obey God, the less you rely on Him.

There is nothing wrong with relying on God, or with recognizing the importance of experience in our Christian lives. But if experience

2. Meister Eckhart, *Meister Eckhart*, trans. C. de B. Evans, 2 vols. (London: John M. Watkins, 1924), 1:220.

is our primary way to God, or if it begins to take the place of our efforts to understand what God has said in His Word, we are moving toward a mystical view of Christianity.

Here is the paradox: A true, biblical view of mystery has its roots not in a lack of understanding, but in the teaching of Scripture. As a matter of fact, it is just the teaching of Scripture that gives us the biblical *truth* of that which we hold to be mysterious. A biblical view of mystery, in other words, is full of truth. It is truth that has real and glorious content. That content includes truths that we must affirm as well as falsehoods that we must deny, statements that are necessarily a part of a biblical understanding of mystery as well as exclamations that point us to its truth. So mystery, if we understand it biblically, is infused through and through with the truth that is found in the Word of God. Mystery is the lifeblood of the truth that we have in God's revelation; it flows through every truth that God gives us.

A MANY-SIDED THING

But perhaps we are not tempted by rationalistic deism or by mysticism. Maybe the views of Locke or Toland or Eckhart do not appeal to us. There is, however, a more insidious and subtle problem among many Christians today. It is a problem that has reached epidemic proportions in our culture and has seeped into the church, although we might not have noticed. The problem has its focus in the paucity of *thinking* and *knowing* in our Christian walk. The Lord is concerned that we *think, learn about,* and *know* Him. This is a significant part of Christian obedience. But for many of us, the obedient use of the *mind* might be something of a foreign idea.

On one occasion, Jesus was responding (as was His custom) to a number of His detractors (Mark 12:13–34ff.). They had come to trap Him and to show their superior knowledge of Scripture (i.e., the Old Testament) over His. The Sadducees and Scribes came to ask Him questions that were, for them, doctrinal conundrums. The Sadducees, who did not believe in the resurrection from the dead, asked Jesus to explain to them how the notion of resurrection could be made compatible, in the afterlife, with (their view of) marriage.

Jesus said to them, in very plain terms, that they were wrong. But they were not simply wrong about some minor matters; Jesus was not rebuking them for getting details wrong. Rather, he made plain that they were wrong about Scripture, and they were wrong about God (Mark 12:24).

Not to be deterred, one of the scribes, who had overheard Jesus' answer and was impressed by it, decided he would enter the discussion:

> And one of the scribes came up and heard them disputing with one another, and seeing that he answered them well, asked him, "Which commandment is the most important of all?" Jesus answered, "The most important is, 'Hear, O Israel: The Lord our God, the Lord is one. And you shall love the Lord your God with all your heart and with all your soul and with all your mind and with all your strength' " (Mark 12:28-30).

Most Christians are well aware of Jesus' answer here. And most are aware of the reason that this answer is given. It does indeed sum up our responsibility toward God. If we have a love for God that includes the entirety of who we are as people, then the rest of what Scripture says will be solidly in place in our lives. What is sometimes overlooked, or minimized, in this greatest command, however, is that in loving God with all of our being, we must love Him *with our minds*.

In our overly romanticized culture and context, "love" and "mind" do not readily go together. We cannot imagine a love story where the boy says to the girl, "I love you with all of my mind." Nor could we find a Hallmark card that trumpeted the depth of someone's mental love for someone else.

The mind, so we tend to think, is the realm of the abstract, the cold, the calculated, the aloof. It is the polar opposite of the typical view of the "heart." The mind, we may think, dwells in cool detachment from the "real world." It may concern itself with sports statistics or recipes. Beyond that, the mind is more a hindrance to love than a help.

But we are commanded to love God with everything that we are — with our hearts, our souls, our strength, *and with our minds*. Our love for God is to permeate every aspect of who we are as people. If we love God with only part of who we are, then we really do not love Him as we should. Suppose, for example, that we commit to love God with all our strength, but that we neglect completely to love Him with our hearts. What would that love look like? It would be an external, vacuous love, a love that might work hard and long, but a love in which, literally, our hearts were not in it. That kind of love is not biblical love; it is a perversion of it.

So also if we neglect to love God with our minds. But what does it mean to love God with our minds? At minimum, this means that we are to *know* God—that is, we are to read and understand what Scripture says about God, and to submit intellectually (and otherwise) to that teaching. We are to think God's thoughts after Him. Those thoughts are found in God's revelation.[3] When we read Scripture, when we study it, we are to see it as the only true description of what reality is like. We are to reorient our thinking, so that the things around us, and within us, take on the truth that God has spoken.

This requires intellectual effort. But, we should recognize, it *does not* require advanced academic degrees. What it requires is that the "people of the Book" be those who think about, who meditate on, and who long to understand just exactly what "the Book" is saying to us— about God, and about everything else.

Here is a test. If you're reading this brief section on loving God with your mind, and your initial reaction is, "But we shouldn't make Christianity overly intellectual," then you are probably more entangled with the spirit of the age than you might think. The spirit of the age is largely anti-intellectual. It is, we could say, more in line with the game show *Wheel of Fortune* than with *Jeopardy*. In *Jeopardy* the use of the mind is required. Without it, one cannot even be considered a contestant. In *Wheel of Fortune* on the other hand, all that is required is the luck of the spinning wheel, knowledge of the alphabet, a basic ability to spell, and the enthusiasm to yell, "Big money! Big money!"

Our culture is often more like *Wheel of Fortune* than *Jeopardy*. We have a basic knowledge of the alphabet—enough to send a text message or write an email. Beyond that, life, for many, is the luck of the wheel and a hope that "big money" will come our way.

Has the church imbibed a *Wheel of Fortune* mentality? Are we content with the basic "alphabet" of Christianity? Do we conduct our

---

3. We have to recognize, however, that even those revealed thoughts are accommodated to us as creatures. God's revelation gives us truth, but that truth is creaturely truth, thus always subject to creaturely limits. God's own truth is not subject to such limits, but is always connected to the truth that is revealed.

spiritual lives according to a superficial trust in God and a hope for a big reward in the end?

Remember the lament of the author to the Hebrews? His concern was for the Christian growth, the *holiness*, of his readers. Without that holiness, he warned, they would not even see the Lord (Heb 12:14). But he was deeply disappointed in their level of Christian maturity. He wanted to write to them about the deep things of Christ and His ministry, but he knew them well enough to know that many could not digest the strong meat of biblical truth:

> About this we have much to say, and it is hard to explain, since you have become dull of hearing. For though by this time you ought to be teachers, you need someone to teach you again the basic principles of the oracles of God. You need milk, not solid food, for everyone who lives on milk is unskilled in the word of righteousness, since he is a child. But solid food is for the mature, for those who have their powers of discernment trained by constant practice to distinguish good from evil. Therefore let us leave the elementary doctrine of Christ and go on to maturity (Heb 5:11–6:1).

These professing Christians were in danger of falling away from their expressed faith. One of the reasons they were in danger was that they had not loved God with their minds. They were infants, unable to think, unable to digest the solid meat of the truth of God. This was no incidental malady; it was central to their inability to follow and to know Christ. Notice how the author puts it: If they want to grow in Christ into mature adults, they need to leave the *elementary* doctrines of Christ behind.

This does not mean they leave behind what they know. It means, rather, they move from the church nursery to the sanctuary; they move from the kindergarten of biblical truth to adult education. They are to take the things they know and integrate them more and more fully into the teaching of Scripture. They are to meditate on the things of Christ, in His Word, and think about them in such a way that the Scriptures make more and more sense to them and thus explain more deeply who Christ is—and who they are in Him. They are to probe the depths of Scripture so that they begin to think as adults. All of this probing and thinking is not, however, simply to make them smarter. If they grow into spiritual adults, it will show in how they live. Only then will they be able to be engaged in the "constant practice of discerning good from evil." According to this passage, the mental effort that believers are required to make concerning the truth of God's Word inevitably shifts to the practice of discernment. In thinking properly, in other words, we learn to *live* properly, and thus to glorify God. This takes mental effort; it requires meditation and thought. But it is as essential to Christian maturity as ingesting something besides milk is to growing into adulthood.

But why talk about the importance of Christian thinking in a book that focuses on *mystery*? Isn't mystery, by definition, something that is beyond the bounds of our thinking?

It is. But here is the biblical irony of it all. In order to worship God for His incomprehensibility, it is necessary to *know* Him deeply. Or, to put it differently, in order to confess properly what we *do not* know, we have to be clear about what God has given us to know. The only way to understand what these mysteries are is by understanding, from Scripture, what it is that causes us rightly to confess our inability to fully comprehend them. We have to know in order to know what we cannot know. The only biblical context for what we do *not know* is *knowing*.

If we are influenced by the temptation to ignore the mind in our Christian walk, we may not see—even worse, we may not *want to* see— the majesty of these mysteries. But if that is the case, then we will remain infants, able only and always to take in milk and never able to grow up into the maturity of Christ (see also, for example, 1 Cor 2:6, 14:20; Eph 4:13; Phil 3:15; Col 1:28). In the chapters that follow, we will be challenged to think, and to think deeply. There is no substitute for this. There is no better time than the present to "go on to maturity."

· · · ·

As we think about the biblical view of mystery in the following chapters, we will be addressing questions that are on the lips of many serious Christians (as well as who do not believe): How can God be three and one? How can God take on a human nature? Can an eternal and unchangeable God also act in history? If God planned everything, how can I be responsible? Do my prayers make any difference in God's plan? Will we finally know everything when we get to heaven?

These are questions that recognize some of the mysterious tensions that Scripture presents to us. They are good questions, but wrong answers to good questions can rob us of a full, and fulfilled, Christian life, and they rob God of His proper glory. Proper answers—answers that allow the mystery of God and His ways to shine brightly—will evoke in us proper worship, preparing us for an eternity of worship with Him, in which, because of the majestic mystery of God's triune character, we will be "lost in wonder, love, and praise."

> *Finish, then, Thy new creation;*
> *Pure and spotless let us be.*
> *Let us see Thy great salvation*
> *Perfectly restored in Thee;*
> *Changed from glory into glory,*
> *Till in heaven we take our place,*
> *Till we cast our crowns before Thee,*
> *Lost in wonder, love, and praise.*
>
> —Charles Wesley, "Love Divine, All Loves Excelling"

CHAPTER 2

The Majesty of the Mystery of the Depth of God

Whenever then we enter on a discourse respecting the eternal counsels of God, let a bridle be always set on our thoughts and tongue, so that after having spoken soberly and within the limits of God's word, our reasoning may at last end in admiration.

—John Calvin
Commentary on the Epistle of
Paul the Apostle to the Romans

The great truths about which Paul was writing to the church at Rome caused him to explode in doxological praise in Romans 11:33–36. This praise passage, which exalts the incomprehensibility of God and His ways, carries with it some of the richest truths and teachings in all of Scripture.

OH, THE DEPTH ...

It may help us to think of the epistle to the Romans in terms (roughly, at least) of two distinct but related sections. Generally speaking, chapters 1 through 11 present the *doctrinal data* of the Christian gospel, and chapters 12 through 16 focus on the *practice* of that doctrine. This does not mean that we, or the Bible, artificially separate doctrine from practice. Thinking obediently is as important as—is even a prerequisite for—living obediently. But Paul's "therefore" in Romans 12:1 is a definite movement toward putting into practice those truths that have been so wondrously set forth in previous chapters.

It is remarkable, then, that at the transition point between doctrine and practice, at the place where Paul moves from a more didactic emphasis to a more practical one, he interjects a glorious and majestic doxology:

> Oh, the depth of the riches and wisdom and knowledge of God! How unsearchable are his judgments and how inscrutable his ways!

> "For who has known the mind of the Lord,
>   or who has been his counselor?"
> "Or who has given a gift to him
>   that he might be repaid?"

> For from him and through him and to him are all things.
> To him be glory forever. Amen (Rom 11:33–36).

Notice that the construction of this passage demands that we see it as praise. Paul's "oh!" is an exclamation, a cry of worship and delight in God. Nowhere else in the New Testament does a passage begin with this use of the particular term "oh!" It is a term of joyful and satisfying surprise, and deep wonder. It evokes and initiates an attitude of reverence, awe, and worship. This one term, "oh," has the effect of pointing us to that which is transcendent, that which rises above the normal and the mundane. It causes us immediately to move beyond the immanence of this world and to set our spiritual eyes on the unapproachable light and glory of God Himself. This one word, "oh," sets the tone and tenor for the rest of what Paul says in this doxology. And what he says, he says in praise to the true and Triune God.

There is a reason why the Holy Spirit inspired the apostle Paul to write in this particular way. What would we think, for example, if Paul had said, "The riches of God's wisdom and knowledge are deep"? That would have been perfectly true, of course. Indeed, that is exactly what Paul is saying in 11:33. But simply to state it in that way lacks something; it omits a central and crucial aspect in Paul's communication of God's depth.

Instead of simply stating the truth, Paul *exclaimed* it, beginning his doxology with "oh!" The etymology of the word "exclaim" is "to shout out." In other words, the meaning of Paul's exclamation is embedded in the form of his expression. When we *exclaim*, we do not simply say true things in a matter-of-fact kind of way. Rather, we, metaphorically or actually, "shout out" an exclamation; that's the purpose *and* the meaning of it. We affirm the truth that is contained in the exclamation, but we also call forth a response by the *way* that we state it; an exclamation is a truth that requires, when affirmed, an action. In exclaiming, we are not content simply to *say* something. The exclamation itself, then, as a particular grammatical *style*, communicates the content, but also says much about how we are supposed to *acknowledge* that content. The exclamation tells us reams about *how* we are to think of the content in the statement as it is given to us.

Think, for example, of one of the differences between teaching and preaching. Granted, there are many points of agreement between the two activities. Oftentimes, however, one of the differences can be seen in *how* the truth of God is communicated. If I am teaching a course on the doctrine of God, I may lay out some specific points affirming, say,

God's infinite knowledge, or that He is unchangeable and independent. Or I may say that God's simple knowledge is not added to Him,
but is instead identical with His infinite character and being. Or I
may say that God's knowledge is exhaustive; it lacks nothing. All of
these things are true of God, and they are things that all Christians
should affirm.

If I were to preach on the same subjects (which I have been known
to do while teaching!), however, I would want the congregation to be
taken up with the glory and majesty of such truths.[1] I would want each
person who hears to be moved and committed to embrace the reality of
God's infinity, His simplicity, His exhaustive knowledge. The purpose
of what I say is directly related to *worship*. So, when preaching, I will
present the same truths in exclamatory ways. After affirming God's
infinite knowledge, for example, I might exclaim, "What a glorious
God we serve!," or "How majestic this God is!," or "Oh, there is none
like this God!" These exclamations are specific, grammatical ways of
directing those who hear them as to *how* they are to hold and believe
what they have heard. They are to hold them and believe them not
simply as true statements, but as truths that bring about a response
of worship, adoration, and praise. They focus the mind more on the
person—God Himself—in light of the glorious truth of the content.

The Holy Spirit, through His servant Paul, wrote, "oh" in Romans
11:33 in order to direct us as to *how* we might affirm the truth of what
Paul has said previously, as well as what follows after his exclamation.
He means for us to hold such truths in a way that will issue forth in

---

1. The word "majesty" inevitably has connotations of transcendence. My use of
the word is meant to point to God's "God-ness," including His greatness, holiness,
sovereignty, and incomprehensibility. After a discussion of the divine attributes,
Edward Leigh says this about God's majesty: "From all these before-mentioned
Attributes ariseth the Glory or Majesty of God, which is the infinite excellence
of the Divine Essence, Heb 1:3; Exod. 33:18; Psalm 29:9. This is called *the face of
God*, Exod 33:20 and *light inaccessible*, 1 Tim 6:16 which to acknowledge perfectly
belongs to God alone, yet the revelation and obscurer vision thereof is granted
to us in this life by the ministry of those things which are seen and heard, the
clearer in the life to come, where we shall see God face to face, 1 Cor. 13;12; Matt.
18:10," quoted in Richard A. Muller, *Post-Reformation Reformed Dogmatics: The Rise
and Development of Reformed Orthodoxy*, Vol. 3, *The Divine Essence and Attributes*
(Grand Rapids: Baker Academic, 2003), 543.

praise, wonder, and worship. We are not meant simply to *affirm* what Paul says here, but to affirm *and to praise* the Lord *because of* the mystery and majesty of God and His ways in the world.

Stop and think about the fact that Paul ends this more doctrinal section of Romans with praise and worship. Maybe the structure of Paul's letter here can help us think more biblically about our own Christian walk. Does Christian teaching move us naturally to the worship of God? A now-famous dictum handed down to us from the medieval period says that theology "comes from God, teaches about God *and leads us to God.*"[2] Does what we know about God lead us to Him, or does it lead us simply to more facts, more data? Theology is to be God-centered; it comes from Him, it should teach us more and more about Him, and that teaching should lead us inexorably to praise Him. Does our theology do that? Is it centered on a God whose truth moves us to exclamation?

As crucial as it is for the sake of our holiness to be learning more and more about God, it can be all too easy when one is learning much about God and His Word and His ways in the world to begin to think that, as a matter of fact, we happen to know Him quite well, thank you very much. And once we think we know something well, it is our natural tendency to think we have mastered it, to get bored with it, and to move on.

In a discussion with a few faculty members of an evangelical college a number of years ago, I asked them what they saw as surprising about their current group of students. One of them responded that a number of students were moving to the Roman Catholic Church. In his estimation, the reason for the move was because of the differences these students saw between their own, tired, practice of worship and the Roman Catholic mass.

But worship is not an isolated activity. It carries with it distinct views of who God is, who Christ is, and who we are. Changing denominations simply because of "worship" is like picking a movie based only on the theater. Worship is not simply a context; it is a *response*, meant to flow from our understanding of God. What is all-important

---

2. This can be found, for example, in Francis Turretin, *Institutes of Elenctic Theology*, trans. George Musgrave Giger, ed. James T. Dennison, Jr., vol. 1 (Phillipsburg, NJ: P&R Publishing, 1992–1997), 2.

in worship is the *content* that must be the substance and motivation of our worship. It may very well be that a tendency to change denominations because of worship betrays a spirit that has become complacent in or indifferent to the true knowledge of God. There is a theological *reason* the Catholic mass is what it is, just as there is a theological *reason* that Protestant worship is what it is. The substance of that reason is located in the view of God that is meant to bring us to worship Him in the first place.

Could it be, we might ask, that some who move from church to church have become lax or disinterested in knowing the depths of God, in loving Him with their minds? Our experience of worship is vitally important for our Christian lives. But the motivation for our worship must not be the experience itself. For a Christian, it must run much deeper than that. Worship is supposed to be the natural product of our knowledge and love of God. But if we become lax or disinterested in knowing God better, then we might begin to think that all we need is to change our location of worship. If that is how we are tempted to think, then Paul's doxological declaration will begin to move us back in the right direction. It will help us to see the end goal of all our theology and of our worship, and the foundation of our Christian lives.

So Paul's design in this passage is to provide for us a fitting conclusion and climax to the doctrine that he has, under the inspiration of the Holy Spirit, so eloquently set forth. Moreover, because Romans 11:33–36 is a transition passage (roughly) from doctrine to practice, this doxology provides a fitting foundation and resting place for living out our Christian lives, as well. Paul is overcome with the transcendence, majesty, and incomprehensibility of God as he writes, and he cannot help but exclaim. But what exactly motivated this exclamation? The commentators are not at all sure if what Paul has in mind as he pens this doxology is the entirety of the preceding epistle or just the preceding section in this chapter, but it really doesn't matter. One thing is for sure: that at least what Paul has in mind in verse 33 is verse 32.

In this letter to the church at Rome, Paul has been attempting to discuss the difficult doctrine of the ways of God with respect to the salvation of the Jews first, and also of the Gentiles. And as he concludes that discussion, notice what he says in verse 32:

> For God has consigned all to disobedience, that he may
> have mercy on all.

Now whatever one wants to think about Paul's reasoning in verse 33, whether he has in mind the whole of the book up to this point or just the preceding section, there can be no question that what has occupied the thought of the apostle is the mysterious ways of God in eternity and in the process of salvation—salvation that God has now provided for all his people, "to the Jew first and also to the Greek" (Rom 1:16). More specifically, notice that Paul insists that it is this transcendent and majestic *God* who has shut all men up in disobedience (cf. Rom 1:18ff., 3:9ff.).

We know that Scripture nowhere lays the blame of sin on God. Paul has attempted to make that abundantly clear in this epistle (e.g., Rom 9:19-20). But it is equally true that nowhere does Scripture teach that God is somehow aloof or lacking control when it comes to the intricate details of all that happens in the world, including sin.

How does Paul explain these two? How does he express both God's activity, from eternity-past and into history, as well as our responsibility for all our decisions? We'll peer into this in more detail in coming chapters. For now, though, we see that Paul's solution to this quandary is not simply to tout the mystery of God's character, though that would have been true enough. Paul's solution, first of all, is to proclaim the *mercy* of God. As he says, God has shut up all in disobedience *that he might show mercy to all*. And it is that dual truth of man's disobedience together with God's mercy that causes Paul to begin his doxology.

In other words, Paul is not satisfied simply with the reality of man's universal disobedience. He moves immediately to God's response and action to that disobedience in us—the purpose of disobedience is that God might show mercy to all kinds of people, to the Jew first, and also to the Greek. So it was in times past that God shut the Gentiles up in disobedience that he might show mercy to the Jew. But now, he has shut up all, both Jew and Gentile, in disobedience so that His mercy might be manifest in all, both Jew and Gentile.

It is this mystery (compare Eph 3:6ff.)—the mystery that God has mercifully brought together both Jew and Gentile, in Christ—that motivates Paul's praise. To know God's merciful plan for His people is to praise Him for it.

This truth deserves our thoughtful attention and meditation. Have we meditated on the fact that everything that we are, all that we will be, the hope that is ours in Christ, the justification that comes to us because of Him, the adoption that is given to us in the Spirit, the assurance that we have that nothing will separate us from the love of Christ—all of these are a product of God's sheer, undeserved mercy? None of them are in any way earned by us, nor could they be. None of them came because God looked down on us and saw our worthiness, or our dignity as human beings, or that we were not as bad as some others, or that we had done some "good" things. All that we have from God, we have from His all-merciful and sovereign hand. We have it, we have it for eternity, and we do not, did not, and will not ever, *deserve* it; if we deserve it in any way, *it would not be mercy*.

Can you fathom the depths of that? Paul says you can't. But you can know that it is true. And you can wonder why. As you wonder why, you won't be able to comprehend the mind of God. So we exclaim its truth; we praise Him for that rich and deep truth of His sovereign mercy to us, in Christ.

Paul uses a word in verse 33 for depth (the Greek word *bathos*) not as a superlative, but as a word that is meant to describe a completely different level of existence. Paul does not say here that the riches of God's wisdom and knowledge are the greatest there is. That would put the plan and counsel of God on a continuum with other plans. It would have the effect of saying that there may be plans, some bad, some extremely bad, at one end of the continuum, and others fair, in the middle, but God's is the greatest plan there is. That is not what Paul is saying. This word "depth" is no word of comparison. Rather, Paul is saying that the depth of God is beyond anything in creation. It is of a different quality than any "deep" thing we might envision in creation.

Paul is speaking of a different level of existence. He is speaking of the depth of God's character and ways. And he is not even telling us how deep his character is. Indeed, he *could* not tell us that. The Spirit knows the deep things of God (1 Cor 2:11), but we don't, nor can we as finite creatures. So Paul is exclaiming that God's riches are deep, *so* deep that one should think of and proclaim that depth, in doxology, as an affirmation of its truth.

A number of years ago, a chess match was set up between Garry Kasparov, the reigning chess champion at the time, and a new IBM computer. The computer was called "Deep Blue" and it was able to calculate two hundred million chess moves per second. Can you fathom that? Two hundred million moves per second. It is virtually incomprehensible. But the fact of the matter is that it *can* be calculated. At two hundred million moves per second, that's two billion moves every 10 seconds. Not that we can accomplish that ourselves, but we can understand something of it by putting an accurate number to it.

But the depth of God's riches of wisdom and knowledge is deeper than Deep Blue. The depth of God's character is so deep that it cannot be calculated, or even accurately estimated. God's depth is beyond anything created. And when something is beyond anything created it is, by definition, beyond *us*. That's what Paul means us to understand here.

Think about it. Paul is not saying that there are a multitude of things that we know about God, so we praise Him for those things. We certainly *do* praise Him for those things, and Scripture gives us myriad examples of such things. But Paul's point is almost counterintuitive. Paul is praising God for what we do not and *cannot* know! The focus of our praise, if we are to think biblically, is on the very fact that God cannot be comprehended, ever, by any creature—not in this life and not in eternity.

Paul goes on to reflect on just what that wisdom and knowledge of God include.

> How unsearchable are his judgments and how inscruta
> ble his ways (Rom 11:33)!

After a general exclamation of praise, we are now directed to the depth of God's wisdom. When we think of wisdom, we are thinking of what God *determines* to do. The wisdom of God just is His knowledge, but, like human wisdom, it is knowledge that is put into action.

So also are His judgments and His ways. God determines what He will do, and then He acts to accomplish what He has determined. Both His judgments and ways go together. And Scripture is expressing here—again, by way of exclamation—that God's judgments cannot be searched out! With all of the searching power of Google at our disposal, it is not possible to type "God's judgments" into your Internet search box and produce a satisfactory answer. As creatures of God, we are unable to search out the majestic, infinite, glorious character of the Triune God. "Whatever the LORD pleases, he does, in heaven and on earth" (Psa 135:6; cf. Psa 115:3). When we cannot tell why the Lord does what He does, we rest content that He does what pleases Him, and we praise Him for that.

IT'S A SECRET

There is a fundamental, and monumentally important, biblical principle here that will guide the whole of what we are setting forth in this book, and that should guide the whole of our Christian worship and living. It is given to us concisely in Deuteronomy 29:29:

> The secret things belong to the LORD our God, but the things that are revealed belong to us and to our children forever, that we may do all the words of this law.

Here we see, in summary form, two basic aspects of God's ways with us. There are things revealed by God, and those things belong to us and to our children forever. They are covenantally directed by God. That is, they are given by the covenant God to covenant families, and they belong to the Lord's people "that we may do all the words of this law." They belong to us in order that we might glorify God as we live according to His character (law). In other words, they are meant to produce and promote holiness in us.

Then there are those things that belong only and wholly to the Lord our God—Father, Son, and Holy Spirit. These are secret things. God has told us all He wants to tell us at this point. He will tell us more later, when Christ comes back and we live with Him for eternity. For now, though, God has told us all that we *need* to know in order that, in this life, we might please Him. But it may be that He has not told us all that we might *want* to know. What are we to do when we find ourselves wanting to know those secret things?

Why, for example, did God decide to create anything at all? Or what was God doing before he created? Augustine supposed this latter question, and had a ready answer for it:

> I answer him that asketh, "What did God before He made heaven and earth?" I answer not as one is said to have

done merrily (eluding the pressure of the question), "He was preparing hell (saith he) for pryers into mysteries."[3]

The sarcasm of Augustine's answer notwithstanding, the substance of his response is crucial for us to see. Those who would want to pry into the mysteries of God are actually denying Him of His own prerogatives *as God*. They are wanting what God has chosen not to give, and thus are, at bottom, in danger of a subtle rebellion against Him.

Part of what Paul is saying in the doxological text of Romans 11:33–36 is that it is not for us to ask questions that God has determined not to answer. John Calvin made a similar point:

> Let us, I say, allow the Christian to unlock his mind and ears to all the words of God which are addressed to him, provided he do it with this moderation, viz., that whenever the Lord shuts his sacred mouth, he also desists from inquiry.[4]

There are, in other words, questions that should not be asked. They should not be asked because the questions themselves attempt to impinge on and undermine the majesty and mystery of God's glorious character. To ask them, we could say, is to betray in our own thinking a less-than-majestic understanding of who God is. The better part of holiness, Calvin is saying, is to "desist from inquiry." God's judgments and His ways are beyond our ability, or our right, to discover. They are contained in "the secret things." The word translated "inscrutable" in Romans 11:33 carries the idea of footprints that cannot be tracked. In other words, there is no way to look at the evidence around us, and then, by that evidence, to find out exactly what God is up to and why. God leaves no footprints behind as He works in the world. His ways cannot be traced. He determines and He acts according to His own sovereign plan, and that plan, though complete, remains fundamentally top-secret to us. It is for God's eyes only, and not for ours. We cannot trace the works of God from here to His infinite wisdom.

---

3. Saint Augustine, *The Confessions of St. Augustine*, trans. Edward Bouverie Pusey (Oxford: John Henry Parker, 1860), 233.

4. John Calvin, *Institutes of the Christian Religion*, ed. Henry Beveridge, trans. Henry Beveridge (Grand Rapids: Eerdmans, 1957), 3.21.3.

In his doxological praise of God's character, Paul goes on to ask a series of questions:

> For who has known the mind of the Lord, or who has been his counselor? Or who has given a gift to him that he might be repaid? (Rom 11:34–35).

The questions are, of course, rhetorical; the unspoken answer is supposed to be obvious. But it would help us to pause and think for a minute about what Paul is saying in these questions.

In an allusion to Isaiah 40:13, Scripture turns our attention both to the knowledge and wisdom of God (referring back to Romans 11:33). "Who has known the mind of the Lord?" is a question requiring the following affirmation: "No one is able to know God's own knowledge." No one, that is, except God Himself (see, for example, Matt 11:27; Rom 8:26–27).

The passage from Isaiah 40 is instructive for understanding the scope of Paul's thinking here. Just after exclaiming, "Behold your God!" (Isa 40:9), Isaiah lifts our thoughts up to the transcendence of God's glory (40:12):

> Who has measured the waters in the hollow of his hand
> and marked off the heavens with a span,
> enclosed the dust of the earth in a measure
> and weighed the mountains in scales
> and the hills in a balance?

In using vast and almost immeasurable aspects of creation, Isaiah is giving us a picture of the vast and immeasurable glory of God's character—again, by using rhetorical questions. The picture Isaiah is giving us is this: Gather every speck of dust on the face of the earth and place it in one container. Or take every mountain that now stands across the globe and place them all on a scale to be weighed. When you've accomplished this, you have a small glimpse of God's majesty.

The only way such things could be accomplished is if there was one who so transcended every aspect of creation—the small (dust) as well as the great (mountains)—that he had masterful, meticulous, and mighty control over every single aspect of creation. But what kind of might and power would have to be involved for such things to happen?

What does this power and might look like? Isaiah's answer: "Behold your God!"

This is what the Lord wants us to see in this passage. As Paul quotes from Isaiah he wants his readers—many of whom would have been quite familiar with the truth and context of Isaiah's prophecy—to be overwhelmed with the majestic mystery of God and His ways (see also 1 Cor 2:16).

Not only so, but just before the passage quoted above, Isaiah says this:

> He will tend his flock like a shepherd;
>   he will gather the lambs in his arms;
> he will carry them in his bosom,
>   and gently lead those that are with young (Isa 40:11).

Remember what motivates Paul's praise? It is his amazement at the ways in which God is carrying out His perfect plan of salvation (cf. Psa 77:10ff.). So also, even as Isaiah turns our attention to the majesty of God, even as he points us to God's utter transcendence, he reminds us that God's transcendence is what it is in the context of His determination to be *with us* to save. That is to say, the majestic God, while always transcendent, while able to measure the dust and weigh the mountains, is also able to be our Shepherd; He is able gently to lead the lambs and carry them in His bosom.

Can you fathom that? Can you see in your mind's eye One who is both transcendent, high and lifted up, and who at the same time is gently leading His lambs to their verdant pastures? Paul and Isaiah express what all true Christians must declare when we think on such things. We must be moved to doxological exclamation.

The next quotation that Paul uses (in Romans 11:35) carries with it the same wonder and amazement as the passage in Isaiah. Paul, thinking of this transcendent aspect of God's character, references Job 41.

We will remember from the book of Job that Job is inflicted with almost-unimaginable suffering. Toward the end of the book, Job wants to meet with God in order to find out why God does what He does to Job. So God meets with Job from a whirlwind and begins to remind Job of His majestic character. One of the questions God asks Job is this: "Who has first given to me, that I should repay him?" (Job 41:11).

It seems that Job had assumed that God *owed* him an answer to his questions. Instead, as God asks Job a series of penetrating questions, He turns Job back to His glory and majesty. God's response to Job was that, even in the midst of intense suffering, he must remember who God is. As Paul quotes Job 41:11, he is reminding us all that God *owes* us nothing; He is no one's debtor.

The point that Paul is making should not be seen as a kind of cold, abrupt, and unsympathetic reply. He is not saying that God doesn't care if we understand His ways or not. Remember the context. The question Paul asks in Romans 11:35 is designed to turn our attention away from what we think we deserve to the awe-inspiring uniqueness of the depth of the riches of God's knowledge and wisdom. As Paul says elsewhere (1 Cor 1:25):

> For the foolishness of God is wiser than men, and the weakness of God is stronger than men.

The clear implication is that "wisdom" is not on a continuum, with man's at one end and God's at the highest end. What Paul is saying is much more radical than that. He is saying that the highest of man's wisdom does not even compare to that which is "foolish" in God. Of course, God's foolishness is actually the mystery of the gospel, as Paul makes clear to the Corinthians. But the point Paul is making to the Corinthians is a similar point to the one he is making in Romans 11:33–36. He is telling us again that we are incapable of reaching into the deep recesses of God's wisdom—to such an extent that God's wisdom appears to us (apart from Christ) as utter foolishness.

This has deep and abiding implications for our understanding and communication of the gospel. Because of the depth of God's majesty, we should not expect that we will ever be able fully to comprehend just why it is, or how it is, that God has decided to do what He does in creation (from the beginning and into eternity). But, as we have seen, confession of our innate and total finitude should move us to praise; it should not be an obstacle to our belief.

As a matter of fact, there are really only two possible responses to "the secret things" of God. We can be agitated, angry, confused, and insistent before God. We can refuse to acknowledge what we do not understand. This is not a Christian option. It succumbs to the rationalism that we discussed in the previous chapter. Moreover, it takes that rationalistic response and turns it into an occasion for rebellion.

The other reaction is the Christian reaction. It is a response of praise and wonder at the sheer greatness of God's infinite character. The Christian response is to take those mysteries that God has revealed to us and to recognize them as stark evidence of our finite, sinful creatureliness. Once we see that clearly, we cannot help but respond in worship and doxology.

Finally, Paul ends his doxology with a statement of praise that should put to rest any self-centered, rationalistic view of God, the world, or anything else. He makes abundantly plain the comprehensive scope of God's own wisdom. Whatever we do not know—and there is an infinite amount of knowledge we lack—this much we do know:

> For from him and through him and to him are all things.
> To him be glory forever. Amen (Rom 11:36).

These two statements alone are worth a lifetime of Christian meditation. The Triune God is the *origin* of all things (from), the *continuation* of all things (through), and the *goal* of all things (to). And the reason that His wisdom comprehends absolutely everything is so that all glory will be His and no one else's.

So, in the midst of so much that we do not and cannot know or understand, this much we can know without question—all of it is to the glory of God. This means, at least, that all of it is meant to show us more and more of who God is, to declare to us more and more of His character, to point us, always and in all ways, to the unsurpassed and matchless glory that God has shown us in His revelation.

Are you able to say "amen" to that? As a Christian, to say "amen!" to this truth is your glorious duty, and it is your greatest privilege, in this life and in the next, for eternity.

· · · ·

In the coming chapters we will think carefully about what we *do* know about God and His ways in order to highlight how majestically mysterious His ways and judgments are. Specifically, the next five chapters—as we think about the Trinity, the incarnation, the covenant,

God's eternal plan for creation, and God's providence—will require us to focus our thoughts and minds as carefully as we can. We will want to think deeply about each of these glorious truths by looking at the biblical development of them in Scripture. We will then see how to bring the biblical teaching together as we highlight the biblical doctrine of these teachings. Once we have the doctrine before us, we will set out some biblical distinctions that are important to remember. Lastly, all of this should lead us to biblical doxology as we recognize the mystery at the root of it all. The last two chapters—on prayer and our eternal joy—will give us a practical perspective on the mystery of Christianity, as that mystery reaches its climax in the new heaven and new earth.

Our thoughts of God must ever increase, so that our worship of Him will be ever growing. In that way, we find ourselves better prepared for our eternal existence with Him, in the new heaven and the new earth. There, too, from Him, through Him, and to Him will be all things, to His eternal glory, and for our eternal praise.

> God moves in a mysterious way
> His wonders to perform;
> He plants His footsteps in the sea
> And rides upon the storm.
> Deep in unfathomable mines
> Of never failing skill
> He treasures up His bright designs
> And works His sov'reign will.

> —William Cowper, "God Moves in A Mysterious Way"

CHAPTER 3

The Majesty of the Mystery of the Three-in-One

But whether it be the Father, or the Son, or the Holy Spirit He is perfect, and God the Father the Son and the Holy Spirit is perfect; and therefore He is a Trinity rather than triple.

—Augustine of Hippo

On the Trinity

There is nothing more unique and more fundamental to the teaching of Christianity than the doctrine of the Trinity. If we think of the various religious cults that have come into existence—Mormonism or Jehovah's Witnesses, for example—as well as of other religions such as Islam or Judaism, none of these teach or affirm anything close to a Christian understanding of the Trinity. As a matter of fact, most are outwardly hostile to it.

There are various reasons for this. As we saw previously, anything that does not fit neatly into our normal ways of thinking is often rejected out of hand. If our minds aren't able to contain a certain teaching, then surely, some think, it simply cannot be true. But, for the Christian, the fact of God's triunity *has* to be true. There is no Christianity without it. Christianity without the Trinity is like a book without words—useless and completely devoid of all content.

When we confess that God is triune we mean to say that He is one God, not three, but that as one God He is three distinct persons. As with most things we confess in Christianity, we have to be careful with the words that we use. Nowhere is this more important than in our confession of the Trinity.

I remember teaching a catechism class to a group of small children one day in church. I began by asking these toddlers to tell me what we mean by the Trinity. One of them blurted out, "Three men in God's head!" Not bad for a three-year-old, but wholly inadequate as a proper grasp of this central mystery of the Christian faith.

The words that we use to describe the Trinity can vary, but whatever words we use have to be consistent with biblical truth. We cannot say that there are three gods; neither can we say that God "has" three persons, or that he is made up of three parts that we call "persons." What God "is" is not something that He "has," and God is not "made up" of any part at all. God doesn't take certain external qualities to Himself *in order to be* the Triune God. We will return to this idea later.

For now, it is enough to remember that God's triunity is what He *is*; it is not something that *composes* Him. And this triunity requires us to affirm that, as three persons, He is one God.

John Calvin was insistent that the Church recognize the central importance of confessing this most mysterious and glorious teaching. But, even though it is crucial to express God's triunity accurately, Calvin was not unduly tied to only one way of expressing its truth. In speaking of the typical terms used to describe the Trinity, he says:

> If, therefore, these terms were not rashly invented, we ought to beware lest by repudiating them we be accused of overweening rashness. Indeed, I could wish they were buried, if only among all men this faith were agreed on: that Father and Son and Spirit are one God, yet the Son is not the Father, nor the Spirit the Son, but that they are differentiated by a peculiar quality.[1]

The terms we use are meant only to express in a more concise way what we confess of God's triunity. We must make sure that we use terms that adequately express what Scripture teaches us about God's triunity. But, more importantly, we must be aware of just exactly what the terms that we use mean.

But just *what is it*, exactly, that we're saying when we confess that God is Three-in-One?

BIBLICAL DEVELOPMENT

> Long ago, at many times and in many ways, God spoke to our fathers by the prophets, but in these last days he has spoken to us by his Son, whom he appointed the heir of all things, through whom also he created the world (Heb 1:1–2).

It is important to recognize that God revealed Himself, more and more, as history advanced. That special, progressive, redemptive revelation of God has now ceased until Christ comes back, but it was advancing

---

1. John Calvin, *Institutes of the Christian Religion*, ed. John T. McNeill, trans. Ford Lewis Battles, vol. 1, The Library of Christian Classics (Louisville, KY: Westminster John Knox Press, 2011), 125–26.

throughout history until the Son Himself appeared with a human nature. So, as the author to the Hebrews reminds us, God chose different prophets, "at many times and in various ways," to communicate Himself to His people. But he also tells us that God's communication reaches its climax *in His Son*. The point the author is making is not simply that God has used various people at various times in order to reveal His Word. Rather, God's Word-revelation has been moving forward, advancing like an army of soldiers, toward a final and ultimate destination. That destination is the Word-revelation that has come in the Son, who Himself is fully God.[2]

As God's revelation advanced in history, so also did the knowledge that the Lord's people had of God. God chose not to give as complete and full a revelation of His character and plan at the beginning of history as He would give as history moved on. To be sure, He gave all that was *needed* at each particular time in history, but, from the beginning, there was more to come as time moved forward (even as there is still more to come when Christ comes back—see 1 Corinthians 13:12, for example).

So it is with the doctrine of the Trinity. It is a distinctly *Christian* doctrine, because it is most fully revealed, in history, with the coming of *Christ*. It was not fully revealed in the Old Testament; instead, it was given in shadows. B. B. Warfield expresses the development and progression of God's revelation of His triunity in history this way:

> The Old Testament may be likened to a chamber richly furnished but dimly lighted; the introduction of light brings into it nothing which was not in it before; but it brings out into clearer view much of what is in it but was only dimly or even not at all perceived before. The mystery of the Trinity is not revealed in the Old Testament; but the mystery of the Trinity underlies the Old Testament revelation, and here and there almost comes into view. Thus the Old Testament revelation of God is not corrected by

---

2. The character of the Son becomes the author's concern in the rest of this chapter, and beyond, as he describes Him as "the radiance of the glory of God and the exact imprint of his nature, and he upholds the universe by the word of his power" (Heb 1:3).

the fuller revelation which follows it, but only perfected, extended and enlarged.[3]

This is a perfect analogy. The Old Testament is like a dimly lit but richly furnished room. All the furniture is there; no more is needed. What is needed is more light so that the furniture can be seen for what it is and where it is.

As Warfield notes, the Trinity "here and there almost comes into view" in the Old Testament. At the beginning of creation, we see God taking counsel with Himself. God says, "Let us make man in our image, after our likeness" (Gen 1:26). This could, of course, be God talking to Himself, but it isn't likely since He says, "Let *us*" and not "I think *I* ..." Clearly there seem to be multiple persons included in this discussion.

But there is not enough "light" available to see that the "us" is three, and not two or 20. And there surely isn't enough to see that the three are Father, Son, and Holy Spirit. But the Trinity "almost comes into view" in this passage.

There are also a number of passages in the Old Testament where "God as Father" is stated or implied. In Exodus 4:22, the LORD refers to Israel as His son; in Deuteronomy 8:5, Israel is not only referred to as the Lord's son, but the Lord promises to discipline Israel in its sins— clearly a *fatherly* activity. More explicitly, the "covenant formula" is given to Israel in the form of a father/son relationship. The Lord says to David through the prophet Nathan, "I will be to him a father, and he shall be to me a son" (2 Sam 7:14). But references to the fatherhood of God are scarce in the Old Testament, and in places where it is mentioned, the reference to His son is usually a reference to His people, not to *the* Son. So, again, there is no explicit teaching about God's triune character during that long span of history, though we do begin to see the personal, fatherly character of the one God.

By the time we get to the New Testament, however, the "lights" come on, because the Light Himself has come. With the advent of Jesus Christ, the Son of God, the fullest revelation of God in history comes to light, so that the Fatherhood of God is seen and shown for what it is.

---

3. B. B. Warfield, *Biblical Doctrines*, vol. 2, The Works of Benjamin Breckinridge Warfield (1929; repr., Grand Rapids: Baker, 2000), 141–42.

At the beginning of Christ's messianic ministry, for example, we see the Trinity involved:

> And when Jesus was baptized, immediately he went up from the water, and behold, the heavens were opened to him, and he saw the Spirit of God descending like a dove and coming to rest on him; and behold, a voice from heaven said, "This is my beloved Son, with whom I am well pleased" (Matt 3:16–17).

There is, in this passage, no clear indication that the "Spirit of God" is personal, but there can be no question that the voice from heaven, speaking about the Son, requires at least two persons; there is One who is baptized, and then there is One who calls Him "Son" and who is well pleased with Him. We now see, in Christ's own ministry, that there is more than one person involved. The inauguration of Christ's messianic ministry begins to shine the spotlight on the triunity of God.

Even if the "bright lights" were not shining on the "furniture" of the Old Testament (to use Warfield's analogy), it was, nevertheless, clear to the Jews that anyone who would claim to be God's true Son would be making Himself equal to God. So, as Jesus was teaching about His work and its relationship to the work of the Father, John tells us:

> This was why the Jews were seeking all the more to kill him, because not only was he breaking the Sabbath, but he was even calling God his own Father, making himself equal with God (John 5:18).

Clearly, there was enough light in the Old Testament for the Jews to recognize what it would mean for someone to be *the* Son of God. The anger of the Jews in seeking to kill Christ was due in part to Christ's own teaching about His identity with His Father. The Jews understood His claim, and they refused to believe it.

In John's Gospel, as Jesus pulls away from the crowd and looks toward His death and departure, He spends the bulk of His time in the upper room explaining to His disciples the relationship of the Father, Son, and Holy Spirit (John 13–17). The Trinity was so important to Christ that it was the final thing He wanted His disciples to recognize before He left them. Surely, the doctrine of the Trinity was deemed to be centrally important to Christ and to the ministry and comfort of His disciples.

Most explicit in the Gospels, however, is that last great commission that Jesus leaves to His disciples and to the Church:

> And Jesus came and said to them, "All authority in heaven and on earth has been given to me. Go therefore and make disciples of all nations, baptizing them in the name of the Father and of the Son and of the Holy Spirit, teaching them to observe all that I have commanded you. And behold, I am with you always, to the end of the age" (Matt 28:18–20).

Notice that the *name* of God is given to the Lord's people in baptism. We know from the rest of Scripture how important the *name* of God is. When we think about and discuss the character of God, we do so, initially, by way of the names that God gives himself in Scripture.

We will look at this later on, but at this point we should recognize two things: First, the name of God that takes a certain precedence over all, in that it describes God *as God*, and not, in the first place, as related to His creation, is the name "Yahweh." That name, initially interpreted by God Himself in Exodus 3:14–16, tells us of the absolute independence of God. God's interpretation of His name (and character) is profound in its simplicity, "I AM WHO I AM" (Exod 3:14). He alone is who He is. Jesus Christ applies this name—"I AM"—to Himself, and when He does so, the Jews want to stone Him to death. They recognize that if it is not true, it is utter blasphemy (John 8:58–59).

Second, the reason the Jews interpreted what Christ said to them as blasphemy (though it was, in fact, the truth!) is that God had set aside, among the top 10 commandments that He had given, the holiness and sacredness of His *name*:

> You shall not take the name of the LORD your God in vain, for the LORD will not hold him guiltless who takes his name in vain (Exod 20:7).

This shows us how important the name of God is to God Himself and to our understanding of His character. This commandment is a commandment of our speech about God. What we say may seem, at first glance, to be relatively insignificant. But this is not the case with God's name. *What* we say with respect to that name and *how* we use that name in our speech is of deep and abiding concern to God Himself. Our speech can be offensive to God, or it can please Him.

We can see how monumental it is, then, when Christ Himself, toward the end of His earthly ministry, announced the final, climactic name of God to His disciples and to the world (Matt 28:19). "From now on," Jesus is saying, "the pronunciation of the name of God—a name which will mark My people in the Church—is the *one* name of 'Father, Son, and Holy Spirit.' " It is crucial to recognize that what Jesus says is *not* "baptizing them in the *names* ... ." The language He uses is clear and explicit. Baptism is to be in the *one name* of Father, Son, and Holy Spirit.

With the coming of Christ the climactic and majestic name of the one God—Father, Son, and Holy Spirit—takes center stage in redemptive history and into eternity. Apart from that name, salvation is now impossible. That triune name of God is the centerpiece of all that we are to think and do as Christ's own people. It is a name that now identifies *us*.

There are a multitude of passages in the New Testament that show the majesty of the Trinity in specific ways. The Apostle Peter, just to use one example, eventually came to understand what Christ was saying to him and the other 11 disciples when He promised guidance from the Holy Spirit (John 16:13). When Peter began his first epistle, the Trinity was the first thing on his mind:

> Peter, an apostle of Jesus Christ,
> To those who are elect exiles of the Dispersion in Pontus, Galatia, Cappadocia, Asia, and Bithynia, according to the foreknowledge of God the Father, in the sanctification of the Spirit, for obedience to Jesus Christ and for sprinkling with his blood:
> May grace and peace be multiplied to you (1 Pet 1:1–2).

Peter recognizes the various roles of the three persons; it is the Father who foreknew, the Spirit who sanctifies, and it is Christ we obey as we are sprinkled with His atoning blood. Clearly, the fullness of our salvation can only be understood in the context of the fullness of God's tri-personal character.

As we see the Trinity taught in the New Testament, it is incumbent on us now, as it has been on the Church since the New Testament was written, to take the various truths of that teaching that are given in Scripture and formulate a biblical *doctrine* of the Trinity.

BIBLICAL DOCTRINE

It has been rightly said that the word "Trinity" never occurs in the Bible. Anti-Trinitarians are quick to remind Christians of that fact, and it is a fact. This fact, however, is no argument against the Trinity, unless what we mean by the *word* is contrary to what Scripture *teaches*. The word "Trinity" is simply a shorthand way of expressing what Scripture teaches about God. The doctrine itself would not suffer if the word was rejected. Instead of saying "Trinity," we could just as easily say that we believe in the *one* God whose *one* name is Father, Son, and Holy Spirit, and that this one name is the identity marker of every Christian (Matt 28:19). In other words, the *doctrine* of the Trinity is produced when we take the unified teaching of many passages in Holy Scripture and express that teaching in more general terms.

The *doctrine* of the Trinity, then, is a product of systematic theology. We use the word "Trinity" in order to designate the clear teaching of Scripture that God is one, and that the one God is three persons, each of whom is fully, exhaustively, and completely the one God. Because the doctrine of the Trinity is a central part of orthodox theology, we can begin to see just how crucial and important systematic theology is for orthodoxy. Even if the *word* "Trinity" is never used, the *doctrine* must be confessed if one is to be and remain biblical. The *name* of God, given climactically by Christ Himself, is all-important for the Church's identity.

This New Testament reality of God's "new" name—the name of God as Father, Son, and Holy Spirit—was a bombshell for the church in its infancy. Consider the church's plight in those early days. For thousands of years, the biblical tradition and confession was both clear and adamant—"Hear, O Israel: The LORD our God, the LORD is *one*" (Deut 6:4). This confessional statement—called the "Shema," from the Hebrew word for "hear"—was central to Israel's life and to its relationship to God. To worship or go after any other gods was, by definition, to forsake the *one* only true and living God. This would be met with swift and certain judgment.

But something monumental had happened. Someone came who Himself was God, and who claimed to be equal to the Father. He came to build a Church that would include all who confessed Him (Matt 16:16–19). How, then, was this "new" Church supposed to understand the significance and importance of worshiping *one* God in the face of the One who had come and said *He* was God? The early church immediately recognized that, given what Christ Himself said, and given what the rest of this "New" Testament said, this One who came must, somehow, be incorporated into the life and worship of the Lord's people. How is the Church supposed to understand this?

This was no ivory-tower question; it was a question, ultimately, about worship. The questions about the identity of Christ were questions, in the first place, not simply about correct doctrine, but about thinking properly in order to *worship* properly. The church was not concerned about doctrine for doctrine's sake, nor should we be. Instead, they were intent on worshiping the one, true God as He had revealed Himself; to worship any other god would be to worship a false god, not the true God of history and of redemption. So the questions asked about Christ's identity, and the answers given, were, for the most part, attempts to ensure that the worship of God in His church was "in spirit and in *truth*."

One of the most predominant and persuasive early answers to the question of Christ's identity was given by a church leader named Arius (c. AD 250–336). Arius concluded that the only way to continue to worship the *one* God, in light of this Jesus Christ who had come, was to recognize that Christ, though divine in some way, was in no way *fully* God. Instead, He was created, even though He was created in eternity and out of nothing. He himself, then, was the agent of everything else that was created. In that way, He had an exalted status, but He simply could not be equal to the one God.

Christ was thought by Arius and his followers to be midway between God and creation. He could not be, they argued, "of the same substance" of the one God. If He were, then we would be caught in a rational predicament. We would have to affirm that the one God was, in fact, two. And this kind of affirmation, argued the Arians, was no part of biblical religion. Polytheism (many gods) was, by definition, pagan. Monotheism (one God) is the clear and explicit teaching of Scripture. Arius and his followers mounted some significant arguments against the full deity of Jesus Christ.

The history of Arianism, and its opposition, is fascinating and could occupy us for some time. What is astonishing, however, is the way that the church responded to the teachings of Arius and his followers. Because Arius' teachings were causing significant controversy in the church, Emperor Constantine, in AD 325, somewhat reluctantly finally determined that the church needed to address these Arian teachings. Constantine called a council of church leaders to come together to debate and resolve the problem of Christ's identity and deity. That council met in Nicea and produced the first ecumenical creed of the church, the Nicene Creed. The purpose of this, as with all creeds, was that the church confess as one body what it believed. The purpose was to restore unity in the church.

In the Nicene Creed, Arianism is declared to be a heresy. Here is what these church leaders concluded:

> We believe in one God, the Father Almighty, Creator of all things visible and invisible; and in one Lord Jesus Christ, the Son of God, only-begotten of the Father, that is, of the substance of the Father. God of God, light of light, very God of very God, begotten, not made, being of the same substance with the Father, by whom all things were made in heaven and in earth, who for us men and for our salvation came down from heaven, was incarnate, was made man, suffered, rose again the third day, ascended into the heavens, and He will come to judge the living and the dead. And in the Holy Ghost. Those who say, There was a time when He was not, and He was not before He was begotten, and He was made of nothing (He was created), or who say that He is of another hypostasis, or of another substance (than the Father), or that the Son of God is created, that He is mutable, or subject to change, the Catholic Church anathematizes."[4]

---

4. Charles Joseph Hefele, *A History of the Councils of the Church*, trans. William R. Clark, vol. 1 (Edinburgh: T&T Clark, 1871), 294-95.

In this creed, the language used is all-important. When the church confesses that Jesus Christ is "of the substance *of* the Father" and "of the same substance *with* the Father," it is saying as explicitly as it can that Jesus Christ is fully and entirely equal to God. The language of "substance" was used to denominate the essential character of God. It was a word that had its roots in philosophy and that was taken into the language of theology in order to signify God's absolute character. Substance indicates something that exists in and of itself, without needing anything else.

When the Nicene Creed affirms Jesus Christ to be of the same substance, which is *one* substance, with the Father, it is teaching that Jesus Christ, like the Father, is fully God. He is not dependent on anything—not the Father and certainly not an act of creation—in order to be who He is *as God.* This does not mean that, *as the Son,* He was not begotten. The creed affirms that the Son's begotten-ness is what it means to be Son. But begotten-ness is articulated negatively in the creed as "not made." So insistent is the creed, against the Arians, that Christ was not made that it "anathematizes" (that is, excludes from the Church) any who would say or think that being begotten means being created. The Nicene Creed set orthodoxy in stone with respect to Christ's deity and, thus, with respect to the Trinity. It declares the teaching of Scripture so that for a church to be orthodox it must reject Arianism and affirm that the One who came down and became man was, at the same time, fully God. This did not end the Arian controversy, but it established the doctrine needed to oppose it.

Over a relatively short period of time, the Church would confess that the Holy Spirit, together with the Father and the Son, is also to be worshiped and glorified. Thus, the Church, since its New Testament beginning, has confessed and maintained that God is one, and that this one God is three distinct persons, each of whom is fully, exhaustively, and completely God.

This is a striking occasion in the early days of the Church. We should recognize that the Nicene Creed can be affirmed only in the context of the *mystery* of God's triune character. In affirming it, we also confess that we cannot *comprehend* what we must *acknowledge.* In the providence of God and by His grace, the Church's commitment in its formulation of Trinitarian doctrine was to affirm what Scripture teaches, even if that affirmation was impossible to grasp with our minds. It was not just that the Church affirmed God's incomprehensibility. Most theists would agree that God is incomprehensible. But the Church was committed to *confessing the content* of that incomprehensibility, to the extent that God's revelation would allow.

In other words, given the incomprehensibility of God, it seems natural that when God reveals Himself He would do so in a way that would allow us to *say* and *believe* certain truths about Him, truths that would rise above our minds, even above creation itself. Our confession of God *as triune* is the fullest expression—this side of heaven—of the glory of our incomprehensible God. We simply cannot understand *how* it can be that God is one and three, but we affirm it with all of the vigor and certainty that Scripture requires of us.

BIBLICAL DISTINCTIONS

As soon as we recognize that Scripture teaches that God is three (persons) in one (God), we also recognize the need to make another, crucially important, distinction. We know that "when the fullness of time had come, God sent forth his Son, born of a woman, born under the law" (Gal 4:4). This passage, and others like it, tell us that the Second Person of the Trinity, the Son of God Himself, *was sent* by God, to be born of a woman, born under the law, in order to redeem a people.

This truth moves us to acknowledge that there are truths about the Trinity that pertain to creation (and redemption) that do not pertain to the Trinity, in and of itself. In other words, it was *the Son* who was sent, and His "sending" included His coming down to creation and participating in it in a way that the Triune God—in and of Himself—does not.

We have to keep in mind a basic distinction, then, when we confess that God is triune. When we think and speak of the Trinity, we must be careful to recognize that the Trinity is just who God is, *as God*. That is the first and primary confession of the Church. But we must also see that this Triune God involved Himself in creation and, therefore, in His historical plan of redemption. In other words, we confess the Triune God *as God*, and we confess the Triune God *as related to, and involved in, creation*.

There are two terms that have come to be used as the standard way of expressing this distinction, and the terms themselves might not be a familiar part of our everyday vocabulary. When speaking of the

Triune God *in Himself*, the term often used is "ontological." In this case, "ontological" means the Trinity with reference to the "Being" ("*ontos*" is a Greek word for "being") of God, without any reference at all to creation. The ontological Trinity is the Triune God *in Himself*. It is a term that signifies the one God—as Father (eternally begetting), Son (eternally begotten), and Spirit (eternally proceeding).

Whenever we focus on the three persons of the Trinity *as they relate to creation and redemption*, however, we are thinking of God as related to something outside of Himself. The term used for this activity is the "economic" Trinity. The word "economic" can be confusing here because it is almost always used in a much different way. When we hear the word "economic," we usually think of a financial or monetary context. In theology, however, the Greek word, *oikonomia*, meant something like "arrangement" and was used to designate the activity of the Triune God in the arrangement of His plan of creation and of redemption. So the "economic" Trinity refers to God the Father, the Son, and the Holy Spirit in their respective roles in creation and redemption.

This does not, of course, mean that there are two trinities, nor does it mean that what the Triune God does in creation and redemption is completely contrary to who He is *in Himself*. What it *does* mean, however, is that it was the Triune God's plan to communicate His ontological character in a way that would relate to His creation. In doing so, His character is expressed differently—because *outwardly*—than it was before creation, when the expression of His character was only within Himself. Once He creates, those characteristics and qualities are seen in His relationship to, as well as His actions in and with, His creation.

So, for example, the Father *sends* the Son to redeem. Apart from creation, there was no need for the Son to be sent; indeed, when there was no creation, there was no "place" to which the Son *could* be sent! Not only so, but the Father's wrath was poured out on the Son as He hung on the cross (cf. Gal 3:13). Apart from creation and the entrance of sin, there was no need or occasion for the wrath of God; in that sense, the wrath of God is not an expression of the *ontological* Trinity (that is, of God in relation to Himself). Moreover, the Holy Spirit, we learn from Scripture, can be grieved because of our sin (Eph 4:30). With respect to God in Himself, though, there is no occasion or reason for any person of the Godhead to be grieving. All of this "economic" activity and work of the Triune God does *not* mean that God changes from who He is in Himself to who He is in creation. What it *does* mean is that God is able to remain who He is in Himself *even as* He expresses His character by interacting in and with His creation, for eternity! (In further chapters, we will introduce a way to categorize these biblical truths.)

The mystery of the Triune God includes the mystery of the relationship between the Triune God in Himself and the Triune God in creation, and in accomplishing redemption. There are, we need to recognize, characteristics of one that help us see the rationale for the other. For example, when the Nicene Creed says that the Son was "only-begotten of the Father," it is confessing the reality of God in Himself (i.e., ontological reality). The Son, therefore, is eternally begotten of the Father. Thus, as the one begotten, it seems natural that the Son would be the one who was *sent* by the Father. There is a biblical logic to the fact that the One begotten is also the One sent, since in both cases (ontological and economic) the Son is *from* the Father. Since, in the Godhead itself, the Father is unbegotten and the Son is, as Son, from the Father, it would not befit the Father to be the One sent; as the ontological begetter, the Father is the economic sender. So also, since the Spirit is eternally proceeding from the Father and the Son, it is fitting that He should be sent from the Father and the Son as the Spirit comes to apply to God's people what the Father has initiated, and what the Son has accomplished, in history and in redemption.

This distinction, as mysterious as it is, has guided the church for almost two millennia. Without it, either the Triune God remains distant and aloof from His creation (if the Trinity is *only* ontological, without relating to creation), or He is dependent on creation and redemption to be who He is (if the Trinity is *only* economic). Both aspects of God's triunity have to be affirmed.

As they are affirmed, we should recognize that the economic flows *from* the ontological. That is, God's disposition toward creation is what it is *because* of who He is in His being. This affirmation in no way makes what is incomprehensible comprehensible to us. Instead, it only increases, and *enhances*, that incomprehensibility, and thus it enhances our biblically informed worship of the Triune God!

BIBLICAL DOXOLOGY

In light of our focus on the majesty of mystery, we need to chew slowly in order better to digest exactly what happened in the early church as it developed a biblical doctrine of the Trinity. This doctrine was not simply touted and accepted by all in those early days. It was not a doctrine that floated down effortlessly onto the Church's creedal statements. As a matter of fact, we can more easily think of reasons why one should *not* believe in God as triune.

If the goal of the church, or of individuals in the church, was to create a statement that would fit with the way we typically think, the church would have affirmed Arius' position. It would have written a creed that confessed a belief in "God, the Father Almighty," and then, like Arius (and because polytheism was not an option), the church would have concluded that Jesus Christ could not be fully God. Then, there would be no confession of a triunity; there would be no Three-in-One to confess. There would only be "One." That "One" would have, perhaps, some kind of special relationship to Jesus and to the Spirit. Or, if the church leaders had wanted to be even more radical at Nicea, they could have affirmed that the Father is God and the Son is God, so that the church was now to confess (at least) two "Gods." But this would have violated the clear teaching of Scripture as well.

Even though the temptation might have been present in those early days of the Church, there was no way such things could be affirmed and confessed if *Scripture* was to be the Church's guide. The Shema of God's Word could not be contradicted. That was clear enough; God was, and must be, only *one*. But this One who identified Himself as Yahweh (cf. John 8:58), yet who came to obey His Father, had to be *worshiped* as well (see, for example, John 20:28; Heb 1:6). Any Christian who read the Scriptures—or heard them read, in those early days— was compelled to recognize that this Christ, who is Himself the Son of God, was both distinct from, even as He was identical to, God Himself (cf. John 1:1).

As we have seen in our previous chapters, it is just this mystery of God that explains and enhances His transcendent majesty. Far from being avoided, this majestic mystery of the Trinity will be personally, enthusiastically, and passionately embraced by every Bible-believing

Christian. This embrace will sanctify us and prepare us for the life to come.

One of the greatest (if not *the* greatest) Puritan pastors was John Owen. His writing can be dense, but it is so well worth the effort to read it that I want to include a quotation from him that helps us to see the majesty of the Trinity (and doctrines like it). Read Owen here slowly and carefully:

> There are some doctrines of the Scripture, some revelations in it, *so sublimely glorious*, of *so profound and mysterious an excellency*, that at the first proposal of them, nature startles, shrinks, and is taken with horror, meeting with that which is above it, too great and too excellent for it, which it could desirously avoid and decline; but yet, gathering itself up to them, it yields, and finds that unless they are accepted and submitted unto, though unsearchable, not only all that hath been received must be rejected, but also the whole dependence of the creature on God be dissolved, or rendered only dreadful, terrible, and destructive to nature itself. Such are the doctrines of the Trinity, of the incarnation of the Son of God, of the resurrection of the dead, of the new birth, and the like. At the first revelation of these things nature is amazed, cries, "How can these things be?" or gathers up itself to opposition. ... But when the eyes of reason are a little confirmed, though it can never clearly behold the glory of this sun, yet it confesseth a glory to be in it above all that it is able to apprehend ... namely, though great above and beyond the reach of reason, yet, upon search, found to be such, as, without submission to them, the whole covenant relation between God and man must needs be dissolved.[5]

Owen expresses well the majesty of the Trinity. Nature (i.e. "Reason") does indeed, initially, "startle, shrink, and is taken with horror" when such incomprehensible and transcendent truths come to light. When embraced, however, we recognize that without these

---

5. John Owen, *The Works of John Owen*, ed. William H. Goold (Edinburgh: T&T Clark, 1862), 16:339–40.

glorious truths "the whole comfortable relation between God and man must needs be dissolved." We embrace the majesty of the mystery of the Trinity because in that mystery is God Himself, and without it there is no relation of God to His creation and to His people.

The majesty of God's incomprehensible triune character advanced throughout redemptive history. And to whom much is given will much be required. It reaches its majestic climax in the life, death, resurrection, ascension, and exaltation of the Son. By the grace of the Triune God, the Church has seen this from its inception. So, in God's gracious providence, the practice of the Church, since those early days, has been to sing of the Trinity in worship. To the question "How can it be that God is both one and three?" the Christian response has to be "We cannot comprehend it." And then we add, "But this truth, and its incomprehensibility, is the focus of our worship, the center of our praise, and the entirety of our lives."

The "*Gloria patri*" has been sung in the Church at least since the fourth century, usually at the end of a reading of a psalm. When we sing it, we revel in the majesty of the mystery of God's triunity:

> *Glory be to the Father, and to the Son and to the Holy Ghost*
> *As it was in the beginning, is now and ever shall be*
> *World without end. Amen.*

CHAPTER 4

The Majesty of the Mystery of the Incarnation

While he was God; when he abode "in the form of God," and was "equal with God," then he "took upon him the form of a servant." This is that glorious condescension of Christ, which is the greatest of all gospel mysteries, which is the life and soul of the church. He that is God can no more cease to be God, by any act of his own, or act upon him, than he that is not God can become God by any act of his own, or any act upon him. Christ could not cease to be God. ... We say, Christ, being God, was made man for our sakes.

—John Owen

The Humiliation and Condescension of Christ

T he first thing that we confess as Christians is the mystery of the incarnation. We may not know the theological terms and concepts, but when we first profess our Christian faith, we profess that we are putting our trust in One who is both fully God and fully man. In that way, we *enter* Christianity through the majestic gate of mystery; mystery is not something that is seen later on as we mature as Christians. It comes with our initial Christian profession. As we profess Christ, we also confess something that our minds are unable to understand. We profess as true that which we cannot grasp. We profess it happily, and it moves us to worship. That is as it should be. But it is also the case that an exploration into the mystery of the incarnation will further ground and grow our own holiness and worship.

In his introduction to Athanasius' book *On the Incarnation of the Word of God*, C. S. Lewis bemoans the fact that, especially in theology, modern books are more preferred over ancient ones, and the more specialized books are rarely read by any but the specialists. This practice contributes heartily to spiritual impoverishment of the soul. Lewis puts it this way:

> I believe that many who find that "nothing happens"
> when they sit down, or kneel down, to a book of devotion,
> would find their heart sings unbidden while they are
> working their way through a tough bit of theology with a
> pipe in their teeth and pencil in their hands.[1]

Many Christians would find, or have found, Lewis' words to be accurate. Digging deeply into the truth of Scripture always repays rich dividends in the development of a Christian mind and heart. Christian

---

1. C. S. Lewis, Introduction to *The Incarnation of the Word, Being the Treatise of St. Athanasius, De Incarnatione Verbi Dei*, by Saint Athanasius (London: Geoffrey Bles: The Centenary Press, 1944), 13–14.

maturity is a product of Christian meditation; sanctification is a result of the study of Scripture.

It is fitting that Lewis wrote these words as he was commending a work on the incarnation. Along with a biblical understanding of the Trinity, nothing will motivate a Christian more toward deep and abiding worship than a deep and abiding reflection on the glorious mystery that is the person of Jesus Christ.

BIBLICAL DEVELOPMENT

There are so many passages in Scripture that testify to the reality of the God-man that it is impossible to cover them all here. As B. B. Warfield puts it, "The proper subject of the New Testament is Christ. Every page of it, or perhaps we might better say every line of it, has its place in the portrait which is drawn of Him by the whole."[2] Redemptive history is replete with evidence for the incarnation; it can be seen on almost every page of Holy Scripture. The account of God coming to man that the Lord gives us in His Word is, when recognized for what it is, enough to evoke wonder and awe in all who read with eyes to see.

As we read about the incarnation at the beginning of the New Testament, we see that the coming of Christ was not as serene and idyllic as our Christmas cards might suggest. The announcement of Christ's coming began with an enigma for Joseph, who initially thought it might be best to disassociate from his fiancée, Mary (Matt 1:19). When Zechariah was told that he would have a son to prepare the way for Christ, that announcement came with his disbelief and subsequent punishment (Luke 1:18–23). Even Mary, whose announcement from the angel was only positive, was nevertheless troubled and struck with fear as she tried to contemplate what it all meant (Luke 1:26–38).

What these accounts show us is that the announcement of the coming of the Messiah was, for those involved, quite literally, incredible. That is, what they were being told and what they were meant to affirm

---

2. Benjamin B. Warfield, *The Lord of Glory: A Study of the Designations of Our Lord in the New Testament with Especial Reference to His Deity* (New York: American Tract Society, 1907), 1.

was something that they, at first hearing, simply could not believe. The announcement brought fear, confusion, and anxiety of heart.

While the Old Testament is filled with the reality of God's condescension to man (more on that below), it does not specify *exactly how* God will come to redeem a people. *That* He will come to redeem is beyond question, but some of the details are left hidden until the proper time.

But as soon as it began to dawn on the Lord's people that He would provide salvation to all the nations by becoming one of us, fear and confusion turned to praise:

> And Mary said,
>
> "My soul magnifies the Lord,
>> and my spirit rejoices in God my Savior,
> for he has looked on the humble estate of his servant.
>> For behold, from now on all generations will call me blessed;
> for he who is mighty has done great things for me,
>> and holy is his name.
> And his mercy is for those who fear him
>> from generation to generation.
> He has shown strength with his arm;
>> he has scattered the proud in the thoughts of their hearts;
> he has brought down the mighty from their thrones
>> and exalted those of humble estate;
> he has filled the hungry with good things,
>> and the rich he has sent away empty.
> He has helped his servant Israel,
>> in remembrance of his mercy,
> as he spoke to our fathers,
>> to Abraham and to his offspring forever." (Luke 1:46–55)

Zechariah, the father of John the Baptist, was struck dumb because he initially disbelieved the angel's report. As soon as his voice returned, he spoke with praise and prophecy:

> And his father Zechariah was filled with the Holy Spirit
> and prophesied, saying,

"Blessed be the Lord God of Israel,
for he has visited and redeemed his people
and has raised up a horn of salvation for us
in the house of his servant David,
as he spoke by the mouth of his holy prophets from of old,
that we should be saved from our enemies
and from the hand of all who hate us;
to show the mercy promised to our fathers
and to remember his holy covenant,
the oath that he swore to our father Abraham, to grant us
that we, being delivered from the hand of our enemies,
might serve him without fear,
in holiness and righteousness before him all our days."
(Luke 1:67–75)

It became clear that God would accomplish His redemptive purposes, not simply by coming down to commune with man as He had
been doing from the beginning of creation, but by coming down and
taking to Himself a human nature—permanently and paradoxically—
in order to accomplish what man could not accomplish. Redemption
would be provided, not through a cooperation between God and man,
but wholly by God, and by God doing something that no one could
have imagined.

When the angel announced to the shepherds, "For unto you is born
this day in the city of David a Savior, who is Christ *the Lord*" (Luke 2:11),
anyone who understood from the Old Testament what the word "Lord"
meant would have recognized that this announced Savior was God
Himself. The Greek word *kyrios*, which is translated "Lord" in the New
Testament, is equivalent to the word "Yahweh" in the Old Testament.
Whenever the word "Lord" appears in capital letters in the Old
Testament (in many of our English Bibles), the Hebrew word behind
that translation is what we call the Tetragrammaton (which means
"four letters"). The Tetragrammaton is the four-letter Hebrew word
יְהֹוָה (*yhwh*), which God Himself used as His own name and which, as
we have seen, He Himself interpreted (see Exodus 3:14–16). God said
to Moses that His name was "I am." The Hebrew word translated as
"Lord" is taken from that name, Yahweh. Yahweh, and He alone, is "I
am who I am."

When the Savior came and embarked on His ministry as the long-expected Messiah, He identified Himself as the One who spoke to Moses on the mountain that day:

> "Your father Abraham rejoiced that he would see my day. He saw it and was glad." So the Jews said to him, "You are not yet fifty years old, and have you seen Abraham?" Jesus said to them, "Truly, truly, I say to you, before Abraham was, *I am*." So they picked up stones to throw at him, but Jesus hid himself and went out of the temple. (John 8:56–59)

As we saw in the previous chapter, the Pharisees understood clearly what Jesus was claiming; He was claiming to be the "I AM" who spoke to Moses on the mountain, and who had been with His people throughout the history of creation. They knew that if the statement wasn't true, it was blasphemy, so they picked up stones to kill him (Lev 24:10–16).

Beyond the Gospels, other passages in the New Testament refer to Yahweh in the Old Testament and are applied to Jesus Christ. Many could be mentioned, but we will restrict ourselves to three.

In Romans 10:13, the apostle Paul writes,

> For "everyone who calls on the name of the Lord will be saved."

In this verse Paul is clearly referring to Christ, but the verse he quotes from, Joel 2:32, just as clearly refers to Yahweh:

> And it shall come to pass that everyone who calls on the name of the LORD shall be saved. For in Mount Zion and in Jerusalem there shall be those who escape, as the LORD has said, and among the survivors shall be those whom the LORD calls.

For centuries, "the name of the LORD" was given to the Lord's people as "Yahweh." Now, almost seamlessly, the New Testament takes this name and applies it directly to Christ. In the New Testament, we are to confess with our mouths that *Jesus* is Lord (Rom 10:9).

In 1 Peter 3:14–15, Peter alludes specifically to Isaiah 8:12–13, which says:

> Do not call conspiracy all that this people calls conspiracy,
> and do not fear what they fear, nor be in dread. But the
> LORD of hosts, him you shall honor as holy.

This passage refers specifically to Yahweh (the LORD) as the one to be regarded as holy. In 1 Peter 3:14-15, Peter interprets Isaiah as referring to Christ:

> Have no fear of them, nor be troubled, but in your hearts
> honor Christ the Lord as holy.

It is significant that Peter can, without explanation or apology, take an Old Testament passage like this one, referring as it does to Yahweh, and apply it to Christ. It seems to be taken for granted that the Christ of the New Testament is the Yahweh of redemptive history who had been with His people from the beginning.

Jude, likely the brother of Jesus, explicitly interprets the exodus of Israel as the work of Christ Himself:

> Now I want to remind you, although you once fully knew
> it, that Jesus, who saved a people out of the land of Egypt,
> afterward destroyed those who did not believe (Jude 1:5).

It would be a rich and rewarding exercise to read through the New Testament and to pick out all of the passages and references that identify Jesus Christ as Yahweh. What would become clear in such an exercise is that the movement from Old Testament to New was not at all a change of direction or of content. Rather, those events and occasions in the Old Testament where Yahweh is with and for His people, fighting with them and claiming them for Himself, all reach their climax in the New Testament when this Yahweh permanently and climactically takes to Himself a human nature—an act theologians call "condescension."

The word "condescend" is a spatial metaphor. It does not mean that God "came down" to a place that He did not otherwise occupy. He completely occupies *every place* in the universe (because He is omnipresent). So "condescend" must mean something else. But what? Generally speaking, it means that God "lowered" Himself. To "come down" is to move to a lower place. But how does God lower Himself? He does so not by any change in Him (which would be impossible), but by establishing a relationship in which His character, *as God*, would be evident in a "relational" way. God had been condescending all throughout history, but the hints in the Old Testament were signs and types, pointing the Lord's people to the condescension of the Son—a unique, monumental moment in history. The great Princeton theologian Geerhardus Vos put it this way:

> Sacramental condescensions on God's part include his appearing in human/visible form. ... Behind the Angel speaking as God, and who embodied in Himself all the condescension of God to meet the frailty and limitations of man, there existed at the same time another aspect of God, in which he could not be seen and materially received after such a fashion, the very God of whom the Angel spoke in the third person. ... The form in which the Angel appeared was a form assumed for the moment, laid aside again as soon as the purpose of its assumption had been served.[3]

Vos calls these condescensions "sacramental" in order to highlight their function of *signifying* what was to come. As the "Angel," who is the Second Person of the Trinity, comes down in Old Testament times, He assumes a created form *for the moment*, pointing to that time when He would *permanently* assume an entire human nature—from conception to ascension—at the proper time.

But God's condescension in the Son—and at times as the Angel of the LORD, who is Himself the LORD—did not begin in the New Testament; it majestically reached its climax there. So, says Calvin (commenting on Acts 7:30):

> *So let us first establish that from the outset there was no communication between God and man other than through Christ.* We have nothing to do with God unless the Mediator is present to purchase his favor for us. This passage, then, abundantly proves Christ's divinity and teaches that he is of the same essence as the Father. Furthermore, he is

---

3. Geerhardus Vos, *Biblical Theology, Old and New Testaments* (Grand Rapids: Eerdmans, 1948), 74–75.

called an angel not only because he was always accompanied by the angels as his officers, so to speak, but also because the people's deliverance foreshadowed the redemption of us all. Christ was sent by his Father to take the form of a servant in a human body. Indeed, it is certain that God never appeared to men as he is, but only under some form they were capable of apprehending.[4]

The entire Old Testament included, even as it looked forward to, the condescension of the Second Person of the Trinity, the Son of God Himself. This One who had been appearing to the saints throughout redemptive history, *when the time had fully come*, now came as the God-man, permanently taking a human nature.

This is unmistakable in the New Testament. The One who had been active in redeeming His people throughout history, since Genesis 3, had now come down permanently, because He would now be, from the incarnation into eternity-future, fully God (as He had always been) and fully man, in order that we might be fully and eternally a redeemed people.

There was, then, in redemptive history a *development* of God's condescension, as it was meant, through the entire Old Testament, to point to that one climactic moment when God would become fully man. It was foreshadowed in the Old Testament; it was present there in types and shadows, but it only became a permanent reality at the time of the incarnation. Those who were true Israelites understood this; every Christian since has gladly confessed its glory. Aside from that confession, no redemption is possible.

BIBLICAL DOCTRINE

Though the New Testament is clear about the deity of Jesus Christ, we saw in the last chapter that His deity was not universally affirmed. Arius and his followers were intent on convincing the church that Jesus was special in some ways, but He could not be fully God. If the New Testament is so clear about Christ's deity, what would motivate someone to doubt it? Here is one explanation:

---

4. John Calvin, *Acts*, Crossway Classic Commentaries 7 (Wheaton, IL: Crossway, 1995), 30; my emphasis.

> First among the doctrinal disputes which troubled
> Christians after Constantine had recognized the Church
> in A.D. 313, and the parent of many more during some
> three centuries, Arianism occupies a large place in eccle-
> siastical history. ... We shall better grasp its meaning if
> we term it an Eastern attempt *to rationalize the creed by
> stripping it of mystery* so far as the relation of Christ to God
> was concerned.[5]

A *significant* part of the reason that so many wanted to deny the
deity of Christ was that it simply did not conform to our normal
ways of thinking. So, as this quote recognizes, there was an attempt
to *rationalize* the biblical teaching concerning the person of Christ.
To "rationalize" means to develop a doctrine of Christ that would fit
comfortably with the way we normally think about things. It would
not contain concepts or categories that were beyond our intellectual
ability to grasp.

As we have already seen, the problem with the appearance of
Christ and His claims to deity was that the Old Testament was clear
that there was only *one* true God. If Christ *was* this God, then so much
of what the Old Testament said about God—that He was sovereign,
omnipresent, Creator of all—was difficult to believe about this man
from Nazareth who was born in Bethlehem. But it was also obvious to
the church that this man identified Himself with—even while He distinguished Himself from—the God of the Old Testament. Not only so,
but the inspired writings of the New Testament describe this Christ as
both truly God *and* truly man.

This, of course, is beyond our intellectual grasp. How could one
person have *two* full, distinct natures, while remaining *one* person?
Wouldn't two natures *require* that there be two persons? How, for
example, would the mind of one nature interact with the mind of the
other? More specifically, how could the infinite knowledge that Christ
has as God be united with the finite, developing knowledge that Christ
has as man?

---

5. W. Barry, "Arianism," in *The Catholic Encyclopedia* (New York: Robert Appleton
Company, 1907), accessed at http://www.newadvent.org/cathen/01707c.htm; my
emphasis.

In the early days of the church, there were a number of different theories proposed concerning the person of Christ. Maybe the nature of God *merged* with the human nature, so that Christ was neither God nor man but some kind of mixture of the two. Given the confession of Christ as the God-man, what *exactly is* a God-man? There were, as we noted above, attempts to rationalize his character in order to remove any mystery that might be taught in Scripture.

Initially, there were two rationalizing theories proposed about this God-man. The first position taught that if Christ were two natures, He must be two completely different personalities; in effect, Christ was thought to be two different beings. This view was labeled "Nestorianism" after its purported founder, Nestorius. The specifics of this heresy can be complex and technical, but the general problem was that this theory argued that the Second Person of the Trinity took to Himself not a human *nature*, but a *man*. The Nestorians were rightly opposed to the Arian heresy, but in their opposition they moved in the wrong direction. They began to teach that there were two personalities, or even two persons, in this One who had come—a view, perhaps, easier to grasp intellectually, but full of biblical difficulties.

A position also surfaced in reaction to Nestorianism, called "Eutychianism" after its purported founder, Eutyches. This theory urged people to think not in terms of two natures (thus, two persons) in Christ, but in terms of one nature *only*. The Eutychians were also called "Monophysites," which means "one nature." As the church was exposed to this view, it was encouraged to believe that the union of the two natures meant that Christ had only one nature. How could there be a *union* of the two natures if *two* natures remained? What kind of union would that be? So the God-man must have a "God-man" nature, whatever that might be.

Volumes have been written about the details of these theories and their resolutions in the church. Without getting into those details, we can summarize the church's response to these theories by referring to another ecumenical creed. In AD 451 an ecumenical council was called in Chalcedon in order to deal with the problems that had arisen in the church concerning the person of Christ. Nestorianism and Eutychianism had to be assessed in light of the church's understanding of Scripture. Building on the Nicene Creed, which had responded to Arianism by affirming the full deity of Christ, the creed that was written at Chalcedon was more specifically tasked with explaining, as concisely as possible, the biblical teaching of the incarnation. That is, given that Christ is fully God (as the Nicene Creed affirms), how are we to think of this divine nature in light of Christ's obvious humanity? Does the divine nature merge with the human nature so that there is only one nature (Eutychianism), or was it actually a man with whom the divine nature united (Nestorianism), resulting in two distinct persons (or personalities)? Or is there another option that must be affirmed?

The Chalcedonian Creed rejected these two heresies and explained the incarnation this way:

> We, then, following the holy Fathers, all with one consent, teach men to confess one and the same Son, our Lord Jesus Christ, the same perfect in Godhead and also perfect in manhood; truly God and truly man, of a reasonable soul and body; consubstantial with the Father according to the Godhead, and consubstantial with us according to the Manhood; in all things like unto us, without sin; begotten before all ages of the Father according to the Godhead, and in these latter days, for us and for our salvation, born of the Virgin Mary, the Mother of God, according to the Manhood; one and the same Christ, Son, Lord, Only-begotten, *to be acknowledged in two natures, inconfusedly, unchangeably, indivisibly, inseparably; the distinction of natures being by no means taken away by the union, but rather the property of each nature being preserved, and concurring in one Person and one Subsistence, not parted or divided into two persons, but one and the same Son, and only begotten, God the Word, the Lord Jesus Christ.*[6]

This creed is masterful in its simplicity and depth. It has been the hallmark of Christian orthodoxy since it was written.

The entire section quoted above is important, but we can focus on the latter, italicized, portion of this creed for a moment. In that

---

6. Philip Schaff, *The Creeds of Christendom, with a History and Critical Notes: The Greek and Latin Creeds, with Translations,* Vol. 2 (New York: Harper & Brothers, 1890), 63; my emphasis.

portion, the creed is affirming that when we think of the person of Christ, we are to acknowledge that He has two natures, not one. Thus, Eutychianism is denied. But the creed needed to say more than that. It needed to say something positive about the incarnation in order to quell the controversies that resulted from Nestorianism and Eutychianism. The only way to do that was to set out how best to think of the relation of the two natures in Christ.

Notice the four adverbs that the creed uses. It affirms, first, that the two natures are *not confused* and *not changed*. These two terms are designed to reject the Eutychian heresy. The two natures, as they exist in Christ, have not merged and become something other than what they are as natures. They are not "confused" or mixed together; nor is either nature changed into something other than what it is. So, against the "one nature" sect, it had to be affirmed in the creed that the two natures, as they reside in the one Person of Christ, nevertheless remain what they are.

The two latter terms—"indivisibly" and "inseparably"—were directed against the Nestorians. There can be no way that the two natures should be spoken of as two separate personalities or persons. They cannot be divided from the person in whom they reside, nor can they be separated from Him in any way. To be divided might suggest two personalities; to be separated would allow for two persons. Neither position is biblical, so both must be rejected.

As important as the negative adverbs in the Chalcedonian Creed are, its affirmation of what we now call in theology the "hypostatic union" is equally important. The creed says that "the distinction of natures being by no means taken away by the union, but rather the property of each nature being preserved, and *concurring in one Person and one Subsistence*, not parted or divided into two persons, but one and the same Son, and only begotten, God the Word, the Lord Jesus Christ."

This part of the creed reiterates that the two natures that Christ has remain what they are. Not only so, but these natures are "concurring in one Person and one Subsistence." The point of this affirmation is that the Person who Himself is incarnate remains the *same person* (hypostasis); He does not become someone else when He takes to Himself a human nature. This is a key point that we will say more about in the next section. At this point, it is crucial to see that the creed recognizes that Christ is "the same Son, and only begotten, God the Word," even after He takes on a human nature.

What we mean, then, by a hypostatic (or personal) union is that the incarnation did not result in the production of *another* person. How could it? If the One who is incarnate were another person, then we would have four persons in the Trinity—Father, Son, Spirit, and Jesus—not three (which would mean God would be a "Quadrinity" rather than a Trinity). So, though we affirm the reality and immutability of those two natures, we must also affirm that they exist in one Person, who is the same Person He has always been, the eternal Son of God. The notion of a "hypostatic" union places the emphasis on the *person*, rather than on the natures.

As we saw in the previous section, there are various biblical passages one could refer to when seeking to set out the doctrine of what kind of person Christ is. It is impossible to say that only one or two Scripture passages are definitive in our understanding of the person of Christ. However, there are a couple of passages that concisely and clearly support what the rest of Scripture shows us about the incarnation, and they were key passages during these early discussions. A brief look at these will have to suffice.

It may be that we are so familiar with the opening verses of the Gospel of John (i.e., the prologue) that its impact on us has been muted. If so, we should read them again with fresh eyes. One of the reasons that the Chalcedonian Creed uses the phrase "God the Word" is that it is referring us to the opening verses of John's Gospel.[7] John begins by alluding to the account of creation in Genesis 1:1. Instead of "in the beginning, God," however, John says, "In the beginning was *the Word*." Anyone who knew the opening verses of the Old Testament would have recognized immediately what John was saying here. He was telling his readers that the One who is the Word is the One who was active in creation "in the beginning." Lest there be any doubt about that, John makes it abundantly clear: "All things were made through him, and without him was not any thing made that was made" (John

7. It should go without saying, but unfortunately cannot, that when I say "John" (or "Paul" or "Peter") writes or says something, it presupposes that such things are said by virtue of the inspiration of the Holy Spirit. It is, in fact, *God* saying these things, not simply human authors.

1:3). So John identifies "the Word" with the One who was "in the beginning" and through whom creation came to be.

But John also gives us two phrases that can only be understood in the context of the Trinity (as we discussed in the previous chapter). John says that this Word, who *was* in the beginning, was Himself "with God" even as He Himself "was God."

What we see in these two clauses is that there is both a *distinction* between the Word and God—He is One who is "with God"—and an *identity* of the Word and God—He "was God." He is *both* distinct, *and* He is identical. We begin to see here how it is that the church had to respond to such passages by affirming the Three-in-One character of God. Since there can only be one God, this One who Himself is God, yet is in some way(s) distinct from God, must Himself be the one God, though He is also the Word (and not the Father or the Spirit).

In these opening verses of John, then, we have a clear declaration that there is One who is God and who also is distinct. As the Gospel continues, we find that "the Word became flesh and dwelt among us" (John 1:14). The identity of the Word is now made abundantly clear: This One who is God, while also being distinct, is the One who took on a human nature and who walked on the earth. He is the One who Himself is "at the Father's side" even as He is "the only God." He alone has "seen God" and thus has come to "make Him known" (1:18).

As these initial verses show, and as the rest of this Gospel (and of Scripture!) will make clear, there is no hint here that this Word ever ceased to be who He is. He did not take on flesh *by* giving up His deity. Such a thing is impossible (cf. 2 Tim 2:13)! Rather, as the One who is God and who also is distinct, He came to reveal God to us, and to save His people from their sins (Matt 1:21). He did not become another person; neither did He become a blend of God and man (whatever that might mean), but He remained "God the Word" even as He was "the Lord Jesus Christ." This is what Chalcedon expresses so clearly. There is a union in the Person because "the Word became flesh." He did not take to Himself another *man*, but He took on "flesh" (i.e., a human nature) in order, as man, to dwell among us.

The other passage that deserves mention in our discussion of the incarnation is Philippians 2:5-7 (especially vv. 6-7):

> Have this mind among yourselves, which is yours in
> Christ Jesus, who, though he was in the form of God, did
> not count equality with God a thing to be grasped, but
> emptied himself, by taking the form of a servant, being
> born in the likeness of men.

We can only scratch the surface of this magnificent passage here.

Two important points from Paul's discussion here must be remembered. First, as Paul is exhorting the church to be selfless, he uses the supreme example of selflessness, which is the incarnation of Christ. Secondly, tucked in the middle of this encouragement to be "other-centered" is some of the deepest and richest theology in all of Scripture.

There are some difficult interpretive themes in this passage, which we must overlook for the sake of simplicity. Those difficulties, however, do nothing to mute the majesty of Christ as explained in this text.

As Paul is thinking of the incarnation, he wants us to see that its initiation is from the One who was "in the form of God." Like other words in this short section, here Paul uses a word (*morphē*, "form"), that is used nowhere else in Scripture. In attempting to understand "one-time" words like this, then, the context in which they're used becomes all-important.

What is clear in the first phrase, "form of God," is that it is meant to be interpreted by the next and similar phrase that refers to Christ: "equality with God." "Form of God," therefore, means the same thing as—because it is interpreted by—the phrase "equality with God." So, the first thing Scripture affirms here is that "Christ Jesus" is one who is equal to God, which can only mean He Himself is God. No one who is less than God could be described in terms of "equality with God."

The intent of Paul's discussion here of the incarnation is his encouragement that the church have the mind of Christ. Scripture tells us here that this One who was equal to God "did not count equality with God as a thing to be grasped." Again, the language here can be difficult to interpret. Aside from those difficulties, Paul clearly affirms here that Christ has a particular status—a status that only *He* could have; He is fully God. He is God's equal. But, says Paul, even *as* God, He did not hold so tightly to His rightful status as to ignore and shun the plight of others. In other words, the point Paul is making is *not* that since the Son did not consider equality with God a thing to be grasped, He ceased to be equal to God. That is not even a biblical possibility.

The result of not grasping equality with God was not inequality, but humility. The Son was willing to humble Himself instead of "grasping" all the prerogatives that are rightfully His as God. He agreed to be a humble servant, instead of *only* exercising His rightful status as Lord of all. What did this "humbling" look like? Again, some have thought that the "humbling" included the Son's decision to cease to be fully God. But that is not possible.

Paul describes this humbling by saying that the Son "emptied Himself." This word "emptied" translates the Greek word *ekenōsen*. The reason that word is important is that some have wanted to understand this passage as teaching that, in emptying Himself, Christ actually gave up His deity; He ceased to be God. This is called a "kenotic" theory of Christ, taken from that Greek word, and it denies the biblical, orthodox teaching of who Christ is.

It is impossible for God to cease to be God; He cannot deny Himself. If Christ were to give up His deity, He would not be the Son of God. In other words, we could think of it this way: If Christ were not God, there would be no Trinity; there would be the Father who is God and the Spirit who is God, but no Son (and *how* could there even be a Father without a Son?). This could not at all be what Paul has in mind.

Fortunately, Scripture tells us exactly what is meant when it says Christ "emptied Himself." The next two clauses interpret what "emptying" means. How did the Son empty Himself? Paul explains: "By taking the form of a servant, being born in the likeness of men" (Phil 2:7). John Calvin understands it this way:

> Christ, indeed, could not divest himself of Godhead; but he kept it concealed for a time, that it might not be seen, under the weakness of the flesh. Hence he laid aside his glory in the view of men, *not by lessening it, but by concealing it*.[8]

---

8. John Calvin, *Commentaries on the Epistles of Paul the Apostle to the Philippians, Colossians, and Thessalonians*, trans. John Pringle (Edinburgh: Calvin Translation Society, 1851), 56–57; my emphasis.

The Son could not cease to be fully God, but He could cover, or veil, His deity in a way that would exhibit His humanity. That is what He did in the incarnation. So, His emptying was not by virtue of *subtracting* something from Himself. Instead, His emptying, as Paul characterizes it, was by *addition*. Christ "took the form of a servant"; He added to Himself an entire human nature, while remaining fully God. There is no other way that He could come to Earth, live an obedient life, and die an obedient death, except by this humbling. This is the wonder and majesty of the gospel! *God Himself* has come. He has come, not only to be with us, but He has come as *one of us*. He is not simply with us when we suffer; *He himself* suffered in our place.

Through all of this—His conception, birth, life, death, resurrection, and ascension—at no time did Christ cease to be fully God as the Son of God. It is *God Himself*, therefore, who has accomplished all that was needed for our salvation. That accomplishment came at a great price—the ultimate price. And the price was paid *to God, by God*. No wonder, then, that no other religion in the history of the world has conceived of such a thing. It is, in a very real sense, beyond imagining. It is utterly mysterious, even while it is the bedrock and primary Christian truth that every true Christian confesses.

BIBLICAL DISTINCTIONS

In our thinking about the incarnation, there remains a biblical distinction that is crucial to recognize, as it informs the way we must think about all of these biblical mysteries. Because Scripture urges us to affirm two distinct natures in Christ, it is tempting to think that two natures combined to "produce" or "create" one Person, Jesus Christ. If we think this way, it is a very short step to affirming that Jesus Christ is Himself a completely new Person. But we cannot think this way—and we can *avoid* thinking this way if we recognize the centrality of the Person in the incarnation, rather than focusing only on the two "natures."

When we speak of two natures in Christ, we are not to think of the natures as equal "partners" that come together to compose the Person. Instead, we have to make an important distinction. We are to see the nature of *deity* as intrinsic and essential to the Person. In other words, Christ, as the Son of God, has always been, and cannot but be, fully

God. Because He is the Son, He is God, whether or not He takes on a human nature. Of course, He decided He would humble Himself and become man, but He did not have to do that. He did it as an act of free and unmerited grace and favor to man. But His deity is essential to who He is as the Son of God.

But His human nature, unlike His divine nature, is *freely* taken by Him. He voluntarily decided to assume that nature so that we might be redeemed. The nature taken is not like His essential nature as God. It is taken at a point in history—"when the fullness of time had come" (Gal 4:4). His human nature, therefore, has a beginning point (though, once taken, it is taken for eternity). It is not, in that way, essential to who He is *as Son*.

There are significant and important differences, then, between the two natures in Christ. What is central in the incarnation is not the natures, but the *Person*. It is the Person of the Son, even while He remained fully and completely the Son of God, who took to Himself a human nature in order to accomplish the salvation that we could not accomplish. The divine "nature" of the Son of God, therefore, is essential to who He is; the "nature" of man is who He is only because He freely decided He would take it.

This makes the truth and reality of the gospel all the more majestic and mysterious. Why would this One, who needed nothing, who had perfect fellowship with the Father and the Spirit, submit Himself to utter humiliation, even to the point of being forsaken by His Father? The best answer we have from Scripture is simply because He loved us and so determined to do what we were unable to do—to break the chains of our sin in order that we might cheerfully serve and worship Him for eternity.

In line with our previous discussion about the Trinity, we should recognize here that this is another instance when God, this time in the Person of the Son, assumes certain characteristics—in the incarnation, a human nature—in order to relate Himself to His creation and to us. This is similar (but *not* identical) to what we saw in our distinction between the ontological and the economic Trinity, and it is what we see now in the Son. Ever since creation, God has been intent on relating Himself to that which He has made, and He has done that in every case *not* by ceasing to be who He is as God, but by expressing who He is in characteristics that ensure such a relationship could take place.

In this regard, it is important to see that, though the incarnation was a unique event, nevertheless the Son of God had been assuming, *temporarily*, certain characteristics and qualities ever since creation, in order to relate to us. Herman Bavinck puts it this way:

> This relation between Father and Son, though most clearly manifest during Christ's sojourn on earth, *was not first initiated at the time of the incarnation*, for the incarnation itself is already included in the execution of the work assigned to the Son, but occurs in eternity and therefore also existed already during the time of the Old Testament. Scripture also clearly attests this fact when it attributes the leadership of Israel to the Angel of Yahweh (Exod. 3:2f.; 13:21; 14:19; 23:20–23; 32:34; 33:2; Num. 20:16; Isa. 63:8–9), and sees Christ also functioning officially already in the days of the Old Testament (John 8:56; 1 Cor. 10:4, 9; 1 Pet. 1:11; 3:19). For there is but one mediator between God and [man] (John 14:6; Acts 4:12; 1 Tim. 2:5), who is the same yesterday and today and forever (Heb. 13:8), who was chosen as Mediator from eternity (Isa. 42:1; 43:10; Matt. 12:18; Luke 24:26; Acts 2:23; 4:28; 1 Pet. 1:20; Rev. 13:8), and as Logos existed from eternity as well (John 1:1, 3; 8:58; Rom. 8:3; 2 Cor. 8:9; Gal. 4:4; Phil. 2:6; etc.).[9]

The Son of God had been appearing to the saints throughout redemptive history. He did that by *temporarily* taking on various qualities and characteristics in order to be with His people, to speak to Moses and the prophets, etc. But he never *permanently* took on a human nature until the point of His conception.

This helps us recognize both the continuities and the discontinuities of the incarnation throughout redemptive history. One of the continuities is in the truth that the Son had been condescending— really and truly, but temporarily and partially, in types and shadows— all throughout covenant history. One of the discontinuities is that the

---

9. Herman Bavinck, *Reformed Dogmatics: Sin and Salvation in Christ*, ed. John Bolt, trans. John Vriend, Vol. 3 (Grand Rapids: Baker Academic, 2006), 214; my emphasis.

incarnation was a *complete* and *perpetual* addition of a human nature to the Son. It was the climax to which the rest of covenant history had been pointing all along.

So now we begin to see the "model of majestic mystery" as it is given to us in Scripture; *it is God's covenantal condescension.* As we saw with the Trinity, now also with the incarnation. In order to relate Himself to His creation, the Persons of the Godhead express God's character in certain characteristics and qualities of that relationship, without in any way impinging on the full and comprehensive deity that is their essence, as they freely condescend to be with us. This model of majestic mystery is almost ineffable in its glory, but that is exactly what we would expect from One who is so infinitely glorious! Without this covenantal condescension, we would know nothing of the mysteries of God and His character. Because of it, we are able to worship Him for who He is.

BIBLICAL DOXOLOGY

As the Apostle John is transported to the throne room of heaven in Revelation 4, we see there, through John's words, "the Lord God Almighty" (4:8) who sits on the throne and to whom belongs all "glory and honor and power" (4:11).

Then, in chapter 5, there is a scroll, fully sealed. Someone is needed who can break the seals of this comprehensive scroll and execute its entire contents. Initially, no one is found in the whole universe who is worthy to carry out the plan of God. But then John is directed to look and see "the Lion of the tribe of Judah," who alone has conquered and who can, therefore, break open the scroll and carry out its plan (5:5). John turns to look at this Lion, and he sees "a Lamb standing, as though it had been slain" (5:6). This Lamb, who is the Lion, takes the scroll from the right hand of the One who sits on the throne, and immediately the entire throne room of heaven breaks out in worship to this Lamb.

John pictures for us in this chapter the coronation of the Lamb of God. It is the fulfillment of Psalm 110:1 (see also Luke 20:45; Acts 2:34–35; Heb 1:13; 10:13):

> The LORD says to my Lord:
>   "Sit at my right hand,
>   until I make your enemies your footstool."

The picture of this fulfillment, and of Christ's redemptive ministry, is given to us in Revelation 5. There we see the Messiah ascended, having perfectly accomplished all that the Father gave Him to do. Because He was humiliated, God has now highly exalted Him and given Him a "name that is above every name" (Phil 2:9), so that He is now both Lord and Christ (see Acts 2:34–36).

The One who is "the Lord God Almighty" in Revelation 4 has now given the name "Lord," finally and consummately, to His Son, who has perfectly fulfilled His mission and task. The One who is, and always has been, Lord has now been *exalted* as Lord; the One who is the only begotten Son is now declared to be the Son of God by virtue of His resurrection (Rom 1:4). So all of heaven turns its gaze on this Lion/Lamb, and falls down and worships Him.

The lesson of the incarnation is that only the Triune God could save us from ourselves. Man brought about his own ruin and the ruin of all of creation. This ruin was so deep and devastating that there was no way for human beings to solve the problem they had created; only God could do that. He had to do that, not by a simple wave of the hand or by a mere declaration. He had to do it by becoming one of us, even while He remained who He is.

We should never minimize the sufferings and trials of Jesus Christ. We should never think to ourselves, "Well, it's easy enough to suffer and die when you're God; who you *really* are remains unaffected. It's only the humanity that suffers." This would be to think wrongly about the reality of what the Son of God did. He really did become man. His sufferings and trials were just as real and painful and trying as are ours. He took His human nature for just that purpose.

But He conquered. He overcame it all. He resisted temptation and obeyed. He alone perfectly pleased His heavenly Father. So the One who was forsaken at the cross was exalted to the very throne of God and was declared to be, by virtue of His perfect obedience, the Lord of redemption who would bring His own to Himself—the Son of God, who would bring many sons to glory (Heb 2:10). This is the model of majestic mystery that we see in the incarnation. It is the climax of covenantal condescension.

The *Messiah*, by George Frideric Handel, is the most popular oratorio in history. It was composed by Handel in a little over three weeks in order to raise money for a few charities in Dublin, Ireland. Handel's librettist, Charles Jennens, was charged with putting words to Handel's music. With its initial performance in 1742, it was an instant success and judged at the time by one newspaper in Dublin to be the finest composition of words and music ever written. A year later, in London, a controversy arose when the oratorio was performed in a theater rather than a church. The *Messiah*, some thought, was meant to be an "act of religion" and was not fit simply for the amusement of the masses.

For many who know the *Messiah*, it is difficult to hear or read some passages in Scripture without immediately pairing them with Handel's music:

> For unto us a child is born, unto us a son is given: and the government shall be upon his shoulder: and his name shall be called Wonderful, Counsellor, The mighty God, The everlasting Father, The Prince of Peace (Isa 9:6 KJV)!

Perhaps the most famous segment of the *Messiah* (part 2, scene 7) is the "Hallelujah" chorus. The scene is titled "God's Ultimate Victory," and it combines passages from Revelation 19:6; 11:15; and 19:16. Tradition tells us that, at the oratorio's London debut in 1743, as soon as the chorus began to sing "hallelujah," King George II stood up and remained standing until the chorus was finished. The rest of the audience stood with him, beginning a tradition that continues to this day.

Since its initial performance, Handel's *Messiah* has been performed for the masses countless times—in churches, concert halls, and theaters. Millions of people, whether they believe the words or not, have risen to their feet for the "Hallelujah" chorus. Handel could not have imagined the breadth of its impact.

The *Messiah* is, indeed, an "act of religion." It is a two-hour doxology. Because of Charles Jennens' work, it is filled with the praise of Christ. Due to its sweeping and obvious outline of redemptive history, it would be natural to think that the "Hallelujah" chorus is the finale of the oratorio, especially given the title that Jennens gave that scene and the Scripture passages used in it.[10] But the "Hallelujah" chorus is

---

10. Historical information on the *Messiah* is summarized from James M. Keller, *Handel's* Messiah: *Notes on the Program* (New York: New York Philharmonic, December 2014), program.

only the end of part 2. The third and final part is titled by Jennens, "An Anthem of Thanksgiving for the Defeat of Death." Part 3 ends with scene 4, "The Acclamation of the Messiah." In that final scene, Jennens takes the words of Revelation 5:12–13 as his concluding chorus:

> Worthy is the Lamb that was slain to receive power, and riches, and wisdom, and strength, and honour, and glory, and blessing. And every creature which is in heaven, and on the earth, and under the earth, and such as are in the sea, and all that are in them, heard I saying, Blessing, and honour, and glory, and power, be unto him that sitteth upon the throne, and unto the Lamb for ever and ever (Rev 5:12–13 KJV).

It is fitting that an oratorio titled *Messiah* should end not with the "Hallelujah" chorus, but with these verses. The "Hallelujah" chorus is prophetic; it points to the praise of the Lamb in Revelation 5. That praise speaks, quite literally, of the crowning achievement of the Messiah, Jesus Christ. Handel's *Messiah* points the chorus of hallelujahs to the coronation of the Lamb in Revelation 5.

The only proper response to this glorious mystery of the Son's condescension, climactically in the flesh, is doxology. We worship the Son not only because He, with the Father and the Spirit, is God and therefore He fully deserves all our worship and praise, but also because He has finished what the Father gave Him to do—and He completed it not for His own sake, but for us, in order that our praise would redound to Him for eternity. Meditate on this model of majestic mystery that just is the incarnation, and you will never be the same. Worthy is the Lamb!

> 'Tis mystery all: th'Immortal dies:
> *Who can explore His strange design?*
> *In vain the firstborn seraph tries*
> *To sound the depths of love divine.*
> *'Tis mercy all! Let earth adore,*
> *Let angel minds inquire no more.*
> *Amazing love! How can it be,*
> *That Thou, my God, shouldst die for me?*
>
> —Charles Wesley, "And Can It Be That I Should Gain"

CHAPTER 5

The Majesty of the Mystery of God's Relationship to His People

Now, a covenant between God and man is a thing great and marvellous, whether we consider the nature of it or the ends of it. ... How infinite, how unspeakable must needs the grace and condescension of God in this matter be! For what is poor miserable man, that God should set his heart upon him—that he should, as it were, give bounds to his sovereignty over him, and enter into terms of agreement with him?

—John Owen

Exposition on Psalm 130

B y now, we should have an initial grasp of the wonderful mystery that is embedded in our Christian faith and practice. As the "lifeblood" of our walk with God, the mystery of God's character and ways should inform our thinking and our living at every step. To acknowledge this permeation of Christian mystery is to frame our Christian experience with the proper picture. It is, first of all, the proper picture of God. But now we will see that, increasing the mystery, this proper picture of God—as triune, as incarnate in the Son—also includes *us*! How can this be?

In previous chapters, we have been thinking, almost exclusively, about the mysteries that surround God and His character. We have witnessed the wonder of His majestic being; we have pulled back the curtain and seen that He is not simply a blank or ineffable one, but that He is, from eternity, One-in-Three; we have shone the light of revelation on the Light of the World Himself, who, while remaining God, took on a human nature in order to solve the problem of sin.

To ponder these mysteries is to enhance and increase our worship of this incomprehensible, Triune God. As a matter of fact, the more we consider these inexhaustible truths, the more they seem to escape our intellectual grasp. As we turn these truths over and over in our minds—that God is eternal and infinite, that He is Three who are One, that the Son of God is fully God and fully man—they seem to become more and more elusive to us. They slip from our mind's eye even as we set our sights on them. The closer we hold them, the more transcendent they become. This is how it is meant to be; it is the proper and praiseworthy paradox of mystery.

BIBLICAL DEVELOPMENT

We now turn to consider this incomprehensible and mysterious Triune God and the unimaginable wonder of His relationship with us. Here we explore mystery on mystery. For us, it is a veiled truth how

God can be who He is; we cannot see through it. How He relates to us enhances and deepens the mystery of it all, and that should increase our devotion and praise to Him.

In his *Institutes of the Christian Religion*, a masterful work written to increase the piety and holiness of each and every Christian, John Calvin begins this way:

> Our wisdom, in so far as it ought to be deemed true and solid wisdom, consists almost entirely of two parts: the knowledge of God and of ourselves.[1]

We have concentrated so far almost exclusively on the first part of "our wisdom"—i.e., the knowledge of God. In this chapter, with the first part now in view, we can begin to open up the second part of wisdom, which is the true knowledge of God's relationship *to us*. As we do, we also begin to see the glorious mystery of what it means that this personal Triune God determined to relate Himself to His creation, and to us, for eternity.

The fact that God has established a relationship with creation in general, and with man in particular, may not strike most of us as mysterious at all. "I open my Bible," someone might say, "and I read that God created all things in the beginning and began a relationship with Adam and Eve. What's so mysterious about that?" This is, in one sense, a natural way to think. The God who made everything is certainly capable of relating Himself to what He has made. God is capable of doing anything He wants to do! Surely, since creation is *His*, it imposes no boundary on who He is or on what He can do.

However, when we begin to think about God's character *as God*, puzzles might begin to appear. If we think about who God is, what kind of characteristics He must have in order to be God, we can begin to see the dilemma. The *Westminster Confession of Faith* has a clear and concise description of God's character.[2] Chapter two of the confession begins this way:

---

1. John Calvin and Henry Beveridge, *Institutes of the Christian Religion*, Vol. 1 (Edinburgh: The Calvin Translation Society, 1845), 47.
2. Excerpts from the *Westminster Confession of Faith* appear in the Appendix. This confession, together with the Larger and Shorter Catechisms, was produced over a five-year period (1643–1648). A number of pastors and theologians were called

> There is but one only, living, and true God, who is infinite
> in being and perfection, a most pure spirit, invisible,
> without body, parts, or passions; immutable, immense,
> eternal, incomprehensible, almighty, most wise, most
> holy, most free, most absolute ...

This statement is a wonderful summary of God's character with which any orthodox Christian should agree. This is the proper place to begin to think about God because it highlights His character as God. But we miss the majesty of mystery if we simply affirm this description of God without thinking, also, in terms of God's relationship to us. As a matter of fact, it is just this exalted character of God that establishes His relationship to us.

In the interest of time, let's consider just three of the characteristics mentioned by the confession. When the confession says that God is "a most pure spirit, invisible, without body, parts, or passions," it is pointing us to God's independence. He is Spirit and has no parts. He cannot be limited in any way; unlike us, there are no spatial boundaries to His character, so that we could point to a place and say, "There is God."

The confession also affirms that God is eternal, which means there is no temporal succession on which He depends in order to be who He is. Again, unlike us, God is not subject to the passing of moments; He had no beginning, and He has no end. His life is not a life consisting of a temporal duration.

Along with that, we recognize God to be immutable (including as well His impassability—i.e., "without passions"). He does not, because He cannot, undergo change in Himself. How could He change? He could not change into something greater, because, by definition, nothing is greater than Him. He could not change into something less because He would then cease to be God, which is impossible (2 Tim 2:13). So, when we affirm that God is God, we are affirming that all of those characteristics that distinguish Him as God *must always* characterize Him. There is no possibility that God will become less

---

by order of the English Parliament to provide advice to the Protestant churches on matters of theology, worship, and Christian conduct. For further study on this confession, see B.B. Warfield, *The Westminster Assembly and Its Work* (New York: Oxford University Press, 1931).

than God by being subject, in His essential nature, to spatial limits or to time, or that He will change into something or someone else.

The reason we affirm these characteristics of God is that they are embedded in God's own revelation of Himself. We do not affirm these things based on some rational or purely deductive principle or idea. Any rational or deductive principle could only move within the limitations of creation, thus concluding for a finite god. We have no experience of infinity or of eternity, so there is no way to affirm something of infinity or eternity unless it is given to us by One who understands, and who is, such things.

As we have seen, one of the primary ways that God's revelation points us to His character is by way of the names that God gives Himself in Scripture. We have seen as well that the clearest pronouncement of God's name, in the Old Testament, is the name "Yahweh." This truth bears repeating because it unfortunately has become neglected in many discussions about God's character. There is a mountain of material that can be pursued about this name of God, but we need to remember a couple of things here as we think about God's character in relation to creation:

1. The name "Yahweh," used over 5,000 times in the Old Testament, is taken from God's own interpretation of His character. In Exodus 3, when Moses asks God to tell him His name (Exod 3:13), he is asking specifically about God's *character*. Unlike today, names in Scripture were often given to designate a person's character. This is why God changes the names of significant people in Scripture as He calls them to particular tasks in redemptive history (cf. Gen 17:5, 15; 32:28; John 1:42; Acts 13:9). So Moses isn't simply asking what he should call God; he is asking about the character of the One who is about to confront Pharaoh.

As we have seen, God's answer to Moses was that His name is "I AM WHO I AM" (Exod 3:14). We can summarize what God intends by this name with a couple of helpful comments. The Old Testament commentators Keil and Delitzsch note (and this is a key point):

> The repetition of the verb in the same form [i.e., "I am"], and connected only by the relative [i.e., "Who"], signifies that the being or act of the subject expressed in the verb *is determined only by the subject itself.*" ... So far then as the

words ["I AM WHO I AM"] are condensed into a proper name in [Yahweh] ... God, therefore, "is He who is," inasmuch as in His being ... He is the self-determining one.[3]

In his commentary on Exodus 3:14, and with respect to the revelation of God's name, Calvin notes:

Therefore ... contrary to grammatical usage, he used the same verb in the first person as a substantive, annexing it to a verb in the third person; that our minds may be filled with admiration *as often as his incomprehensible essence is mentioned*.[4]

The name that God gives to Himself, as Keil and Delitzsch note, means that He is utterly and completely independent and self-defined. He is in need of nothing else in order to be God. Calvin recognizes that the grammar of the name is meant to express God's incomprehensibility, in order to fill us with admiration. Worship is meant to flow from the mystery of God's self-referential character, which is given to us in Scripture "as often as his incomprehensible essence is mentioned."

2. As we have seen, the meaning of the name that God gave to Moses can be summed up as "self-existence" or absolute "independence." The technical term for God's independence is His "aseity." It comes from the Latin *a se* ("of Himself") and means that God depends on *nothing* in order to be who He is. He does not depend on space in order to be somewhere, or on time in order to be, or on a process in order to become. God, simply, is who He is. He is utterly and completely *self*-dependent. He exists of Himself, lives of Himself, defines Himself, and exhaustively knows Himself, without reference to anything outside of Himself. He alone *is who He is*.

We need to be reminded of these two crucial aspects of God's character as we begin, in this chapter, to consider the mystery of this "I AM" in relation to us. We need to think about God and these independent

---

3. C. F. Keil and F. Delitzsch, *Commentary on the Old Testament in Ten Volumes: The Pentateuch*, trans. James Martin, Vol. 1 (Grand Rapids: Eerdmans, 1980), 74–75; my emphasis.

4. John Calvin, *Commentaries on the Four Last Books of Moses Arranged in the Form of a Harmony*, trans. and ed. Charles William Bingham (Edinburgh: Calvin Translation Society, 1852), 1:73; my emphasis.

characteristics in light of what Scripture teaches us about our relationship to Him.

The minute we open our Bibles, we see immediately that the One who is "I AM WHO I AM" begins to create. He speaks, and things that were nonexistent begin to exist. We also see that God not only speaks *about* what He has created (e.g., Gen 1:5, 8), but, on the sixth day, He speaks *to* what He has made—to man (male and female), whom He has made *in His image* (Gen 1:28)!

God begins a relationship with those made in His image. He gives them commands and thus makes them responsible in their obedience, or disobedience, to those commands. In the context of God's sovereign rule over them, it is up to them to keep, or break, those commands, and that responsibility brings consequences that will follow their decisions.

The terms and conditions of this "beginning" relationship would change because of Adam's decision to sin. Prior to sin, Adam and Eve were responsible to *maintain* their created status of fellowship with God by *obeying* what God had commanded (Gen 2:9, 16–17). After Adam and Eve sinned, the punishment of death was set in place. But God graciously intervened to change the corrupt nature of those born after Adam so that fellowship with God might be restored. So, before the fall into sin, obedience qualified the relationship between God and man. After the fall, there had to be an intervention of God's saving grace if man was going to be in fellowship with God again.

But, with each and every individual, from the first man to the last one in history, there is, *even into eternity*, a relationship to God. For those who come to Christ in faith, that relationship is characterized by God's grace. For those who continue to rebel against God, that relationship is characterized by His wrath. The relationship of grace continues in the new heaven and the new earth; the relationship of wrath continues in hell. But there is always, forevermore, a relationship.

This relationship of the Triune God to man characterizes the entirety of God's revelation, from beginning to end. It may seem to some, therefore, that we are creating problems that don't exist if we lay out the tensions involved in this relationship.

But questions about God's relationship to us come naturally from Scripture. How can One who is eternal speak to Adam and Eve at a particular *time*? How can One who is infinite be in the garden? Not only so, but one cannot read the account of the fall into sin in Genesis 3, for example, without asking questions such as, "Did the fall into sin take God by surprise? Why did God create if He knew that things would turn out so poorly? Was God in control of Adam's decision to sin, or did He give up His control?"

All of these questions and many others highlight the tensions that exist in our thinking between God's *a se* character and His relationship to us. As we rightly confess that God is infinite, eternal, impassable, and unchangeable, we also see God meeting with, talking to, and interacting with, the people that He has made.

For example, in Genesis 18:1-3, the LORD meets with Abraham at Mamre; in Genesis 32:30, Jacob claims to have seen God; in Exodus 3:2-4:17, the LORD appears to Moses in a burning bush; in Deuteronomy 31:14-23, the LORD appears to Moses and Joshua; in Joshua 5:13-15, Joshua meets, and worships, the Divine Warrior, God Himself. And on and on it goes throughout redemptive history. We see numerous passages in Scripture that tell us that the Lord has come down to meet with His people (e.g., Gen 11:5; Exod 3:8; 34:5; Num 11:1-3; 12:5, etc.).

All of these passages, virtually every text on every page of Scripture, assume that the Lord is with His creation, and interacting with His people. It is natural, therefore, that we would begin to ask how it can be that the One who is infinite, eternal, and unchangeable, can be *in* Mamre, or *seen by* Jacob, or *come down*. Wouldn't the Lord's defined presence in a certain place contradict His infinity? Wouldn't Jacob seeing the Lord contradict His invisibility? Wouldn't the Lord coming down contradict His immutability? Wouldn't His impassability contradict His anger?

All of these examples of God being with His people reach their climax in the New Testament. Given what we saw in the previous chapter, we can begin to see how best to think of God's presence with His people throughout history. As we saw in the incarnation, God, in the person of the Son, "comes down" to us by taking to Himself a human nature, even while He always remains who He is as God.

Could it be, therefore, that what we have in other "appearances" of God in history—especially when those appearances include human characteristics—are temporary but obvious signs pointing to what God will do permanently in Christ?

Not only *could* this be, but it *is* what God is teaching us throughout His revelation to us. When we read our Bibles and see there that God has "come down" to relate to His creation, to the world, to His people, we are meant to see also that He is pointing us, in each and every case, to Christ Himself, who is the climactic example of "God with us"—Emmanuel.

As a matter of fact, the New Testament tells us, we will remember, to read the Old Testament in exactly that way. As we saw in the previous chapter, the New Testament is full of references from the Old Testament that the New Testament attributes to Christ.

So, the biblical development of God's relationship with creation and with His people includes those *temporary* and *signal* appearances of (the Son of) God throughout the Old Testament, all of which find their *permanent* resting place in the incarnation. Or, we could say, as the Son came down temporarily throughout the Old Testament (pointing *to* His climactic redemptive work), He came down permanently in His incarnation (to *accomplish* His redemptive work) and into eternity.

Throughout God's revelation, we see God—focused in the Person of the Son—relating Himself to creation generally and to His people more specifically. Until the incarnation, the characteristics that the Son would take on were temporary, pointing to the greater, redemptive moment of the incarnation. But they are all examples of God coming down to reveal and to redeem.

In his commentary on John 1:3, John Calvin put it this way:

> Now the design of the Evangelist is, as I have already said, to show that *no sooner was the world created than the Speech of God* [i.e., "the Word"] *came forth into external operation*; for having formerly been incomprehensible in his essence, he then became publicly known by the effect of his power.[5]

In other words, from the point of creation onward, the Word came forth, revealing God and relating to what He had made and to those

---

5. John Calvin, *Commentary on the Gospel according to John*, trans. William Pringle (Edinburgh: Calvin Translation Society), 1:31; my emphasis.

creatures made in His image. That revelation and relating was not redemptive before the fall into sin but was, nevertheless, covenant condescension. However God related to Adam and Eve before the fall (and we have little information about that), he condescended to relate to them. Thus, the Triune God becomes "publicly known" by coming down to, in, and with His creation. All of Scripture, therefore, is pointing us to God's relationship to creation, which has its focus in and through the Son. In the words of John Owen:

> After the fall there is nothing spoken of God in the Old Testament, nothing of his institutions, nothing of the way and manner of dealing with the church, but what hath respect unto the future incarnation of Christ. And it had been absurd to bring in God under perpetual anthropopathies, as grieving, repenting, being angry, well pleased, and the like, were it not but that the divine person intended was to take on him the nature wherein such affections do dwell.[6]

BIBLICAL DOCTRINE

Now that we have some of the biblical data in place, we will seek to understand the theological terms and concepts that help us better to recognize what God has done by, in, and through His creative activity.

As we have seen, God is "a most pure spirit, invisible." We have asked how it can be that One who is a spirit and invisible can *walk* with Adam and Eve in the Garden (Gen 3:8–10) and *appear* to Abraham (Gen 18:1), Moses (Exod 3:1–4:17; 6:2–3), Joshua (Joshua 5:13–15), etc.—especially when we recognize that God has no body and no parts? How can One who is a spirit, with no body, *walk* and *appear*?

God is also infinite, eternal, and immutable. As we read our Bibles, the question will arise as to how One who is not constrained by space or subject to its limitations can *be in the garden* with Adam and Eve, or *by the oaks of Mamre* with Abraham, or *on Mount Horeb* with Moses?

---

6. John Owen, *The Works of John Owen*, ed. William H. Goold (Edinburgh: T&T Clark, 1862), 1:350; my emphasis. Thanks to Mark Jones for bringing this quote to my attention.

Don't these appearances all require that God be located at a particular place, instead of being infinite? It is certainly the case that some have concluded that God cannot be infinite, eternal, or unchangeable. Instead, He simply becomes "one of us." Others have argued that these "appearances" are simply "activities" of God that do not require Him to be located in any place or any time.

But these are not options available to us as we read Scripture, any more than it is an option to change God's *name*! The *a se* characteristics of God are tied inextricably to the name He gives Himself; that alone is reason enough for us always to affirm those characteristics. Not only so, but if we reduce our reading of Scripture simply to "activities" that God accomplishes, then we have much difficulty believing that God is, really and truly, *with* us.

So if God is eternal, and thus not subject to temporal succession, how can He be with Adam and Eve, Abraham, Moses, Joshua, and a host of others at a particular time of the day, month, and year in history?

If God is immutable, how can He *walk* in the garden, *speak* different words to different people, all the while never changing? Doesn't His walking imply a change of location, and His speaking a change of utterances?

We also affirm, with the confession, that God is "without passions." How, then, can He be a jealous God (for example, in Exod 20:5), or angry with sin (for example, Exod 4:14; Num 11:10; Deut 6:15; Josh 7:1; 2 Sam 6:7; Psa 106:40; Isa 5:25), or loving to His people, even while hating those who are not His own (for example, Mal 1:3; Rom 9:13). How can these things be? Is Scripture giving us two different gods here? Is there a god who is infinite and a god who is located in different places in creation, or a god who is without passions and another god that loves, has mercy and compassion, hates and gets angry?

There is an abundance of literature that deals with these issues, much of which can be pursued with great profit. However, even some of the best theologians in the history of the church misstep when pressed with questions like the ones above. Unfortunately, examples are almost too numerous to list. But we'll give a few examples as representative and typical of how many great theological thinkers have tried to address the questions above.

Perhaps the greatest of all church fathers, Augustine (AD 354–430), in contemplating the character of God as eternal and infinite in light of Scripture's affirmation of God's jealousy and "regret," said this:

> [Scripture] has borrowed many things from the spiritual creature, whereby to signify *that which indeed is not so*, but must needs so be said: as, for instance, "I the Lord thy God am a jealous God;" [Exod 20:5; cf. Exod 34:14; Deut 4:24; 5:9; 6:15; Josh 24:19; Ezra 36:6; Nah 1:2] and, "It repenteth me that I have made man" [Gen 6:7].[7]

We need to pause over Augustine's words here and notice what he says. He says that Scripture borrows aspects from the creature in order to signify something about God. But he also says that what Scripture is signifying to us "indeed is not so." In other words, when Scripture ascribes something "creaturely" to God, it is not telling us what God is like; it is saying something that is not the case.

Stephen Charnock (1628–1680), a brilliant Puritan theologian, thinks of God's relationship to creation this way:

> God is not changed, when of loving to any creatures he becomes angry with them, or of angry he becomes appeased. The change in these cases is in the creatures; according to the alteration in the creature, it stands in a various relation to God.[8]

According to Charnock, when Scripture says, for example, that we "were by nature children of wrath" but that we became children of grace (cf. Eph 2:1–10), we should not think that God's disposition toward us has changed at all. How could it, if God is eternal and immutable? Instead, the change is only in *us*. Perhaps we simply *believe* that we were under wrath, and then we begin to believe that we are under grace.

---

7. Augustine, *On the Trinity*, trans. Rev. Arthur West Haddon (New York: Christian Literature Publishing Co., 1887), I.1.2; my emphasis.

8. Stephen Charnock, *The Existence and Attributes of God*, 2 vols. (Grand Rapids: Baker, 1979), 1:345.

The greatest Dutch systematic theologian, Herman Bavinck (1854–1921)—whose *Reformed Dogmatics* is without peer, in my opinion—says this about God's will:

> We can almost never tell why God willed one thing rather than another, and are therefore compelled to believe that he could just as well have willed one thing as another. *But in God there is actually no such thing as choice* inasmuch as it always presupposes uncertainty, doubt, and deliberation.[9]

What are we to make of Bavinck's assertion, in light of Scripture? When the Bible tells us that God chose us before the foundation of the world, are we to think that "in God there is actually no such thing as choice"? Is God's choice of us, in fact, *not* a choice? How can we make sense of what Scripture says, given these explanations?

These few examples, and a multitude of others like them, all stem from the same admirable motive. They are expressed this way in order to affirm, as strongly as possible, the fact of God's independent character. That character, we should recognize, must always be affirmed, no matter what else we say concerning God's revelation of Himself.

These authors want, rightly, to ensure that no one thinks that God is anything less than infinite, eternal, immutable, without body, parts, or passions, etc. They recognize, perhaps, the tendency of so many to try to "bring God down" to the level of creation, making Him little more than a super-man. Their view of God is such that something like jealousy or regret or wrath or choice is beneath Him. Surely One who is the "I AM," who is complete in Himself, who is in need of nothing, who knows and plans the end from the beginning, would never be caught in a situation where He becomes jealous or is angry because of something that happens in creation. This would mean that God is nothing but a fellow actor, even a *reactor*, on the stage of creation, rather than the infinite, eternal, immutable sovereign Creator of all that is.

As admirable as these motives are, however, it is not in keeping with biblical language and emphases to think, speak, or write in such

9. Herman Bavinck, *Reformed Dogmatics*, ed. John Bolt, trans. John Vriend, 4 vols. (Grand Rapids: Baker Academic, 2003–2008), 2:239–40; my emphasis.

ways as these great theologians have done. We have to find a better way to interpret biblical passages dealing with God and His relation to the world. If we say, in order to affirm God's eternity and immutability, that what God says in His word "indeed is not so," as we see above, then we are in danger of undermining the very revelation that tells us of God's eternity and immutability!

If we say that "in God there is no such thing as choice," in spite of the fact that Scripture clearly says, just to use one example, that God chose a people for Himself, then we separate what God says of Himself from who He "really" is. Thus, we would conclude that God's own revelation, in accommodating itself to our capacity, in fact doesn't tell us who God "really" is, only what we should believe about Him, whether true or not.

These interpretations of the character of God, though prominent and prolific in some of the Christian tradition, in the end lack biblical support. By that, I mean that they provide no satisfactory way of affirming what the Bible *clearly* teaches about God. As a matter of fact, the quotes above encourage us to contradict what Scripture, in fact, says. Theology simply cannot be accomplished this way. Fortunately, there is a better way to think theologically about God and about God's revelation of Himself. It finds its roots in God's covenant and in the way the covenant is initially defined. The *Westminster Confession of Faith*, chapter 7, is entitled, "Of God's Covenant with Man." The bulk of the chapter helpfully sets out the nature of the "Covenant of Works" that God made with Adam and Eve and the "Covenant of Grace" that God made with His people after the entrance of sin.

But the first section of this chapter helps us to see how best to think of God's covenant more generally:

> The distance between God and the creature is so great, that although reasonable creatures do owe obedience unto him as their Creator, yet they could never have any fruition of him as their blessedness and reward, but by some voluntary condescension on God's part, which he hath been pleased to express by way of covenant.

This first section of chapter 7 should be read as a preamble to the sections that follow. It is affirming that obedience is owed to God but that the terms of obedience can be understood only if God communicates them to us. It also is affirming that the only way we can attain or maintain a right relationship to God (i.e., "fruition") is if God determines to bring it about. However, the focus of this section is not on the obedience or fruition that the creature might gain; that focus comes in the other sections. Rather the focus here is on how God established the relationship between Himself and "reasonable creatures" in order that fruition and obedience might be had by us.

There are two clues that point to this "how" focus. The first clue is in the language that the confession uses in this section. It begins by alerting us to a "distance" between God and the creature. We have to pause here and ask what this distance is. It may be so obvious to us that the question might seem pointless.

But if we ask the question, we recognize that the word "distance" cannot mean a spatial distance. Christians have always confessed that God is omnipresent; there is no place where He is not. So, whatever is meant by "distance," it cannot be a spatial distance, because God is always and everywhere present.

The distance that the confession has in view is a relational distance. How can it be that One who is infinite, eternal, unchangeable, and who is not dependent on anything in order to be who He is relates to something that is finite, temporal, and completely dependent? In other words, the first section of chapter 7 of the confession has in view the affirmations of chapter 2, which we saw above. If God is "infinite in being and perfection, a most pure spirit, invisible, without body, parts, or passions; immutable, immense, eternal, incomprehensible," *how* can such a God establish a relationship with "reasonable creatures" who possess none of these characteristics? There is, then, a distance of *being* between God and man. How can the Infinite One relate to finite creatures?

The second clue that points us to the "how" emphasis of this section of the confession is in the Scripture references that are appended to it.[10] The Scripture references that those who wrote this confession included in this first section, in this order, were these: Isaiah 40:13–17;

---

10. The Scripture references were not originally part of the confession, but were placed there by the Westminster Assembly, by order of Parliament, after it was written (1648).

Job 9:32–33; 1 Samuel 2:25; Psalms 113:5–6; 100:2–3; Job 22:2–3; 35:7–8; Luke 17:10; and Acts 17:24–25.

A quick perusal of these verses shows what the writers of the confession had in mind in this section. Notice:

> Who has measured the Spirit of the Lord,
>   or what man shows him his counsel?
> Whom did he consult,
>   and who made him understand?
> Who taught him the path of justice,
>   and taught him knowledge,
>   and showed him the way of understanding?
> Behold, the nations are like a drop from a bucket,
>   and are accounted as the dust on the scales;
>   behold, he takes up the coastlands like fine dust.
> Lebanon would not suffice for fuel,
>   nor are its beasts enough for a burnt offering.
> All the nations are as nothing before him,
>   they are accounted by him as less than nothing and emptiness (Isa 40:13–17).

> For he is not a man, as I am, that I might answer him,
>   that we should come to trial together.
> There is no arbiter between us,
>   who might lay his hand on us both (Job 9:32–33).

> If someone sins against a man, God will mediate for him,
> but if someone sins against the LORD, who can intercede
> for him (1 Sam 2:25)?

> Who is like the LORD our God,
>   who is seated on high,
> who looks far down
>   on the heavens and the earth? (Psa 113:5–6).

> Serve the LORD with gladness!
> Come into his presence with singing!

> Know that the LORD, he is God!
>   It is he who made us, and we are his;
>   we are his people, and the sheep of his pasture (Psa 100:2–3).

Can a man be profitable to God?
  Surely he who is wise is profitable to himself.
Is it any pleasure to the Almighty if you are in the right,
    or is it gain to him if you make your ways blameless?
      (Job 22:2–3).

If you are righteous, what do you give to him?
  Or what does he receive from your hand?
Your wickedness concerns a man like yourself,
  and your righteousness a son of man (Job 35:7–8).

So you also, when you have done all that you were commanded, say, "We are unworthy servants; we have only
done what was our duty" (Luke 17:10).

The God who made the world and everything in it, being
Lord of heaven and earth, does not live in temples made
by man, nor is he served by human hands, as though he
needed anything, since he himself gives to all mankind
life and breath and everything (Acts 17:24–25).

It is important to list these verses in order to see the progression of this section of the confession in light of these biblical texts.
The Scripture passages begin with the distance between God and His
creation in Isaiah 40 and then move from that to the reality that there
can be no "automatic" relationship between One so utterly independent and the rest of creation. Because of God's independence—no one
can measure Him, no one has taught Him understanding or knowledge, the nations are like a drop in a bucket, etc.—there can be no
arbiter between God and man. Because God is seated on high, there is
nothing we can do that would be gain to Him.

In other words, the progression of these appended Scripture passages shows us the problem (for us, not for God) of the distance of God,
which distance constitutes a boundary between the being of God and
the being of creation.

The confession is clear that, because God is so utterly independent,
and creation is not, there could be no relationship between the two
unless the One who is infinite, eternal, and unchangeable determined
that He would "voluntarily condescend" to that which He had made.

As with the word "distance," it is important to pause over these two words in order to understand them properly.

When the confession says that God's condescension was "voluntary," it is making an important and central theological point. The point is that creation, including God's act to create, was not *necessary*. For something to be necessary, it means it has to be and there is no possibility that it could not be. A square *has to be* an object with four sides; it cannot be a square unless there are four sides (as well as other qualities). But creation did not *have* to be. There is nothing in the character of God that *required* that He create. There would have been nothing amiss, nothing lacking in God, if He had determined that He would not create. He was complete and sufficient unto Himself. Therefore, we have to recognize that the Triune God *freely* determined to create. He was not compelled to create, but He freely decided that He would.

What He decided to do is condescend. As we noted above, that condescension initiates a relationship; it means that God "comes down" to relate to His creation. Since creation could not ascend to the heights of His transcendence, God decides to be with us.

In other words, what God determines to do in creation *reflects* His character as God, even as it relates to creaturely and created things. God *speaking* to Adam and Eve reflects His character *as the eternal Word*; His walking in the garden is a relational reflection of His character *as omnipresent*. Appearing to Moses on a certain day and at a certain time is a relational reflection of His character as *eternal*.

This may be difficult, initially, to grasp. We are accustomed to think of eternity as the *opposite* of time and local presence as the *opposite* of omnipresence. But this kind of "opposition" does not apply to God and His relationship to creation. Instead, since it is the eternal and infinite God who creates, and who then locates Himself at a time and a place, God's character—as *a se*, as eternal, as invisible, as infinite, etc.—establishes the reality of God's relationship to creation.

This is biblical logic in all of its beauty and depth. What we initially might think to be opposites are, as a matter of fact, organic and coherent aspects of God and the expression of His relation to creation. The biblical logic of this truth, then, is that because of what God is *in Himself* He can and does express Himself, in a necessarily limited and accommodated way, in His interaction with creation. But this limited and accommodated expression of God's character is just as *real* as is His character *as God*, because the former flows from the latter.[11] Thus, in relating Himself to creation, God determines to reveal Himself through "relational" characteristics and qualities that are revealed in order to establish and maintain a relationship with His human creatures.

So, for example, when we read (in Genesis 3:8) that Adam and Eve "heard the sound of the LORD God walking in the garden" we recognize that, in order for that to happen, God would take to Himself human characteristics so that He could be in the garden and walk and talk with Adam and Eve. This takes place in order to relate to, and in this case to judge, Adam and Eve. It is the first recorded redemptive appearance of God in history.[12] From this point on, God's condescension has a specifically redemptive focus.

According to the confession, it is this "voluntary condescension" that characterizes the biblical notion of "covenant." In other words, God—Father, Son, and Holy Spirit—exhibits these characteristics and qualities (as we saw in our discussion of the economic Trinity) in order to relate Himself to His creation, and that relationship is best characterized as a *covenant* relationship.[13]

As this chapter of the confession will go on to explain, that covenant relationship was qualified by works with Adam and Eve. They could remain as they were if they *obeyed* God. Once they disobeyed, our relationship to God became characterized by grace. But the first thing we see in chapter 7 of the confession is the covenant principle. Before there was any works principle, or any grace principle, there was a covenant principle as God condescended in order to relate. That condescension established a relationship between God and His

---

11. A technical point that we won't develop here is that this is what is meant when we affirm that God's characteristics are *analogical* to the creature's. It's not simply that His characteristics are His and ours are ours, true though that is. It is, rather, that the (necessarily) eternal, for example, grounds the (contingently) temporal relationship of God to His creatures.

12. God did, in some way, "appear" to Adam and Eve prior to this, as He gave them commands, etc., but we are not told the form of that appearance.

13. A point we must mention, but cannot develop, is that God's relationship to creation has its focus not in His divine *essence* per se, but in the three divine Persons.

creatures, especially His human creatures. That relationship, once established, will never end; it will continue into eternity-future.

The model of majestic mystery, therefore—a model that we have seen displayed in the distinction between the ontological and the economic Trinity, and between the divine nature and the human nature of the Son—as we have said previously, could be labeled "covenantal condescension." It is the free "coming down" of the Triune God in order to establish a covenant relationship to that which He has made, a relationship that begins "in the beginning" and that remains even into eternity-future. Herman Bavinck aptly describes it this way:

> If not just one relation but all relations and all sorts of relations of dependence, submission, obedience, friendship, love, and so forth among humans find their model and achieve their fulfillment in religion, then religion must be the character of a covenant. For then God has to come down from his lofty position, *condescend to his creatures, impart, reveal, and give himself away to human beings; then he who inhabits eternity and dwells in a high and holy place must also dwell with those who are of a humble spirit* (Isa. 57:15). But this set of conditions is nothing other than the description of a covenant. If religion is called a covenant, it is thereby described as the true and genuine religion. This is what no religion has ever understood; *all peoples either pantheistically pull God down into what is creaturely, or deistically elevate him endlessly above it*. In neither case does one arrive at true fellowship, at covenant, at genuine religion.[14]

Notice how Bavinck characterizes all other forms of religion—they either pull God down, so that He is little more than a creature, or they "elevate" him to such an extent that He cannot really relate to what He has made. Christianity affirms neither of these extremes. Because God condescends covenantally, He can both remain who He is as the *a se* Triune God and He can come down to relate to His creation, especially to those made in His image.

---

14. Herman Bavinck, *Reformed Dogmatics, vol. 2, God and Creation*, ed. John Bolt, trans. John Vriend (Grand Rapids: Baker Academic, 2004), 569–70; my emphases.

One further point must be recognized here. The problem of distance and the dilemma of God's relationship to creation is no problem or dilemma for Him. To repeat, the biblical picture is that *because of*—not in spite of—the fact that God is who He is in Himself, He could condescend and relate to us. In other words, He is not denying Himself by this relationship but is rather showing us something of the fullness of who He is by freely deciding to condescend.

BIBLICAL DISTINCTIONS

So far we have seen that God is altogether *a se*; He is independent of all things created and dwells in unapproachable light. He is, in that sense, the antithesis of creation. Much of what characterizes creation, God *is not*. He *is not* limited, He *is not* temporal, He *does not* change. These characteristics of God are impossible for us to comprehend or to understand fully. We have no experience of these qualities, and our minds are unable to grasp them. They remain mysterious to us.

But we have also seen that this God who is infinite, eternal, and unchangeable "comes down" in order to be in a covenant relationship with His human creatures. He does so by expressing Himself in "new" characteristics in order to relate to us. He is located at particular places throughout history; He speaks in sentences, with languages; He comes at particular and specific times in history. When He was walking with Adam in the garden or speaking with Moses on the mountain, it was a specific day in history, and a specific time of day.

How can we reconcile these two—and *true*—pictures of God that God Himself, in His Word, gives us? In the history of theology, there have been various ways to attempt to categorize God's characteristics. Some have said that God has some characteristics that are *incommunicable* and some that are *communicable*. By this is meant that some characteristics of God cannot be "communicated" to creation so that we can know what they are. Such is the case with God's eternity, for example. Other characteristics of God are *communicated* in creation, such as His wisdom, or goodness, or justice.

Other categories that have been proposed to distinguish God's characteristics are "metaphysical and moral" characteristics, or "absolute and relative." All of these categories can be helpful in explaining the differences in God's perfections.

We can consider, however, another way of thinking of God's character, a way that does not negate or deny but hopefully enhances these other ways of describing God's character. This way attempts to shed more light on what we mean when we affirm God's characteristics *as God* (and, thus, quite apart from creation), and what we mean when we affirm God's character as He relates Himself to us. The first set of characteristics we can call "essential." By essential we mean all of those characteristics that God *has* and *is*, whether or not there is creation. They are essential because they point to characteristics without which God would not be God.

If God were not infinite, for example, He would be subject to some kind of limitation. If He were limited, He would depend on whatever limited Him in order to be who He is. This cannot be true of God. So, among the essential characteristics of God we can include His infinity, eternity, immutability (including the fact that He is, as the confession says, "without passions"). All of these characteristics and more are included in a proper understanding of God, whether or not there is creation. Thus, they are essential to Him. These characteristics are primary and must be seen as foundational to anything else that is said of God.

The characteristics that God has because of His voluntary condescension include all of the essential characteristics, but it includes them in terms of God's revelation of Himself *as related* to us—those characteristics that express His commitment to relate to His creatures. These characteristics are secondary, in that sense; they are "relative" in that they describe God in terms of His revelation in relationship to us. So, for example, God's anger and wrath are expressions of His essential holiness. They are characteristics that He expresses because of the presence of sin and rebellion. God's graciousness, similarly, is His unmerited expression of love and kindness in the face of sin.

When there was no creation, there was no anger or wrath of God; without creation, and the entrance of sin, there would be no need for God to be gracious. Because these characteristics present themselves in light of God's voluntary condescension, we can call them "covenantal." They are what they are in light of the model of majestic mystery—i.e., covenantal condescension. Just as condescension presupposes an initial height from which to come down, so the covenantal characteristics presuppose the essential. In this way, the covenantal are not antithetical to the essential, but express, in their various ways, what those essential characteristics *are*, as revealed to us.

One way to think about this might be to recognize the helpful theological distinction between the *essence* of God, on the one hand, and the three *persons*, on the other. This might serve as a helpful analogy of what we are saying. The essence of God simply *is who God is*. God cannot change and always remains who he is. So also each of the persons is *fully* (not partially) that one essence, so that they, too, *must be* who and what they essentially are.

But the persons of the Godhead have their own *distinctive* and *relative* characteristics as well. Each is who He is relative to the others. The Father is unbegotten and does not proceed; He is who He is relative to the Son and the Spirit. The Son is begotten but does not proceed; He is who He is relative to the Father and the Spirit. The Spirit proceeds but is not begotten; He is who He is relative to the Father and the Son. These are all *relative* characteristics of the persons. God's *essential* character, therefore, necessarily includes the *absolute* essence, which is relative to *nothing*, and the *relative* persons, each of whom is distinctively defined relative to the others.

So also, the covenantal characteristics (themselves relative) that are expressed by God are characteristics of the persons (who are relative to each other). In that way, we recognize both the (essential) immutability of God, and the relative (covenantal) difference of the persons. This does not explain the inexplicable; it does not minimize the mystery. But it may help to see how such things as "essential" and "relative" can be what they are. The deeply mysterious and glorious truth is that the absolute and the relative exist, first and foremost, in the Triune God Himself!

An analogy here might help. It is not intended to be sacrilegious or trite; it is simply an analogy, and all analogies break down. Many aspects of our superhero mythologies employ, perhaps unwittingly, a parody of Christian truth. If we think of a typical superhero—say Superman—we recognize a couple of things about him. He is Superman because he is from another planet and thus possesses superpowers. But, when he comes down to Earth from Krypton, he takes on other characteristics in order to relate to mere mortals, in order to be Clark Kent. As Clark Kent, he veils his superpowers, but they're never gone. In a sense, he "condescends" to look like a mere mortal. Just because he drives a car does not mean he has lost his ability to fly. At no point, even as he takes on all the characteristics of Clark Kent, does he cease to be Superman or to have superpowers. So, he is essentially Superman, even as he condescends to be "with us" as Clark Kent—i.e., as one of us.

In an analogous way, God—Father, Son, and Holy Spirit—in His covenantal condescension, even as He reveals His character to us, nevertheless veils many of His essential characteristics as He relates to human creatures. He never gives them up; He *couldn't* give them up. But when the Lord fights the battle against His enemies, He is displaying a covenantal "veiling" of His omnipotence, even as His fighting reveals that omnipotence. In Joshua 5:13–6:3, for example, the Lord appears in (apparently) human form as a warrior in the battle. But even in this appearance, Joshua is commanded to treat that presence of the Lord as an occasion for worship (Josh 5:15; compare Exod 3:5), and he is told that it is this divine warrior who has given His enemies into Joshua's hands.

Does this mean the Divine Warrior does not have the power, then and there, to destroy His enemies? No. Instead it means that His power is *displayed* in the battle; it is a picture of His omnipotence. Thus, we have covenantal characteristics, which both reveal and veil the essential characteristics, pointing to the character of God *as God*. So, though the essential characteristics are not fully on display, they still reveal who God is *as God*. This cannot be comprehended by us in its majestic fullness. Because He is God, He will always be incomprehensible to us. But what is revealed to us is true, and it is real, even if ultimately incomprehensible.

Another way to begin to see this mystery is to reflect on what we discussed in the previous chapter. There we saw that the Son of God, while remaining fully God, took on a human nature in order to redeem a people. This assumption of a human nature did not change who the Son is essentially—He remains infinite, eternal, and unchangeable—even while He became tired (Matt 8:24). He felt compassion (Matt 15:32); He cried (John 11:35); He became indignant (Mark 10:14).[15]

---

15. For a magnificent look at these and other characteristics of our Savior, see Benjamin Breckinridge Warfield, "The Emotional Life of Our Lord," in *The Person and Work of Christ* (Philadelphia: Presbyterian and Reformed, 1950).

How could these experiences of Christ not change God Himself, since He is fully God? We have to confess that we do not know *how*, even as we do not know how He could take to Himself a full human nature without changing who He is as God. *But He did!* And what He did flows from who He is; it does not oppose Him in any way. We cannot properly (biblically) know Christ without recognizing that both things are true of Him; our very salvation and sanctification depend on its truth.

In the incarnation the Son of God *permanently* takes to Himself characteristics that are not "originally" His. But we should not miss the fact that, even from the beginning of God's relationship to man, other characteristics that describe God in His relationship to us came into view in order for Him to be in that relationship. Some of those characteristics are now permanent (e.g., grace, wrath), some only temporary (e.g., theophanies, human forms, appearances as fire, in the Old Testament). God was revealing Himself throughout covenant history, until—finally, redemptively, climactically, and completely— He did so in the incarnation of His Son.

The great and glorious mystery of the incarnation, therefore, is the climax to the great and glorious mystery of God relating Himself to us from the beginning of creation! So we ought not say that when Scripture speaks of God as jealous that "it is not so." God's jealousy is an expression of His condescension to us, culminating as it does in Christ! We should not say, when Scripture says that God is angry, that "the change in these cases is in the creatures." We need not say, when Scripture says that God chose a people for Himself, that "in God there is actually no such thing as choice." We should affirm that God's *jealousy* is a covenantal expression of His lordship (which itself expresses His essential aseity); His anger and His grace are God's covenantal expressions of His holiness (which itself is essential to Him); His choosing of a people is His eternal commitment to condescend to redeem (Eph 1:4).[16]

---

16. "God is therefore called 'the Holy One,' because He exists in Himself and nothing can be compared to Him. The metaphysical gap that exists between Him and the creature is therefore expressed by the concept of holiness." Geerhardus Vos, *Reformed Dogmatics*, ed. Richard B. Gaffin, et al., Vol. 1 (Bellingham, WA: Lexham Press, 2012–2014), 25–26.

There are important differences between the incarnation as the climax of covenantal condescension and the characteristics that God displays, such as wrath and grace. In the incarnation, the Son of God takes on a new, human, nature. Taking on this nature allows us to recognize certain characteristics of the incarnate Son in His relationship to us. God's wrath and grace are not explicable in terms of an assumed human nature. They are, however, like the incarnation, expressions of God's character *in relationship*. They show us something of what God is like when He determines to relate to us.[17]

Attempts to deny God's covenantal characteristics, though understandable, are all, in the end, rationalizations that do an injustice to mystery as the lifeblood of theology. They assume that for God to be and remain God, He cannot also really relate to us.[18] They mute the meaning of what God has told us about Himself. They have the effect of minimizing, if not eclipsing, the wondrous mystery of God's relationship to us, as that relationship reaches its climax in the incarnation.

God *does* become angry; His disposition toward His people *does* move from wrath to grace in history; the Holy Spirit can be, and *is*, grieved. All of these characteristics are true of God, even into eternity! But even as we affirm these truths we must also affirm, as we do in the incarnation, that there is not, because there *cannot be*, a change in God. He does not give up His infinity, eternity, immutability, etc. All of these remain as they are, because they *must*. And they are revealed to us covenantally—that is, in those very characteristics that God reveals in His relationship to us. They are essential to God being

---

17. According to Richard Muller, "As in the case of the other divine affections, the Reformers identify such negative attributions as anger, hate, scorn, or jealousy as metaphors and anthropopathisms, applied to God or even in a sense *'assumed' by God by way of revelation and accommodation to us*—as in the case of the anger of God against a 'stiff-necked' Israel in Exodus 32:10, it is not 'as if God learned by experience' that Israel was recalcitrant." Richard A. Muller, *Post-Reformation Reformed Dogmatics: The Rise and Development of Reformed Orthodoxy*, Vol. 3, *The Divine Essence and Attributes* (Grand Rapids: Baker Academic, 2003), 581; my emphasis.

18. "Note that the orthodox do not deny that, from a temporal perspective, God enters into new relations—they only deny that such 'accidental' properties as external relations belong to the divine being. Since they are not 'in' God, their alteration indicates no change in the divine being." Muller, *Post-Reformation Reformed Dogmatics*, Vol. 3, *The Divine Essence and Attributes*, 317.

God; they provide the necessary foundation for anything else that God does and is. And He comes to us. He fellowships with us. He takes up residence in us, and He does this for eternity.

BIBLICAL DOXOLOGY

It is fitting and proper that we began our discussion of the majesty of the mystery of God with God's incomprehensible triune character. God is to be praised and worshiped *for who He is as God*. Even if He had done nothing to save us or had not extended His grace to one single creature, God is still infinitely worthy of praise. When we sing, "Immortal, invisible, God only wise," we are praising God for His infinite deity. We are praising Him because He is God.

The fact is, though, that much of God's revelation encourages us to praise Him for what He has done. It encourages us to worship God *because* of the relationship that He has established in creation. Why is that? If God is to be praised just because He is God, why does Scripture tell us to praise God for what He has *done*? The answer is that our praise of God for what He has done is not meant to focus simply on what God has done, but is meant to point us back to the majestic character of God Himself! Notice, just to pick out one example, Psalm 104. It begins this way:

> Bless the LORD, O my soul!
>   O LORD my God, you are very great!
> You are clothed with splendor and majesty,
>   covering yourself with light as with a garment,
>   stretching out the heavens like a tent.
> He lays the beams of his chambers on the waters;
> he makes the clouds his chariot;
>   he rides on the wings of the wind;
> he makes his messengers winds,
>   his ministers a flaming fire.
>
> He set the earth on its foundations,
>   so that it should never be moved.
> You covered it with the deep as with a garment;
>   the waters stood above the mountains.

> At your rebuke they fled;
>> at the sound of your thunder they took to flight.
> The mountains rose, the valleys sank down
>> to the place that you appointed for them.
> You set a boundary that they may not pass,
>> so that they might not again cover the earth (Psa 104:1–9).

The contemplation of creation in this psalm leads the psalmist not simply to the wonder of creation, but to the majesty of the Creator. (This is a topic for another book, but one of the things that would promote and encourage a biblical practice of Christian meditation would be to establish the habit of contemplating various aspects of creation in order to see in them the revelation of God's majestic character. Psalm 104 would be a good place to begin, and a perfect example of such contemplation.)

Not only is God to be praised for His creation and His work in it, but He is praised as well for the redemption that He alone is able to provide. After the Lord delivered His people from Egypt, Moses and the people of Israel sang a song of praise:

> I will sing to the LORD, for he has triumphed gloriously;
>> the horse and his rider he has thrown into the sea.
> The LORD is my strength and my song,
>> and he has become my salvation;
> this is my God, and I will praise him,
>> my father's God, and I will exalt him.
> The LORD is a man of war;
>> the LORD is his name.

> Pharaoh's chariots and his host he cast into the sea,
>> and his chosen officers were sunk in the Red Sea.
> The floods covered them;
>> they went down into the depths like a stone.
> Your right hand, O LORD, glorious in power,
>> your right hand, O LORD, shatters the enemy.
> In the greatness of your majesty you overthrow your
>> adversaries;
>> you send out your fury; it consumes them like stubble.

At the blast of your nostrils the waters piled up;
    the floods stood up in a heap;
    the deeps congealed in the heart of the sea.
The enemy said, "I will pursue, I will overtake,
    I will divide the spoil, my desire shall have its fill of them.
    I will draw my sword; my hand shall destroy them."
You blew with your wind; the sea covered them;
    they sank like lead in the mighty waters.

Who is like you, O LORD, among the gods?
    Who is like you, majestic in holiness,
    awesome in glorious deeds, doing wonders?
You stretched out your right hand;
    the earth swallowed them.

You have led in your steadfast love the people whom you have
    redeemed;
    you have guided them by your strength to your holy abode.
The peoples have heard; they tremble;
    pangs have seized the inhabitants of Philistia.
Now are the chiefs of Edom dismayed;
    trembling seizes the leaders of Moab;
    all the inhabitants of Canaan have melted away.
Terror and dread fall upon them;
    because of the greatness of your arm, they are still as a stone,
till your people, O LORD, pass by,
    till the people pass by whom you have purchased.
You will bring them in and plant them on your own mountain,
    the place, O LORD, which you have made for your abode,
    the sanctuary, O Lord, which your hands have established.
The LORD will reign forever and ever (Exod 15:1–18).

This is a praise song of deliverance. But notice how that deliverance is only a means to the end of praising God for who *He* is; God is praised because the deliverance reflects His majestic character—it is the Lord who is "my strength and my song." "Who is like you, O LORD, among the gods? Who is like you, majestic in holiness, awesome in glorious deeds, doing wonders? ... You have led in your steadfast love the people whom you have redeemed." Notice how God's covenantal character does not *oppose*, but *reveals*, who He is as God. The means to the end of worship is God's relationship to us.

So the salvation that the Lord has provided for us is only a means to the end of showing us the glory of His incomprehensible character. We are, of course, thankful to have been delivered from the torments of eternal suffering, but that is secondary to the wonder and magnificence of the Triune God as He is revealed in His accomplishment and application of redemption.

At the end of our last chapter, we saw the saints in heaven singing praise to the Lord God and to the Lamb, because the Lamb alone is worthy. *That* is the message of God's covenant. It is not simply that God has established a relationship with us, mysterious as that is, but it is that the Triune God alone was able, in the person of His Son, to come down and restore a relationship that we had so radically ruined. We praise God that He has saved us, but our praise should never stop there. True praise of our covenant Triune God always reaches up to its loftiest height, as it has in view the majesty of God's holy character.

> Holy, holy, holy! Lord God Almighty!
> *All Thy works shall praise thy name in earth and sky and sea;*
> *Holy, holy, holy! Merciful and mighty!*
> *God in Three Persons, blessed Trinity!*
>
> —Reginald Heber, "Holy, Holy, Holy"

CHAPTER 6

The Majesty of the Mystery of God's Decree and Desire

If God is an intelligent agent, he must
have had a plan; if an eternal, infinitely
wise and powerful and immutable agent,
he must have had one all-comprehensive
plan from the beginning; if he exists as
three Persons, his plan must be mutual—
that is, of the nature of a covenant, to be
executed by the Three in concert.

—Archibald Alexander Hodge
and J. Aspinwall Hodge

*The System of Theology Contained
in the Westminster Shorter Catechism:
Opened and Explained*

In *The Lion, the Witch and the Wardrobe*, Narnia was under the reign of the White Witch. With the White Witch in control of Narnia, it was always winter but never Christmas. But Aslan the lion was on the move. When the Witch and Aslan finally meet, the Witch says to Aslan that one of the children, Edmund, has been found to be a traitor. So Aslan strikes a deal with the Witch and agrees to die in Edmund's place. But then Aslan returns from the dead. After he comes back from the dead, the children are confused:

> "But what does it all mean?" asked Susan when they were somewhat calmer. "It means," said Aslan, "that though the Witch knew the Deep Magic, there is a magic deeper still which she did not know. Her knowledge goes back only to the dawn of time. But if she could have looked a little further back, into the stillness and the darkness before Time dawned, she would have read there a different incantation. She would have known that when a willing victim who had committed no treachery was killed in a traitor's stead, the Table would crack and Death itself would start working backward."[1]

In this chapter, we will strain to peer into the "stillness before time dawned." It was there that the majestic mystery of covenantal condescension began. We will see there that the Father, the Son, and the Holy Spirit consider and agree together to save a people. We will also see that, in "the stillness before time dawned," the Triune God decreed "whatsoever comes to pass."[2] All of history is, then, a manifestation of what God planned in eternity-past.

---

1. C. S. Lewis, *The Lion, the Witch and the Wardrobe* (New York: Scholastic, 1995), 163.
2. *Westminster Confession of Faith* 3.1.

Even as the Triune God planned and decreed all that is, and all that happens, this does not mean, as some might suppose, that He remains aloof and detached from the destinies of His creation and of humanity. He does not simply plan and, as it were, sit back to watch it all happen. Instead, and most mysteriously, the same God who plans it all expresses His own wish and desire in the midst of what He has meticulously planned. He is, for example, deeply desirous that every person come to repentance and faith. The God who planned the end from the beginning and who chose a specific people for Himself, nevertheless takes no delight in the death of the wicked (Ezek 18:23). How can this be? It is the wonder of the mystery of God's decree and His relationship to creation. The "deeper magic," then, will help us to better understand the deeper mystery that is God's eternal decree along with His desire for His creation.

Before we look more closely at God's decree and desire, it might be helpful to briefly sum up the previous chapters. By now we should have in mind the model of majestic mystery that surrounds God, the Trinity, the incarnation, and God's covenant with man. That model includes God's character as triune. It includes the fact that this Triune God is "infinite in being and perfection, a most pure spirit, invisible, without body, parts, or passions; immutable, immense, eternal, incomprehensible." So, as the Athanasian Creed states, we confess that "the Father is eternal, the Son is eternal, and the Holy Spirit is eternal. And yet they are not three eternals: but one eternal."[3]

But, even as we affirm that the Triune God is absolutely independent, we also must affirm the biblical distinction of the "ontological" Trinity and the "economic" Trinity. The difference in the two categories is that, in their economic manifestations, the persons of the Trinity reveal God by expressing relational characteristics for purposes of relating to creation and redemption.

The economic Trinity, therefore, is an example of God's "covenantal condescension." The Father sends the Son and is pleased by Him (cf. John 3:16; Matt 3:17). The Son comes to deliver a people, to redeem His own (cf. John 10:11, 15), and to do the will of the Father

---

3. Philip Schaff, *The Creeds of Christendom, with a History and Critical Notes: The Greek and Latin Creeds, with Translations*, Vol. 2 (New York: Harper & Brothers, 1890), 67.

(cf. Matt 26:42; Heb 10:7). The Holy Spirit comes to brood over creation (Gen 1:2), to initiate the humanity of the Son in the incarnation (Luke 1:35), to convict the world (John 16:8–11), to comfort and be with the Lord's people (John 14:16–18), and to be, with the Son, the life-giver (1 Cor 15:45).

None of these characteristics was in place when there was no creation. There was no need for the Father to send, or for the Son, in obedience to the Father, to be sent, or for the Spirit to comfort and convict. These characteristics are all economic—that is, they assume creation and redemption. They are what they are because of the free and voluntary decision of the Triune God to condescend, to create, and to redeem a people.

So also for the wrath of God, His anger, His mercy, and His grace. All are characteristics that reveal God's character as they are manifest in, and because of, creation, and they will remain into eternity-future. They are not "ontological" characteristics in that they do not apply to God as God; they do, however, reveal God's ontological characteristics. They all presuppose God's relationship to creation.[4] As we have seen, they *reflect* who God is ontologically, though they have their expression in the covenant relation that God has established.

We also saw this covenantal condescension in the Son's activity in creation. As He comes to interact with Adam in the garden, with Moses on the mountain, with Joshua at Jericho, and so forth, He is expressing Himself in light of the covenant relationship that He has established, even to the point of taking *created* (i.e., human) characteristics, temporarily, as He works in redemptive history with His people. All of this looks forward to that once-for-all, permanent, and eternal taking of an entire human nature, from conception into eternity-future, in order to do the will of His Father and to bring His people to Himself.

So while covenantal condescension has its roots and genesis in the Triune God, it has its revelatory focus and climax in God the Son, whose incarnation is the centerpiece of all of redemptive history. Everything

---

4. We should remember that these covenantal characteristics have their foundation in God's ontological character. As such, they are contingent "ways" or "modes" of God that are consistent with His essential character, but are what they are in light of creation.

that led to the Son's incarnation and everything that comes after it, into eternity, is illuminated by that one signal work.

This condescension begins before "the beginning." Covenantal condescension did not have its genesis in Genesis. It did not begin in history. It began in eternity-past. From eternity-past (Eph 1:4) and into eternity-future, Christ is the central focus. Quite apart from creation, and before it began, the Triune God committed Himself to something that would be outside of Him; He decreed everything that would come to pass, from the point of creation into eternity. That decree was *itself* condescension, because it was God's *commitment* to something outside of Himself—i.e., creation and redemption. The majestic mystery of this covenantal condescension is that, in eternity-past, God committed Himself—*bound* Himself—to creation, and to redeem a people.

At that "point" in eternity-past—what Scripture calls "before the foundation of the world"—God determined *everything* that would come to pass in history and into eternity-future.[5] Because of this all-encompassing decree, nothing would ever be the same again with respect to God. In the decree, He permanently attached Himself to His creation and to His human creatures, into eternity-future! God's sovereign decree is initiated in eternity-past, and it encompasses the new heaven and the new earth, as well as the eternal torment of hell, in eternity-future.

BIBLICAL DEVELOPMENT

There are three distinct parts to our discussion in this section—parts that are inextricably linked. The first part helps us to see the eternal beginnings of the covenant relationship that God initiates; the second part focuses on God's all-encompassing decree; the third part affirms God's compassion and desire for all of His human creatures. The three parts are meant to go together, theologically, but they must be kept distinct for our purposes here. The first part is the key that helps us properly to understand the other two.

---

5. Note that "God from all eternity, did, by the most wise and holy counsel of His own will, freely, and unchangeably ordain whatsoever comes to pass: yet so, as thereby neither is God the author of sin, nor is violence offered to the will of the creatures; nor is the liberty or contingency of second causes taken away, but rather established" (*Westminster Confession of Faith*, 3.1).

God's Eternal Love

This first part of our discussion concerns what is typically called the *covenant of redemption* (*pactum salutis*). In this covenant, which has its origin in eternity-past, the Father, Son, and Holy Spirit agree together to create and to redeem a people. In the "stillness before time dawned," the Father chooses for Himself a people (Eph 1:4). He will give those people to the Son, who comes in history to accomplish His work in their behalf (John 17:11), and the Spirit agrees to apply in history the redemption accomplished by the Son to those same people (John 16:12–15). This is God's eternal pact, His covenant with Himself, on behalf of His people. But why think there is such a thing as a covenant of redemption in eternity?

The answer is that Scripture explicitly points us in that direction. We can only introduce, rather than fully develop, the discussion here. The best place to start is to focus on what Peter says about Christ in 1 Peter 1:20. Speaking of Christ, Peter says:

> *He was foreknown before the foundation of the world* but was made manifest in the last times for the sake of you.

On the face of it, it should strike us immediately that Peter's language in the italicized phrase seems strange. What could Scripture mean when it says that Christ was "foreknown before the foundation of the world"? How could it be that God "foreknew" Christ? Did the Father, at some eternal point, *come to know* the Son as Christ? Surely God knows everything, *especially* His triune self!

To begin to answer that question, we can ask how the New Testament uses the word "foreknow." It turns out that the word is used only five other times in the entire New Testament (Rom 8:29; 11:2; 1 Pet 1:2; 2 Pet 3:17; Acts 26:5). The latter two verses in this list (2 Pet 3:17; Acts 26:5) clearly signify something that a person (or persons) knows in the past. The most rudimentary meaning of the word, therefore, is that "foreknow" means to know before, or in the past. However, in the four other occurrences (Rom 8:29; 11:2; 1 Pet 1:2, 20), the object in view is not *something* that is known in the past but, instead, is *someone* or *someones* that were known in *eternity-past*! Other than our passage in 1 Peter, the other two passages that have this meaning are in the book of Romans.

John Murray's comments on Romans 8:29 ("For those whom he foreknew ...") are worth quoting at length, as they will help us understand what Scripture means by Christ being "foreknown" in 1 Peter. On Romans 8:29, Murray says:

> It should be observed that the text says *"whom* he foreknew"; *whom* is the object of the verb and there is no qualifying addition. This, of itself, shows that, unless there is some other compelling reason, the expression "whom he foreknew" contains within itself the differentiation which is presupposed. ... Although the term "foreknow" is used seldom in the New Testament, it is altogether indefensible to ignore the meaning so frequently given to the word "know" in the usage of Scripture; "foreknow" merely adds the thought of "beforehand" to the word "know." Many times in Scripture "know" has a pregnant meaning which goes beyond that of mere cognition. It is used in a sense practically synonymous with "love," to set regard upon, to know with peculiar interest, delight, affection, and action (cf. Gen. 18:19; Exod. 2:25; Psalm 1:6; 144:3; Jer. 1:5; Amos 3:2; Hosea 13:5; Matt. 7:23; 1 Cor. 8:3; Gal. 4:9; 2 Tim. 2:19; 1 John 3:1). There is no reason why this import of the word "know" should not be applied to "foreknow" in this passage, as also in 11:2 where it also occurs in the same kind of construction and where the thought of election is patently present (cf. 11:5, 6). ... It means "whom he set regard upon" or "whom he knew from eternity with distinguishing affection and delight" and is virtually equivalent to "whom he foreloved."[6]

As Murray points out, these texts of Scripture do not say that God knew *something* beforehand; instead, He knew *someone(s)*. To "foreknow," therefore, when the subject of foreknowledge is God, does not mean, simply, that God knew things beforehand. God knows all things, from eternity, so there is no reason to interpose such a word in these three passages in Scripture; the context demands more.

---

6. John Murray, *The Epistle to the Romans*, The New International Commentary on the Old and New Testament (Grand Rapids: Eerdmans, 1968), 1:316–18.

Instead, given that the word "foreknow" in each case is used in the context of salvation, and that the object(s) known are *persons* in each of these four passages, something more specific than omniscience is most definitely in view. What is in view, as Murray says, is God's "fore-love." God sets His loving sights on someone(s) for the purpose of redemption. That is surely the meaning of the word in Romans.

In 1 Peter 1:20, however, we're told that *Christ* was foreknown "before the foundation of the world" and that He was made manifest in these last days for our sake. This passage, too, is speaking about our salvation, since it was for our sake. Given what we have learned about the word "foreknow," however, there must be a "foreloving" of Christ in view here, with the goal being His accomplishment of our redemption.

The fact that Christ was "foreknown" (i.e., foreloved) must mean that there was a special love that the Father expressed toward the Son, with a view toward our redemption. The Son was *foreloved* by His Father because the Son agreed, in eternity-past, to humble Himself in order that we might be saved. This foreloving of the Son, by the Father, through the Spirit, is what is meant by the "covenant of redemption" (also sometimes called the "covenant of peace"). In eternity-past, Father, Son, and Holy Spirit agreed together to redeem a people. That agreement included all that would take place in history, in light of creation, and in light of the redemption that God would graciously provide.

This forelove from the Father to the Son is, no doubt, what Christ had in mind when He prayed to His Father just before His crucifixion:

> The glory that you have given me I have given to them, that they may be one even as we are one, I in them and you in me, that they may become perfectly one, so that the world may know that you sent me and *loved them even as you loved me*. Father, I desire that they also, whom you have given me, may be with me where I am, to see my glory that you have given me *because you loved me before the foundation of the world*. ... I made known to them your name, and I will continue to make it known, that *the love with which you have loved me may be in them*, and I in them. (John 17:22–24, 26)

In this prayer, which Peter himself no doubt heard, the connection between the Father's love for the Son "before the foundation of the world" and God's love for the redeemed are intimately intertwined. Christ prays that the love with which the Father, "before the foundation of the world," loved the Son might be *in us,* as well. This, undoubtedly, is the love of redemption; it is the love that is initiated by the Triune God in eternity-past and that characterizes the "covenant of redemption."

It is, of course, true that the Father, Son, and Spirit have infinite and eternal love in themselves (ontologically) quite apart from the decree and from creation. But Christ's prayer has its focus not in the ontological Trinity, but in the economic and redemptive aspects of the Trinity. That is, He is focused on the agreement in eternity-past that set in stone the glorious salvation that the Triune God would accomplish, in Christ, through the Spirit. Christ prays that the world may know that the Father loves us, *even as He loved Christ.* That love could not be the love of the ontological Trinity; it must be the covenant love, with a view toward our redemption, accomplished by Christ, applied by the Spirit, because agreed to in eternity-past!

This love about which Christ prays before His crucifixion can be nothing other than the foreloving of which Scripture speaks in 1 Peter and which it ascribes to the elect in Romans 8 and 11. It is the eternal, redemptive love of God that initiates, *in eternity,* the salvation that only the Triune God could accomplish. It is applied to all for whom Christ prayed—to those whom the Father gave to Christ (John 17:6), to whom Christ has given His word (17:8, 14), who are not of the world but who remain in the world (17:9, 11, 16), who know that the Father has sent the Son (17:25), and whom Christ desires would be with Him (17:24).

The movement of the covenant of redemption, then, is this: In the "stillness before time dawned," the Triune God agreed to effect and accomplish redemption for the people whom He had chosen. As the Father set His affection on (foreloved) the Son for the purpose of the salvation of His people, so also He, through Christ and in the Spirit, set His eternal affection on all those whom He gave to Christ (17:6, 9, 11, 12), for whom Christ died (17:9; cf. John 10:10ff.; Matt 1:21), and to whom the Spirit was and will be given (14:16-17).

This is another unfathomable mystery in Scripture. Why is it that the Triune God—who is complete in Himself, who lacks nothing, who exists in eternal and infinite bliss, completely and fully self-satisfied—determined to create, and then to redeem, a people for Himself?

As creatures, the apex and yearning of our human existence is to be complete, to be everything that we are meant to be. But God *exists* in that self-complete state; He has no incompleteness in Himself. Of Himself, He yearns for nothing. Yet He decides to take the likes of us to Himself for eternity. In order to do that He decides to condescend, to express Himself in terms of characteristics that He did not have to express, so that He might relate to us on our level. Why? The only and best answer is Romans 11:36: "For from him and through him and to him are all things. To him be glory forever. Amen."

Surely no other religion or man-made system has ever come close to thinking in this way. No cult has a God who is complete in Himself, yet who decides, while remaining who He is, to become "one of us." We would not have thought of such a thing—*unless* God Himself has spoken and has told us these magnificent truths (1 Cor 2:9–10). To Him be glory forever.

God's Decree

The general category under which topics like "the covenant of redemption" and "God's decrees" are normally discussed is "the works of God," because in the eternal covenant, and in God's decree, He is *acting* to do something. This is a proper category, but it should not escape our notice that such a category only enhances the mystery of our Triune God.

The technical Latin term for these works of God in eternity is "*ad intra*." What that means is that these are works of God that take place "within" the Triune God Himself. But how can this be?

We have already seen that God is utterly self-complete and self-sufficient. He lacks nothing and is in need of nothing. We have also seen that God is eternal. This means that He is not subject to the passing of moments in order to be who He is or to have perfect fellowship with Himself. We have no idea, nor can we conceive of, what this kind of existence is like.

But now we see that there was an eternal "point" at which God—Father, Son, and Holy Spirit—agreed together to create all that is and to redeem a people. Wouldn't such a "point" require that there be *some kind of change* in God? As God eternally exists, and as that eternal existence "moves" from "no covenant of redemption" to "covenant of redemption," what else could that be but some kind of eternal change?

The first answer to this question is that, whatever this "point" of an eternal covenant of redemption is, it is *not*, as it *cannot be*, a change in God Himself. It bears repeating again and again that God *cannot* change in Himself. The covenant of redemption did not change God from eternal to temporal or from infinite to finite. Exactly *how* this can be, we simply don't know. But *that* it is, there can be no question. God is, and necessarily remains, immutable.

Once we recognize the first answer, we can move to the second. The second answer to the question moves us to make a distinction. As we think about creation and redemption, we recognize that such things did not have to exist at all. As we have already noted, there was/ is nothing in God that *requires* that He create and, once sin enters His creation, that He redeem.

To illustrate this, we can develop an example here that we mentioned in the previous chapter. Let's say that, for a square to be a square, the following things must be true:

1. It has (exactly) four sides.
2. Each of its sides is straight.
3. It is a closed figure.
4. It lies in a plane.
5. Each of its sides is equal in length to each of the others.
6. Each of its interior angles is equal to the others, at 90 degrees.
7. The sides are joined at their ends.

Now, let's suppose that all but (1) and (6) are true of an object. Is it possible that such an object could be a square? Of course not. A square *must* have four sides, with each angle at 90 degrees. This means that a square is not sufficient to itself. It *needs* other things in order to be a square. It needs lines, planes, angles, equal measurements, etc.

Now, we can ask, "What things does God need in order to be God?" Maybe you are tempted to answer something like this: "God needs *eternity* in order to be God. If He is not eternal, He is not God." Or, "God needs immutability in order to be God. Without immutability, He changes and cannot be God." Or, "God needs goodness in order to be God." Responses like this, however, commit a subtle but important error. The error is that they think of characteristics such as eternity or immutability or goodness as *things* that are, in their origin and existence, somehow independent of God. In our example of the square, things like lines and planes and angles can be independent of squares. Octagons have lines and angles, but are not squares. So these characteristics of squares can exist, even if squares did not exist.

But eternity, immutability, and other essential characteristics of God are not like lines, planes, and angles. They do not exist somehow outside of God so that they could be "applied" to God in order to make up His character. Instead, such essential characteristics of God are just *ways* that He exists *as* the true and triune self-sufficient God. In other words, eternity does not exist independently of God so that it is applied to God to make Him eternal. Rather, one of the *ways* we describe God's existence is *as eternal*. Eternity is not a "thing" (it is not even an "environment" in which God lives, as time is for us); it is an essential characteristic of the Triune God. Eternity is not something God is "in"; it is, rather, an essential characteristic that God *is*. It acknowledges that God's existence has no beginning and no end and is not subject to temporal duration.

What does this have to do with the covenant of redemption and God's decree? It helps us to recognize that both of these things refer us to something that—unlike God's eternity and immutability—did not *have* to be at all. Since God needs nothing in order to be who He is, there was no absolute *need* for God to decree, or to agree to create, or, once sin entered the world, for redemption to be accomplished.

Why, then, do these things exist? Here we need to recognize an important distinction when we consider God's character. Because God is tri-personal, He has *personal* characteristics. His personal characteristics are the foundation for personal characteristics in us. That is part of what it means to be image of God. Included in those personal characteristics is God's ability *to choose*. In other words, God, as tri-personal, is a God who *wills* to do some things and not to do others.

Some things God wills necessarily. He necessarily wills Himself. That is, God necessarily wants to be who He is; His will is an aspect of His essential character. So, like His essential character, it is necessary.

But there are other things that God wills that do/did not *have* to be. These things we attribute to God's free will. By "free," here we mean that whatever is a product of that aspect of God's will is, by definition, contingent. "Contingent" means that something does/did not have to *be* at all. We have seen this already in our discussion of God's "voluntary" condescension; it was a free, *contingent* decision; God did not have to choose to condescend at all. Now we need to recognize that God's covenant of redemption, as well as His decree, *all* originate by His free choice.

This is an important distinction to remember because it provides a proper way to think about God's incomprehensible character. Remember, there are some aspects of God's character that *must* be—such as His infinity, eternity, and immutability—and other aspects of His character that He *freely chose* to express and reveal. He chose to be Creator; He did not have to create.[7] He chose to extend grace; He did not have to be gracious. Since He chose to create, and since Adam brought sin into the world, God's anger and wrath toward sin are due to His free will as well (though, once sin entered the world, God could be nothing but angry and wrathful toward it, given His holiness).

When we think of God's decree, therefore, we are expressing something about God's free choice that took place when there existed nothing but the Triune God Himself. So, though it is an *ad intra* "work" of God, it *refers* to God's relationship to everything that is *ad extra*—that is, outside of God. His decree is something He freely decided to do, and it initiates and establishes a relationship between God and everything else.

When we think of the decree of God, we are thinking of God's plan for creation. That plan is exhaustive; it includes everything that God creates, and God creates everything. One of the biblical terms for God's exhaustive decree is the word "counsel." For example:

> Remember this and stand firm,
>> recall it to mind, you transgressors,
>> remember the former things of old;

---

7. "Attributes which are not related to created reality must be fundamentally distinguished from attributes which are somehow related to creation and thus are principles of divine acts (*operations*)" (Andreas J. Beck, "Gisbertus Voetius (1589–1676): Basic Features of His Doctrine of God," in *Reformation and Scholasticism*, ed. Willem van Asselt and Eef Dekker, 205–26 [Grand Rapids: Baker Academic, 2001], 218).

> for I am God, and there is no other;
> I am God, and there is none like me,
> declaring the end from the beginning
> and from ancient times things not yet done,
> saying, "My counsel shall stand,
> and I will accomplish all my purpose." (Isa 46:8–10)

Notice how the Lord moves from a description of His character ("there is no other," "there is none like me") to an affirmation of His comprehensive plan ("declaring the end from the beginning"). This plan, we are told, is according to God's "counsel," a counsel that will stand and in which God will accomplish His purpose for all of creation.

God's decree includes everything, without exception.[8] However, included in God's decree (though not identical to it, since the decree covers *everything*) is God's eternal predestinating purpose. This is set out concisely for us in Ephesians 1.

Ephesians 1:3–14 is, in the original Greek, one long sentence. It is a sentence of praise—a doxology—that moves from eternity-past, through the entirety of history, and into eternity-future. It begins with praise:

> Blessed be the God and Father of our Lord Jesus Christ,
> who has blessed us in Christ with every spiritual blessing
> in the heavenly places (Eph 1:3).

The rest of this one long sentence (through verse 14 in our English Bibles) is a parade of blessings that should evoke praise in every Christian. These praises are given to Paul by the Spirit of God, who inspires him to pen a panoramic view of God's entire plan, from start to finish. Toward the end of this lengthy sentence, we read that God "works all things according to the counsel of his will" (1:11). The phrase "counsel of his will," we will recognize, refers us again to God's comprehensive decree. "All things" (as we will see in the next chapter) are working "according to" that counsel. His counsel is exhaustive in its scope; it leaves nothing to chance.

But God's comprehensive decree is not the first thing Scripture mentions for which we are to praise God. What is the *first* thing the

---

8. See the *Westminster Confession of Faith* 3.1, in footnote above.

Spirit mentions for which God is to be praised? We are to bless God because "he chose us in him before the foundation of the world, that we should be holy and blameless before him" (Eph 1:4). The first item of praise directs us to eternity-past, what Scripture calls "before the foundation of the world." In eternity-past, God chose a people. The people to whom Ephesians refers are called, collectively, the Church.

Lest there be any confusion, the sentence goes on to encourage praise because "in love he predestined us for adoption as sons through Jesus Christ, according to the purpose of his will" (Eph 1:4–5). The ones who are "chosen" are the ones God has "predestined." And the predestination of God was done "according to the purpose of his will." In other words, God did not predestine a people according to what He knew of us in eternity-past; He did not pick us out *because* He saw that we would pick Him out in history. Nowhere in Scripture is such a view of predestination given.

In Romans 9, for example, the Lord is abundantly clear concerning the *reason* for picking out one person for salvation and not another. The example of Jacob and Esau is given: two boys who are virtually identical in their conception, birth, and lives. But God chose one of them, and not the other. Did He choose Jacob in eternity *because* He saw that Jacob would choose Him in history? No. Nothing in God's choice of Jacob has reference to Jacob's activity or life.

> For he says to Moses, "I will have mercy on whom I have mercy, and I will have compassion on whom I have compassion." So then it depends not on human will or exertion, but on God, who has mercy (Rom 9:15–16).

God does not have mercy on those whom He knows in eternity will choose Him. He certainly knows that, because He knows everything, but the point Scripture makes in this passage concerns the *reason* that God chooses. God chooses whom He will choose. He has mercy on whom He will have mercy. So, as the passage says, our salvation ("it") does not depend on our choice ("human will") nor on what we do ("exertion"), but on God's character alone. We choose God in history *because* He chose us in eternity-past.

Maybe someone will think that if God's decision in eternity-past ensures the salvation of some and passes over others, then the only person responsible for salvation, or the lack of salvation, is God

Himself. How can He blame someone for not believing when believing is dependent on His predestinating choice from eternity-past? It must be God's fault, not ours. The Holy Spirit, as He inspired Paul to write, knew this objection might come:

> You will say to me then, "Why does he still find fault? For who can resist his will?" But who are you, O man, to answer back to God? Will what is molded say to its molder, "Why have you made me like this?" Has the potter no right over the clay, to make out of the same lump one vessel for honorable use and another for dishonorable use? (Rom 9:19–21).

The Spirit of God, writing through the apostle Paul, knew that someone might object that if God chose in eternity-past the ones who would believe, then believing is not up to us, nor is it our fault if we do not choose; it is all up to God. Surely His eternal counsel and will cannot be thwarted.

Notice how Scripture turns this objection into a focus on the character of God. This is something we have been at pains to show throughout each chapter thus far. If we truly recognize the eternal and praiseworthy character of the Triune God, how can we simply think in mundane, earthly ways about *His* ways and *His* judgments in the world (cf. Rom 11:33–36)? The illustration of the potter and the clay is meant to point to God's almighty character as Creator and Sustainer of all that is. He alone has absolute right over what He has made (cf. for example, Isa 29:16; 41:25; Jer 18:6).

In working "all things according to the counsel of His will" (Eph 1:11), therefore, God saw fit to choose us, in Christ, before the foundation of the world. But if this is true (which it is), doesn't it mean that God loved us even before we existed? Of course it does! Romans 8:29 says that those whom God foreknew, He predestined. We have already seen that this foreknowledge is equivalent to God's foreloving. He loved us for no other reason than that He decided that He would.

Conversely, the Triune God, who is the "potter," has sovereign rights over those whom He has not chosen, to make them "vessels of dishonor." "So then he has mercy on whomever he wills, and he hardens whomever he wills" (Rom 9:18). The truth that Scripture clearly displays for us is that, in eternity-past, this sovereign and independent

Triune God took counsel with Himself in order to decree everything in creation into eternity-future and that this decree, including the salvation of a people and the reprobation of the rest of mankind, was nothing other than His own independent decision, based only on the eternal counsel of His will. *For that*, says Scripture, we are not to be agitated, nor to look for ways "around" this truth; instead, we are to praise Him for who He is!

God's Desire

Given what we have said thus far, it would be natural, perhaps, to begin to think this way: "Since, in eternity-past, God has chosen some and passed over others, surely His disposition toward His chosen people in history is *always only* love and grace, and His disposition toward those He has bypassed is *always only* wrath. History is just a working out of God's disposition toward mankind which was set in stone in eternity-past."

If God has "fixed in place" everything that happens, including salvation and reprobation, then it is not possible that things could happen differently than what He has planned. Wouldn't this mean that His relationship to His chosen ones is always nothing but love and grace, and His relationship to those He has not chosen is always nothing but wrath and anger? In other words, because all of history is eternally predetermined, isn't determinism the only Christian way to think?

We will explore this in the next chapter as well, but in light of what we have said above, we need to recognize that what God wills and desires in history is in a different category than what He wills in eternity. This is not to say that God's will *actually* contradicts itself, even though it may look contradictory to our finite minds. It is, rather, to highlight the majestic *mystery* with respect to God's choice(s) in eternity and His relationship to mankind in history.

The tension that we detect between God's purposes toward mankind in eternity (i.e., election and reprobation) in relation to His disposition toward mankind in history has often been discussed under the heading "the free offer of the gospel."[9] "Free offer" does *not* refer

---

9. My discussion here will be dependent on John Murray, "The Free Offer of the Gospel," in *Collected Writings of John Murray*, Vol. 4, *Studies in Theology*

to the offer that Christians make to those outside of Christ (since we cannot know who are elect and who are not). Rather, "free offer" indicates whether or not there can be sincerity in God's offer of His gospel, given His eternal purpose to elect some and pass by others. Some have referred to the "free offer" as the "well-meant offer," which might be a clearer way to think of it. In other words, if God has chosen in eternity-past who will be His and who will not, can we make any sense of a sincere *desire* or *wish* on God's part that *all* people turn to Him and believe?[10]

The motivation for this question is not an abstract one; it comes from Scripture itself. For example, in Ezekiel 33:11, the Lord says to Ezekiel:

> Say to them, As I live, declares the Lord GOD, I have no
> pleasure in the death of the wicked, but that the wicked
> turn from his way and live; turn back, turn back from
> your evil ways, for why will you die, O house of Israel?

This is God's declaration, through the prophet, to Israel. But it does not pertain *only* to Israel. The statement itself is more general than that. God says He takes no pleasure in the death of *the wicked*. This would include any wicked who die in their sins.

John Murray's comments on this passage are helpful. After concluding with a couple of exegetical points, Murray says:

> There will not be any dispute regarding the universal-
> ity of the exhortation and command in the clause, "turn
> ye, turn ye from your evil ways." This is a command that

(Edinburgh: Banner of Truth, 1977). See that chapter for a more detailed exegesis and explanation.

10. With respect to God's "desire," Murray says this: "The word 'desire' has come to be used in the debate, not because it is *necessarily* the most accurate or felicitous word but because it serves to set forth quite sharply a certain implication of the full and free offer of the gospel to all. This implication is that in the free offer there is expressed not simply the bare preceptive will of God but the disposition of lovingkindness on the part of God pointing to the salvation to be gained through compliance with the overtures of gospel grace. In other words, the gospel is not simply an offer or invitation but also implies that God delights that those to whom the offer comes would enjoy what is offered in all its fullness" (Murray, "Free Offer," 113–14).

applies to all men without any discrimination or exception. It expresses therefore the will of God to repentance. *He wills that all should repent.* Nothing less than that is expressed in the universal command. To state the matter more fully, he wills that all should repent and live or be saved. ... The only adequate way of expressing the will implied in the exhortation is the will that all should repent and it is surely that truth that is declared in the oath supported statement, "I have no pleasure in the death of the wicked, but that the wicked turn from his way and live."[11]

Murray also looks at 2 Peter 3:9:

The Lord is not slow to fulfill his promise as some count slowness, but is patient toward you, not wishing that any should perish, but that all should reach repentance.

Again, after moving through some exegetical details, Murray concludes:

The reason or ground for the longsuffering of God until the day of judgment is given in what is said concerning his "willing." He is longsuffering in that, or because, he does not wish that any men should perish, but rather because he wills or wishes that all should come to repentance. Repentance is the condition of life, without repentance men must perish. But the will of God that men be saved expressed here is not conditional. It is not: I will your salvation if you repent, but: *I will that you repent and thus be saved.*[12]

There are other passages that relate to these two (Murray deals with Matt 5:44–48; Acts 14:17; Deut 5:29; 32:29; Psa 81:13ff.; Isa 48:18; Matt 23:37; Ezek 18:23, 32; Isa 45:22), but the sense we get from all of these passages is clear. God takes no pleasure in the wicked who die in their sins. Instead, He *wills* that none should perish, but that all should repent. He sincerely commands such repentance (Acts 17:30).

---

11. Murray, "Free Offer," 125; my emphasis.
12. Murray, "Free Offer," 130–31.

The theological question that we face in passages like this is, "Why does God ordain something in eternity-past that will bring Him displeasure in history, and that seems contrary to what He wills in history?"

BIBLICAL DOCTRINE

By now, given our discussion in previous chapters, the answer to a question like the one above should be closer at hand. Once God condescends to relate to us in history, that which is His, and which pertains to Him, in eternity is often "veiled" (even as it is revealed) so that He might—really, truly, and meaningfully—interact with us covenantally as our God.

As we have already seen in previous chapters, God's condescension includes, for example, the obedience of the Son to the Father, though there is no such obedience in the ontological relationship of the Son to the Father; it includes the covenantal grieving of the Spirit, though that grieving is not included in His ontological character; it includes (the Son of) God locating Himself in history, at a time and place, though He remains infinite and eternal. These covenantal characteristics actually *reveal* God to us. It remains a mystery just exactly *how* God can do this, but *that* He does this is clearly revealed.

Now we see that God's condescension includes God sincerely expressing something—the repentance of all—though His decree does not so will. We should recognize that, as with all of God's modes of condescension, nothing that He does puts Him in conflict with Himself. The "willing" of God in the decree is not identical with the "willing" of God that all would repent. There is tension here, but no contradiction. So, also, the Son of God taking on a human nature did not put that nature in conflict with His divine nature.

It is also true that God's disposition toward those who move from wrath to grace (see Eph 2:1-8) in no way means His ontological character changes. Instead, in some magnificent and mysterious way, the immutable character of God as well as the movement from wrath to grace are harmonious in God, though we cannot understand how. So also here with God's will.

The will of God in His decree is unified with the will of God for mankind in history so that the two are actually one, without either one becoming the other. We could even say that, in eternity-past, as

God willed everything that would be, including the salvation of His people, He also included in His will the sincere expression that everyone repent and be saved. In this, His will in eternity is *revealed* in His will in history. In our next section, we will look briefly at distinctions we can make as we think about these truths. For now, it might be helpful to recognize the theological categories that have been developed to aid the church in its discussion of these two truths.

The typical categories with respect to these two aspects of God's will are His "secret" or "decretive" or "hidden" will, on the one hand, and His "revealed" or "preceptive" or "signified" will, on the other. To simplify, we will use the designations of God's "secret" will and His "revealed" will (see Deut 29:29).

Though these categories have been fairly standard in the history of theology, explanations of them, especially concerning how they relate to each other, have not always been uniform. For example, the great Reformed systematic theologian Herman Bavinck argues that these two wills of God do not, in fact, express any tension, but are wholly united in their expression. After a lengthy and helpful discussion of some theological distinctions of the will of God, this is how Bavinck seeks to explain the two categories:

> God's secret will and his revealed will are not diametrically opposed to each other, as though according to the former God willed sin, but according to the latter he did not; as though according to the former he does not will the salvation of all, but according to the latter he does. Also, according to his secret will God takes no pleasure in sin; it is never the object of his delight. He does not afflict any person for the pleasure of afflicting that person. Conversely, even according to his preceptive will God does not will the salvation of everyone individually.[13]

But there may be a problem with Bavinck's discussion, a problem that goes to the heart of God's majestic mystery. This problem can be illustrated in an incident in the life of our Savior. In Matthew 23:37, Jesus expresses His heartfelt desire for the Jews:

13. Herman Bavinck, *Reformed Dogmatics*, ed. John Bolt, trans. John Vriend (Grand Rapids: Baker Academic, 2004), 2:245.

> O Jerusalem, Jerusalem, the city that kills the prophets
> and stones those who are sent to it! How often would I
> have gathered your children together as a hen gathers her
> brood under her wings, and you were not willing!

Here Jesus is expressing His compassion for Jerusalem, His people. His words express deep desire and frustration. This is no passing glance, but is an intensely disappointed gaze *of* the Lord *on* the Lord's own chosen race of people. Jesus says, "How often would I ... ." It is a statement of His perseverance and longsuffering, of repeated attempts and repeated rejections throughout all of redemptive history. It is a statement of a long and tragic history of God's chosen nation, throughout the Old Testament. And there can be no question that it is a statement of a deep desire in Jesus that has been quelled by Israel's willful rebellion.

The desire Jesus expresses is one that stretches back into the history of God's covenant with Israel. In that covenant, God promised to love His people, to hide them in the shadow of His wings (cf. Pss 17:8; 36:7). Now, standing over Jerusalem, here is (the Son of) God Himself, lamenting that His desires for Israel have been frustrated, because Israel "was not willing."[14]

It might be supposed that what we have here is a demonstration of the two wills of Christ. As one who has taken on an entire human nature, that nature includes his human will. But so does His divine nature. So, in Christ, there is the divine will and the human will (cf. Luke 22:42). Perhaps His lament over Jerusalem is simply a function of His *human* nature and will, a *human* expression of disappointment, quite apart from His deity.

But this explanation seriously undermines the force of Christ's statement. He is not simply speaking according to His human nature here, humanly wishing that Israel had repented. He is speaking as the Messiah, the divine-human Savior. As such, the desire He expresses is inextricably tied to His deity as well as His humanity; to put it better, His desire is a product of His (divine-human) *person*. Murray, in commenting on this passage, is helpful:

---

14. How the fact that they "would not" fits with the election and providence of God will be taken up in the next chapter.

The majesty that belongs to [Christ's] person in this unique capacity shines through the whole episode and it is quite improper to abstract the divine aspect of his person from the capacity in which he gives utterance to this will and from the prerogative in virtue of which he could give expression to the utterance. ... Our Lord in the exercise of his most specific and unique function as the God-man gives expression to a yearning will on his part that responsiveness on the part of the people of Jerusalem would have provided the necessary condition for the bestowal of his saving and protecting love, a responsiveness, nevertheless, which it was not the decretive will of God to create in their hearts. ... And, viewing the matter from the standpoint of revelation, *how would it affect our conception of Jesus as the supreme revelation of the Father if in this case we were not to regard his words as a transcript of the Father's will as well as of his own?* We can readily see the difficulties that face us if we do not grant the truly revelatory significance of our Lord's statement.[15]

In expressing His desire that Jerusalem would have come to Him, Christ, as the God-man, is expressing the covenant desire of the Triune God.

In affirming this, however, we also should recognize that God's own intent in His "secret" will is of a different kind, or mode, than His "revealed" will. What God wills in eternity necessarily happens. His will in eternity ordains "whatsoever comes to pass." But His will, or desire, as He expresses it in the passages above is *not* an ordaining will or desire. Instead, it is God expressing His desire that what He has commanded of us would be carried out by us all.

In that sense, His revealed will is not referring us to His eternal determination but to His expression of what it means for us to be in conformity to God's own character. God commands that His human creatures not be idolaters. Would it even be possible that God *desire* or *wish* that some people be idolaters? This would be completely out of accord with His own character as God. So the tension can be expressed

---

15. Murray, "Free Offer," 120–21; my emphasis.

this way: God delights in the fulfillment of His preceptive will. He does not delight in the death of the wicked because wickedness is in opposition to His character. Yet, His eternal decree includes His ordaining the reality of death and of wickedness; everything is ordained by Him. In all of this, God is not working against Himself. Instead, He is, in the context of His all-encompassing, universal decree, expressing and revealing His own character, in light of what He has given to us in His Word.

But this does not erase the majestic mystery of it all. As Murray says:

> We have found that God himself expresses an ardent desire for the fulfillment of certain things which he has not decreed in his inscrutable counsel to come to pass. This means that there is *a will to the realization of what he has not decretively willed, a pleasure towards that which he has not been pleased to decree. This is indeed mysterious,* and why he has not brought to pass, in the exercise of his omnipotent power and grace, what is his ardent pleasure lies hid in the sovereign counsel of his will. We should not entertain, however, any prejudice against the notion that God desires or has pleasure in the accomplishment of what he does not decretively will.[16]

BIBLICAL DISTINCTIONS

We have covered a good bit of biblical territory thus far in this chapter. We have seen that the Triune God took counsel with Himself in order to decree all things, and, more specifically, in order to plan for the redemption of His people. We have also seen that God decrees "all things" by the "counsel of His own will" (Eph 1:11), and a part of that decree includes the fact that the Triune God also desires the repentance of every sinful person. Thus, He sincerely offers the gospel to all who hear it—it is, indeed, a "well-meant" offer—even though, by His decree, only the elect will respond to it.

There is a crucial point here, a crucially *practical* point, that must be kept in mind in light of this mystery. Whenever we are discussing the

---

16. Murray, "Free Offer," 131; my emphasis.

mystery of God's decree in relation to His desire, we have to remember that each needs to be seen and understood in light of the other. It will not do, for example, simply to see God's decree as His *only* activity in relation to the world. To do so fails to recognize His real desire that none perish. But neither will it do to affirm God's desire and deny His decree. His desire has to be seen in light of His decree.

This point is particularly important here with respect to our preaching and our communication of the gospel. We should never think or act as if God's decree is the *only* word from Him when we preach the gospel. But (and this may be the bigger problem for many Christians) neither should we give the implication that God's desire for none to perish is due to His lack of sovereignty, as if He does not, in fact, ordain "whatsoever comes to pass." In fact, it is just *because* God is sovereign that, in some mysterious way, He takes no delight in the death of the wicked. *All* of it is in accordance with His eternal decree.

When we preach or communicate the gospel, then, both of these truths must be kept in mind. Even if we are not able, at all times, to say all that we can about this tension, it has to be central to our understanding of the good news of the gospel.

Though God's decree and desire need to be seen in a mysterious tandem, we have to recognize the priority of decree over desire. Because God's decree initiates *everything* that comes to pass in and through His creation, it is His sovereign decree that provides the foundation for the "well-meant" offer of the gospel.

Given these three important aspects of God's activity that we have discussed thus far—His covenant of redemption, His decree, and His sincere, or "well-meant," offer of the gospel—we can see them summed up in a remarkable passage in the Gospel of Matthew. In Christ's final appeal to the crowds, just before His crucifixion, He says this:

> At that time Jesus declared, "I thank you, Father, Lord of heaven and earth, that you have hidden these things from the wise and understanding and revealed them to little children; yes, Father, for such was your gracious will. All things have been handed over to me by my Father, and no one knows the Son except the Father, and no one knows the Father except the Son and anyone to whom the Son chooses to reveal him. Come to me, all who labor and

are heavy laden, and I will give you rest. Take my yoke upon you, and learn from me, for I am gentle and lowly in heart, and you will find rest for your souls. For my yoke is easy, and my burden is light" (Matt 11:25–30).

It is remarkable that, in the midst of a crowd, and before He addresses that crowd directly, Jesus looks to His heavenly Father and prays. His prayer is pregnant with biblical truth, including a clear revelation of His identity and of the Trinity (the parallel passage in Luke 10:21 says that Jesus "rejoiced in the Holy Spirit"). We will focus on those aspects of this passage that are directly related to our discussion in this chapter. Notice, first of all, that Jesus is thanking His Father for His eternal, electing purposes. It is God the Father who hides and who reveals "these things" according to His "gracious will." Jesus recognizes and is announcing to the crowd that, in the proclamation of the gospel and the necessity of repentance, God is sovereign. The efficacy of the gospel finds its roots, ultimately, in the sovereign "gracious will" of the Father.

Jesus then turns to the crowd and leaves no question about His identity. He refers them to eternity-past, to that covenant of redemption that originates everything that Jesus does in history, and He says to them that His Father, who hides and reveals, has handed "all things" over to Christ. So, as we saw earlier, when Scripture teaches us that we were "chosen in Christ before the foundation of the world," part of what that means is that the Father who elects also gives to His Son the tasks, duties, and people to whom that election will apply. To choose is the prerogative of the Father; for that divine choosing to occur "in Christ" means that the Father hands the means of His electing purposes over to the Son, that it might all be accomplished in Him.

The reason that this eternal relationship in the covenant of redemption so closely identifies the Father's purpose with the Son's is because, says Jesus, in eternity, only the Father knows the Son. Not only so, but only the Son knows the Father, and that knowledge can only be had by those to whom the Son chooses to reveal it.

In other words, the context for Jesus' entire discussion in these few verses is the eternal relationship of the Triune God; here in this prayer, Jesus, rejoicing in the Spirit, contemplates the reality of redemption. And it is Jesus' task to come to earth, as He had agreed to do in eternity-past, to show and reveal the Father (cf. John 14:8–10) and then to send the Spirit to apply what Jesus had accomplished. Words are insufficient to describe the glory that these statements represent. In a matter of three short verses, Jesus has set forth the magnificent reality of God's eternal covenant and His eternal plan, even while it is nearing the completion of its historical accomplishment in Him.

After these three verses, Jesus appeals to the entire crowd. Here we find the free offer of the gospel. To *all of them,* Jesus says, "Come to me" (Matt 11:28).

God has sovereignly determined who will see the truth and from whom that truth will be hidden. This sovereign purpose originated in eternity-past, when Father, Son, and Spirit agreed to create and to redeem a people. No one could know of this agreement or of this redemption unless the Son came and Himself revealed the Father to His people. Therefore, it is incumbent on all to come to Christ, because there alone will they find rest for their souls. Our entire discussion of God's eternal decree and desire is summed up in these six verses!

Given all that we have said in this chapter, we recognize another distinction that is important to make as we attempt to think biblically about this majestic mystery. As we saw, the covenant of redemption is, as the phrase implies, a *covenant.* It is the Triune God committing Himself to redemption, and thus committing to express His character in ways that He did not have to and that were not needed "prior to" this point. The Father chooses a people; the Son agrees to obey the Father, to come and to die; the Spirit agrees to come as "another Helper" (John 14:16) who will apply what the Son has accomplished. These are all characteristics that require God's decree of creation and redemption. They are not characteristics that are required for God to be God.

When we think, therefore, of characteristics that the Triune God expresses covenantally, we see that there are "eternal" covenantal characteristics, and there are "historical" covenantal characteristics.[17] The latter presuppose the former, of course, but historical covenantal characteristics require, in some cases, a condescension in space and time that are not required of the eternal covenantal character of God.

---

17. Thanks to my colleague Lane Tipton for suggesting these distinctions.

So it may help us to remember that the mystery of God's covenantal condescension is located in the activity of the Triune God's free will. Once God determines to do something that He does not *have to* do, that determination *itself* is a condescension. It is a determination to relate Himself to something that is *not* (nor could it be) God, so that it requires (once determined) a coming down in order to establish that relationship. Once established, that relationship reveals "new" aspects of God's character that are meant to move us back to the majesty of the eternal, Triune God.

But how is it possible for One who Himself is absolutely necessary— who cannot but live, who lacks nothing, and who cannot change—to will something that is *not* necessary? That question, to which there is no answer for us, moves us back to the mystery that is the lifeblood of our theology and of Scripture. We will not, because we *cannot*, figure it out. It is beyond our comprehension, as it will always be. He is God, and there is no other.

BIBLICAL DOXOLOGY

As we have already said, this mystery of God's relationship to us can, if not properly recognized, move us to anger, or frustration, or even unbelief. But to be moved in that direction is to think too highly of ourselves and too little of God. It is, perhaps subtly or unconsciously, to place such importance on our own ways of thinking that we refuse to bow to the majesty of God. But Scripture will not countenance this way of thinking. It repeatedly moves us in the opposite direction.

The doxology that we saw in Ephesians 1:3–14 is a perfect example of this. God is to be praised because He has chosen us in Christ; He has predestined us for adoption; He has made known to us the mystery of His will, according to His purpose, which He set forth in Christ. That one, long sentence is so packed with biblical truth that it carries with it a lifetime of doxology and praise to God.

It would be a worthwhile exercise to read through the book of Psalms, keeping track of all of the reasons for which God is to be praised. When we begin to ponder those reasons, we recognize that even when we praise God for what He has done for us, the reality is— as we saw in the last chapter—that God is to be praised first and foremost not because of *us*, but for who *He* is. When we grasp who He is, we marvel again and again because of what He has done. In His majesty, lacking and needing nothing, He condescended. And in that condescension, He picked us to be with Him for eternity, and He accomplished what is needed so that we could be with Him.

This is what David had in mind in Psalm 8:

> O Lord, our Lord,
>> how majestic is your name in all the earth!
> You have set your glory above the heavens.
>> Out of the mouth of babies and infants,
> you have established strength because of your foes,
>> to still the enemy and the avenger.
>
> When I look at your heavens, the work of your fingers,
>> the moon and the stars, which you have set in place,
> what is man that you are mindful of him,
>> and the son of man that you care for him (Psa 8:1–4)?

Contemplation of God's majesty will immediately and inevitably put us in our proper place. And we will wonder, in that mystery of mysteries, why this majestic God would be mindful of us. And the only answer we will receive is "because He decided to love us, from eternity-past into eternity-future," which will only compound the mystery further, and thus further motivate our praise.

In one of his sermons, B. B. Warfield puts it this way:

> In the depths of eternity our foreseen miseries were a cause of care to Him. In that mysterious intercourse between Father and Son, which is as eternal as the essence of Godhead itself, we—our state, our sin, our helplessness, and the dreadfulness of our condition and end,—were a subject of consideration and solicitude. ... It is not simply that God has taken notice of this sinful, puny creature, that we have to consider; but that the All-Holy and All-Blessed God has felt care and solicitude for his fate and looked not at His own things in comparison with his. What indeed is sinful man that God should love him; and before the foundations of the world should prepare to save him by so inconceivable a plan as to give His only-begotten Son as a ransom for his life! My brethren,

this is not to the glory of man, but to the glory of God; it is not the expression of our dignity and worth, but raises our wondering hearts to the contemplation of the breadth and length, and height and depth of the love of God that passeth knowledge.[18]

Vast the immensity, mirror of majesty,
galaxies spread in a curtain of light;
Lord, your eternity rises in mystery
there where no eye can see, infinite height!

Who can your wisdom scan? Who comprehend your plan?
How can the mind of man your truth embrace?
Here does your Word disclose more than your power shows,
Love that to Calv'ry goes, infinite grace!

Triune your majesty, triune your love to me,
fixed from eternity in heav'n above.
Father, what mystery, in your infinity
you gave your Son for me, infinite love!

> —Edmund P. Clowney, "Vast the Immensity, Mirror of Majesty"

---

18. B. B. Warfield, *The Saviour of the World* (1916; repr., Carlisle, PA: Banner of Truth, 1991), 236.

CHAPTER 7

The Majesty of the Mystery of God's Providence and Our Choices

Every individual has only to look at his life history to discern that there was a higher hand that governed it. At this point faith in God's co-working is most closely connected with our dependence upon Him. He directs even our free acts, and however far above our comprehension may be the manner in which he does that, in any case it must be a co-working, a concursus. Not matter, not fate, not chance can affect us, if our freedom is to be maintained, but only the co-working of God (Psa 104:4; Prov 16:1; 21:1).

—Geerhardus Vos

Reformed Dogmatics

T he nature of God's providence and its relationship to our choices is illustrated in Charles Dickens' *A Christmas Carol*. After the Ghost of Christmas Future beckons for Ebenezer Scrooge to face his own gravestone, Scrooge hesitates:

> "Before I draw nearer to that stone to which you point," said Scrooge, "answer me one question. Are these the shadows of the things that Will be, or are they shadows of things that May be, only?" Still the Ghost pointed downward to the grave by which it stood. "Men's courses will foreshadow certain ends, to which, if persevered in, they must lead," said Scrooge. "But if the courses be departed from, the ends will change. Say it is thus with what you show me!"[1]

How might we answer Scrooge's penetrating question? Is it possible, by choosing one thing rather than another, to alter the course of things as they would have been?

To begin to address Scrooge's question, we need to think about the providence of God, then see how that providence relates to our responsible choices. Our discussion of God's "covenant of redemption" as well as His decrees moves us naturally to a discussion of God's providence.

As usual, the *Westminster Confession of Faith* is a good place to start for a concise explanation of providence.[2] In chapter 5, entitled "Of Providence," section 1, the confession says this:

---

1. Charles Dickens, *A Christmas Carol* (London: Blackie and Son, 1908), 102.
2. It is worth noting the rich, biblical basis for this entire chapter in the confession. The notion of God's providence is replete throughout the Bible. The Scriptures cited, in the order in which they're given in this chapter of the confession, are: Heb 1:3; Dan 4:34–35; Psa 135:6; Acts 17:25–26, 28; Matt 10:29–31; Prov 15:3; Pss 104:24; 145:17; Acts 15:18; Psa 94:8–11; Eph 1:11; Isa 63:14; Eph 3:10; Rom 9:17; Gen

> God the great Creator of all things doth uphold, direct, dispose, and govern all creatures, actions, and things, from the greatest even to the least, by his most wise and holy providence, *according to his infallible foreknowledge, and the free and immutable counsel of his own will*, to the praise of the glory of his wisdom, power, justice, goodness, and mercy.[3]

As we think of God's providence, therefore, we are referring to the fact that God upholds and directs *all things*, and that He does this "according to His infallible foreknowledge, and the free and immutable counsel of His own will." By now, these terms and concepts will be familiar to us. God knows all things in eternity-past, and that knowledge is directed by the "free immutable counsel of His own will." In other words, the providence of God means that God is working out every single detail, and each and every detail is planned in eternity-past.

The confession goes on to say, in section 2, that "in relation to the foreknowledge and decree of God, the first Cause, all things come to pass immutably, and infallibly." In other words, what God plans in eternity will *necessarily* come to pass; once determined, it is impossible that His plan could change or be altered in any way.

So it may look bleak for Scrooge at this point. How could our choices today change the way things are meant to be tomorrow? If God has planned all things, and His plan is comprehensive and immutable, wouldn't the Ghost of Christmas Future be obliged to tell Scrooge that his choices make no difference in how things will proceed in the future?

Can such a notion of God's providence be compatible with the reality of our responsible choices? I purposely left out some key elements

---

45:7; Psa 145:7; Acts 27:31, 44; Isa 55:10–11; Hos 1:7; Matt 4:4; Job 34:10; Rom 9:19–21; 2 Kgs 6:6; Dan 3:27; Rom 11:32–34; 2 Sam 24:1; 1 Chr 21:1; 1 Kgs 22:22–23; 1 Chr 10:4, 13–14; 2 Sam 16:10; Acts 2:23; 14:16; Psa 76:10; 2 Kgs 19:28; Gen 50:20; Isa 10:6–7, 12; Jas 1:13–14, 17; 1 John 2:16; Psa 50:21; 2 Chr 32:25–26, 31; 2 Sam 24:1; 2 Cor 12:7–9; Psa 73; 77:1, 10, 12; Mark 14:66–72; John 21:15–17; 1 Tim 4:10; Amos 9:8–9; Rom 8:28; Isa 43:3–5, 14; Rom 1:24, 26, 28; 11:7–8; Deut 29:4; Matt 13:12; 25:29; Deut 2:30; 2 Kgs 8:12–13; Psa 81:11–12; 2 Thess 2:10–12.

3. My emphasis.

of the quote from section 2 of the confession above. Here is what it says, in its entirety:

> Although, in relation to the foreknowledge and decree of God, the first Cause, all things come to pass immutably, and infallibly; yet, *by the same providence, he ordereth them to fall out, according to the nature of second causes, either necessarily, freely, or contingently.*[4]

So, as God controls all things, the necessity of God's decree and the providence that carries out that decree do not deny or negate the freedom or contingency that is a proper aspect of our life in the world. As a matter of fact, it is providence that *establishes* our freedom!

By now, it should be easier to anticipate how best, biblically, to think about this tension. In our discussion, we will first look at the biblical warrant for God's providence, then the theological (i.e., doctrinal) concepts that help us articulate what Scripture teaches. As in previous chapters, we can then move to biblical distinctions and from there to doxology.

BIBLICAL DEVELOPMENT

The biblical teaching of God's providence is stated or presupposed on every page of Holy Scripture. The Triune God who creates all things and who orders creation in His own perfect way does not, after creation, remove Himself and simply let the universe run on its own. Virtually every Christian would agree with this.

But there is a particular way of thinking that could hinder a full-orbed view of God's providence. This way of thinking can be seen when a biblical view of God's providence is affirmed, but then it is also thought that God is removed from the everyday affairs of the world. This view of God is one in which we would, almost unconsciously, relegate Him to somewhere above all the fray of our day-to-day existence. Instead of recognizing God working in "all creatures great and small," this mindset gives undue, even if unconscious, credence to such concepts as "Mother Nature" or to "animal instinct," so that the fact of God's activity *in* creation is rarely in our minds. This is a view that

---

4. My emphasis.

accepts that the universe and our world run according to (impersonal) laws, and not according to the working of the Triune God. It may be that this is the predominant view among many Christians today.

Perhaps this view is owing to an affirmation of God's transcendence. God is indeed "above" everything, because He is "beyond" all aspects of creation. Creation is finite; He is infinite. Creation is dependent; He is independent. Creation works according to the passing of time; He is eternal. So the transcendence of God is something that every Christian must affirm, and it is good to highlight its truth.

But if we think only of God's transcendence, we miss its complement. We must also affirm that God is immanent. That is, *even as* He is and remains transcendent, He is also in and with everything He has made, without in any way being identical to what He has made. God's presence and activity in creation are exhaustive; there is nothing in creation where God is absent. In that sense, all things are *in* God (see Acts 17:28).[5]

It is the doctrine of God's providence, then, following as it does on the doctrine of creation, that helps us to see God's exhaustive penetration and presence in everything created. The things of this world—the computer I am now using, your heart that now beats, the air that you are breathing, the sounds around you—all of these are evidence of the inexhaustible and immanent working of the Triune God.

Because of what we have already discussed with respect to God's decree, we can be relatively brief in our discussion of the biblical warrant for God's providence. As we saw in the last chapter, as Ephesians 1 moves us from eternity-past to eternity-future, it affirms the fact that God "works all things according to the counsel of his will" (Eph 1:11). We noted in the last chapter that the "counsel of His will" took us back to eternity-past, wherein the Triune God took counsel with Himself and determined whatsoever comes to pass. The decree of God refers to that triune counsel.

But we also recognize that it is *God* who works all things according to that eternal counsel. This *"working* of all things" refers us to the providence of God, who acts in the universe to carry out His decree.

---

5. We should recognize that both transcendence and immanence presuppose creation. Before there was creation, there was nothing but God—and so nothing to transcend or to be in.

The providence of God, as the confession states above, includes the fact that it is God who "upholds, directs, disposes, and governs all creatures, actions, and things." This is God's *work* of providence, and He carries out that work from the beginning of creation into eternity-future. Once begun, it is a work that will never end.

The providence of God is usually discussed under two distinct but inseparable biblical notions. The first notion is God's sovereign *government* over all that is. Again, Scripture either states this or assumes it on every page, but we can illustrate it using one familiar example.

When Joseph's brothers became jealous of him, they determined to kill him. So they threw him in a cistern, and then sold him to some Ishmaelite traders, who then took him to Egypt (Gen 37). In Egypt, Joseph became a man of power under Pharaoh. Eventually, Joseph's brothers had to travel to Egypt, and they met the brother they had harmed. Joseph said to them:

> "I am your brother, Joseph, whom you sold into Egypt. And now do not be distressed or angry with yourselves because you sold me here, for God sent me before you to preserve life. For the famine has been in the land these two years, and there are yet five years in which there will be neither plowing nor harvest. And God sent me before you to preserve for you a remnant on earth, and to keep alive for you many survivors. So it was not you who sent me here, but God" (Gen 45:4–8).

When Joseph affirms that he is in Egypt because it was *God* who sent him, he is acknowledging God's governing providence over everything. When Joseph tells his brothers that "it was not you who sent me here, but God," he does not mean to tell them that they played *no* part in Joseph's presence in Egypt. Instead, Joseph is telling them that God's superintending providence is the final explanation for his being in Egypt. John Calvin's comment on this passage is illuminating:

> This is a remarkable passage, in which we are taught that the right course of events is never so disturbed by the depravity and wickedness of men, but that God can direct them to a good end. We are also instructed in what manner and for what purpose we must consider the providence of

God. When men of inquisitive minds dispute concerning it, they not only mingle and pervert all things without regard to the end designed, but invent every absurdity in their power, in order to sully the justice of God. And this rashness causes some pious and moderate men to wish this portion of doctrine to be concealed from view; *for as soon as it is publicly declared that God holds the government of the whole world, and that nothing is done but by his will and authority, they who think with little reverence of the mysteries of God, break forth into various questions, not only frivolous but injurious.*[6]

The exhaustive and incomprehensible government of God over His creation is, indeed, as Calvin says, one of the mysteries of God. And it might provoke frivolous and injurious questions. But it should not be doubted. The same God who said, "Let there be," and there was, is the God who rules over all, with meticulous detail, such that nothing is outside of His benevolent rule and control. As Joseph, reflecting on the injustice his brothers had caused him, said to them, "As for you, you meant evil against me, but God meant it for good" (Gen 50:20). Even the wicked plot of Joseph's brothers could not thwart the purposes of God in His governing providence.

The second notion that is inextricably tied to God's providence is His *sustaining* everything that exists. Not only does God rule over all, He sustains and maintains all things. In his Areopagus address, the Apostle Paul made this clear to his Athenian audience. When Paul begins his discussion with these Athenians and philosophers, he wants them, first of all, to understand the sovereign authority of God:

The God who made the world and everything in it, being Lord of heaven and earth, does not live in temples made by man, nor is he served by human hands, as though he needed anything, since he himself gives to all mankind life and breath and everything. And he made from one man every nation of mankind to live on all the face of the earth, having determined allotted periods and the

6. John Calvin, *Commentary on the First Book of Moses Called Genesis*, trans. John King (Edinburgh: Calvin Translation Society, 1850), 2:377–78; my emphasis.

> boundaries of their dwelling place, that they should seek
> God, and perhaps feel their way toward him and find him
> (Acts 17:24–27).

God made all things; He is Lord of all things; He is independent of all things; and all things depend on Him.

Once God's meticulous sovereignty is established, Paul uses two quotations from literature that would have been familiar to most of his audience. What was *not* familiar to his audience was the application of those two statements to this God that Paul was proclaiming. The first quote gives us, in a concise way, the *sustaining* aspect of God's providence. Paul says to them:

> In him we live and move and have our being (Acts 17:28).

What Paul is telling the audience on Mars Hill is so sweeping and all-encompassing that we might miss its impact. Unlike the Greek pantheon of gods, who were limited and subject to all kinds of transcendent forces, the God of whom Paul speaks is the One *in whom* we all live, He is the One *in whom* we all move, and He is the One *in whom* we all exist.

In other words, Paul is saying to the Athenians that none of us would be here—living and breathing, listening and thinking—if it were not for the moment-by-moment sustaining of God's providence. Even as these Athenians rejected the true God and made for themselves idols, they were, at the same time, dependent on that same true God for all that they were and for all that they did. They could not move one inch, breathe one breath, think one thought, unless they were *in* God. Their very rejection of Him depended on the reality of His gracious providence![7]

One more passage that concisely sets forth God's sustaining providence is Hebrews 1:3. So much could be said about these initial verses in Hebrews that it is difficult to summarize them. As the author is intent to show that the Son of God, as our great high priest, is greater than the angels, greater than Moses, greater than the Levitical priests,

---

7. For more on the apologetic significance of Paul's address at Athens, see K. Scott Oliphint, *Covenantal Apologetics: Principles and Practice in Defense of Our Faith* (Wheaton, IL: Crossway, 2013), or access it in the Logos Bible Software digital library.

he begins with a glorious description of who this Son is. He is the One whom the Father appointed "the heir of all things, through whom also he created the world. He is the radiance of the glory of God and the exact imprint of his nature, and *he upholds the universe by the word of his power.* After making purification for sins, he sat down at the right hand of the Majesty on high, having become as much superior to angels as the name he has inherited is more excellent than theirs." (Heb 1:2–4)

The Son is the one who upholds all things. If He were to let it go, even for a second, it would completely cease to exist; it would be no more. The only reason things continue on as they do is because of the exhaustive, sustaining power of the Son of God. John Calvin comments on this providence of the Son:

> To uphold or to bear here means to preserve or to continue all that is created in its own state; for he intimates that all things would instantly come to nothing, were they not sustained by his power.[8]

The One who sustains the world is the same One who has come down and made purification of sins for His people.

The Triune God, through the Son, governs and sustains the universe. All of his governing and sustaining is the working out of His eternal decree in history. How, then, does that providence relate to the actual events that take place in the world on a daily basis? Is everything *simply* necessary because it is exhaustively determined in eternity? Does the Ghost of Christmas Future need to tell Scrooge that his choice is meaningless in the end?

BIBLICAL DOCTRINE

God's Providence

There is a deep and abiding mystery when we think of God's providence in relation to our decisions and choices. Before we look at that more closely, we have to get straight just what we mean when we speak of God's providence, *in light of our choices.* We will not be concerned

---

8. John Calvin, *Commentary on the Epistle of Paul the Apostle to the Hebrews,* trans. John Owen (Edinburgh: Calvin Translation Society, 1853), 37–38.

here with events and circumstances that happen that are unrelated to our choices and actions. Those events are no less controlled and ordained by God, but the particular mystery that we are concerned to highlight surrounds God's providence in relation to what we decide.

So, we will briefly set out three predominant views of God's providence, given human choice. These views are all attempts to articulate how it is that God controls all things, given that events seem to happen according to responsible choices that we make. In other words, how does God's providence *work with* human choices, since God's providential control *includes* each and every choice? Here it will be important to remember that God's providence includes both His governance, and His maintaining or sustaining of all things.

We can better understand these three views if we set them out in relation to two propositions:

1. *God causes* everything at every moment (GC).
2. *Humans cause* things to happen in this world (HC).

One view of God's providence is that HC is true, but GC is not. In other words, this view would hold that while God *sustains* everything, He cannot control or govern everything, especially not our choices. This view has been called "preservationism" because it allows *only* for God's preservation of all things, but not His governance of everything. In this view, we are the sole causes of what we choose in this world.

A second view is sometimes called "occasionalism," because what we choose to do in the world is only the *occasion* for God's causal control. In this view, there is no HC; only GC applies. God immediately— always and everywhere—*causes* to happen whatever we choose to happen. This view is sometimes called "continuous creation" because it supposes that each and every thing that happens is, at the point that it happens, *created* by God. God's providence, then, is His perpetual "let there be ..." in the world, at every moment in history.

These two views want to emphasize opposite notions. The first wants human beings to be their own, independent causes, even though God continues to sustain them. The second view wants God to be the *only* cause of each and every effect. Neither of these views is the most predominant view in Christianity.

The third view, usually called the "concursus view," wants to hold that *both* GC and HC apply to God's providence. The word "concursus" is a Latin term that means "to run together." This is the predominant Christian view, and it is the view expressed by the confession above. In this view, God is the original, or first, cause of any choice that we make, and a person is the second, or dependent, cause of that choice. When we choose something, there is a concursus taking place, in that God has ordained and caused that choice, but we also really and responsibly choose. God causes first, but is not responsible for what we choose. Then, concurrent to God's cause, we choose and are, thus, secondary causes. But how can there be a first and second cause involved in my choice, and only the second one be *responsible* for it? Herein lies the mystery.

Human Choices

There is, perhaps, no more explosive a term in theology than the term "free will." Its pedigree in theology goes back at least to the early church fathers. It is a concept that has been discussed and debated throughout the history of the Church.

Fortunately, we need not recount that debate. We can be content to let the *Westminster Confession* frame our discussion. Chapter 9 of the confession is entitled, "Of Free Will." This might be surprising in itself, since many think that a Reformed confession like this one would have no place for such an idea. On the contrary, and as usual, the confession packs mountains of material in a few short sentences and paragraphs. Section 1 of that chapter says this:

> God hath endued the will of man with that *natural liberty*,
> that it is neither forced, nor, by any absolute *necessity of*
> *nature*, determined to good, or evil.[9]

There are key ideas in this statement that need some explanation.

The term "natural liberty" (*voluntati naturalem*) is meant to point us to the fact that when man—male and female—was created, God created them with the ability to choose in such a way that their choices

---

9. My emphases.

would have consequences in the world. This is, in part, what it means to be "image of God."

There are a multitude of things that can be said, and have been said, about what it means to be image of God. Scripture nowhere gives us a concise and obvious definition of what it means. But that does not mean that we do not know what God intended for His image. We can only scratch the surface here of such a deep and rich biblical concept as image of God, but a few salient points can be highlighted:

1. As soon as God determines, by way of His own counsel, to create man (male and female), He assigns *dominion* to them.

> Then God said, "Let us make man in our image, after our likeness. And let them have dominion over the fish of the sea and over the birds of the heavens and over the livestock and over all the earth and over every creeping thing that creeps on the earth" (Gen 1:26).

No other created thing is given this dominion. God creates man to be a "little lord" over the Lord's own "house." Man is to take what God has made and (under God) be ruler over it, to do it good, and to use it for the good of man and to the glory of God.

This dominion command of God to man changes the structure of creation entirely. For five days, creation was God's alone, to use and to organize as He saw fit. But now, on the sixth and crowning day of creation, God makes something that is meant to image His character, and He gives to man the responsibility to rule over His creation. We are given no exact details as to what that rule would look like. We are not privy to the everyday activity of Adam and Eve in the garden. But whatever it is they were doing, they were doing it in the context of their *covenant responsibility* to God.

2. Clearly, then, at the initial act of creation, to be image of God meant that man—male and female (1:27)—was put in a *responsible relationship* to God, a relationship that included man's dominion over what God had made. That which God made for His own enjoyment, was also made for man's responsible rule. In one sense, God gave His creation over to man so that God's enjoyment of it would include the daily work and process of man's obedient dominion over it. That dominion was a *responsible* dominion, which would have consequences.

We can see one of the consequences, for example, in the relationship of God to man in naming the animals. Because man now had dominion over creation, he was given the responsibility of naming the animals. And because this naming process was a responsibility given by God, God's sovereignty over Adam's responsibility was highlighted; it was *God* who brought the animals to Adam to name (Gen 2:19-20). It is not *simply* that Adam was given responsibility to name the animals; rather, it was that Adam was to exercise his dominion over the earth by naming the animals that *God brought* to him. This is a picture of God giving Adam his dominion responsibilities, even while those responsibilities are carried out in relationship to, and within the ultimate control of, the sovereign Lord Himself.

3. God not only shows His sovereignty positively by bringing Adam animals to name, but He shows His own sovereign rule over creation negatively by delimiting one aspect of creation that Adam and Eve could *not* rule over. He set aside one tree in all of the garden and made it clear that it was not a part of their dominion. In doing so, he was also reminding them whose creation it was in the first place. They were to leave that tree alone; it was not to be part of their dominion mandate.

There was, as far as we're told, nothing significant about the tree that God chose. According to the account in Genesis, God simply designated one tree as "the tree of the knowledge of good and evil" (Gen 2:17) and told Adam and Eve that their dominion was restricted by that tree. It was God's sovereign dominion that delimited and designated the dominion of Adam and Eve.

Even as they ruled in the garden, their rule was never meant to be exhaustive; they were not to touch, much less to rule over, that one tree. This was a visible, tangible way that God reminded man that his lordship over creation had its origin and its character in the ultimate Lord of all.

The rest, as they say, is history. We know all too well what happened next. Adam and Eve sinned; they were deceived into thinking that their dominion should extend to *every* part of the garden, even the tree from which God had forbidden them to eat. They rejected God's exhaustive rule and tried to usurp it. When they did, their relationship with God was forever changed, and God's *good* creation itself began to *groan* (see Rom 8:19-22). Man fell from his sinless state, and creation lost its "goodness." Since that first sin, people have continued to attempt to be sovereign over their own lives, with nothing but tragic results. Consequences followed Adam and Eve's choices; consequences follow all of man's choices.

We all no doubt wish things had remained as they were before Adam sinned. But what it means (in part) to be "image of God" is that Adam and Eve, and all human beings after them, are *responsible* to God for their activity in this world. God gives commands to us. Whether we obey or disobey those commands, there will be consequences. Our responsibility is what it is because of the relationship that God established with man on the sixth day. To be responsible to God is to be in a covenant relationship with Him that is unique and radically different from the rest of creation.

The notion of "image," in other words, is by definition a *relational* word. An image requires a relationship to its original. A painting or picture is what it is only because it is the image of the original. It could not be what it is without the original. Without the original, there can be no image. This relationship, as we see in the garden, is characterized by how the image acts toward its original. To the extent that it "mirrors" its original, it is what it is meant to be. To the extent that it tries to hide its origin, it shows itself to be something it was never meant to be. For an image to pretend to be an original is, by definition, a grotesque and horrid distortion of reality; it is a hideous pretense.

4. The relationship that God establishes with His image is founded in God's speech to them. When God created the sea creatures, He blessed them, saying, "Be fruitful and multiply and fill the waters in the seas, and let birds multiply on the earth" (Gen 1:22). When God created Adam and Eve, we get the same kind of language, but with a significant difference:

> And God blessed them. And God said to them, "Be fruitful and multiply and fill the earth and subdue it, and have dominion over the fish of the sea and over the birds of the heavens and over every living thing that moves on the earth." And God said, "Behold, I have given you every plant yielding seed that is on the face of all the earth, and every tree with seed in its fruit. You shall have them for food (Gen 1:28-29).

With the creation of man comes God's blessing. But now, instead of "God said," we read, "God said *to them*." There is now, by virtue of man being created, male and female, in God's image, a relationship in which God speaks to man and establishes the terms of His relationship to them. At no other point in creation is this speech of God relationally and responsibly directed *to* what He has made—only with Adam and Eve. It also was this speech of God that set apart "the tree of the knowledge of good and evil."

God told Adam and Eve what they were to do in and with His creation, and He told them what they were not to do. Embedded in this covenant responsibility to God is the fact that Adam and Eve could either choose to be obedient to God in the garden, or they could choose to disobey. If they chose to obey, they could inherit life eternal with God; if they chose to disobey, death for them would be certain. Either way, it was their choice, and their choice would bring about the requisite consequences.

When the confession says "natural liberty," it is referring to this *ability to choose*, an ability that was given to our first parents in the beginning and which, since we remain the "image of God" even after the fall into sin, we never lose. To have a will, in other words, just means *to choose*. That ability is not lost at the fall. If we retain a will, we retain the natural ability to choose.

A related phrase in the confession's statement in chapter 9 is that our wills are not, by any "absolute necessity of nature, determined to good or evil." What this means is that our choices are never "naturally determined." A *natural* determination would be one that comes from the order of creation itself. But creation does not work out of necessity. In order for a choice to be a choice, *we* are the ones who have to choose. An "absolute necessity of nature" would allow for no choice at all because *nature* (i.e., creation) would itself and alone have *determined* what we do.

Another look at Genesis 1 might help to illustrate this. When God created the birds and the fish, He "blessed them, saying, 'Be fruitful and multiply and fill the waters in the seas, and let birds multiply on the earth'" (Gen 1:22). This command, however, is not one that implies responsible choices on the part of the birds or fish. Unlike when God spoke to man, God is not speaking *to* the birds and fish. Instead, God is *saying* what their behavior in this regard will be. Thus, the propagation of birds and fish is according to a "necessity of nature." There is no free choice involved. It is, rather, a description of how they *must* act.

The commands God gave when man was created, however, were given *to* man, and the consequences of man's choices were made clear. There was, in the command not to eat from the tree of the knowledge of good and evil, no "necessity of nature" with respect to that command. It was man's responsibility to choose, and his choice would bring about certain events, whether good or bad.

Now it looks like Scrooge's quandary might be answered. Remember Scrooge's conundrum as he peered over his grave: "Men's courses will foreshadow certain ends, to which, if persevered in, they must lead. ... But if the courses be departed from, the ends will change." Doesn't this sound like God's command to Adam and Eve?

> And the LORD God commanded the man, saying, "You
> may surely eat of every tree of the garden, but of the tree
> of the knowledge of good and evil you shall not eat, for in
> the day that you eat of it you shall surely die" (Gen 2:16–17).

In other words, eating from the tree will foreshadow death, but to avoid that tree would lead to life eternal. The choices they make will have direct consequences for the direction of their future.

"But wait a minute," someone might protest, "haven't we been saying all along that God ordained whatsoever comes to pass, and that His decree is immutable? Isn't everything that happens already determined in eternity-past?" The answer to these two questions is, "Yes and yes."

BIBLICAL DISTINCTIONS

What Must Be and What Might Be

In order to develop the "yes and yes" answer above, we need to look at another aspect of what it means that God Himself is *necessary* and that His covenant is *contingent* (i.e., freely determined by Him). So far we have two truths that might seem to be in tension: God determines everything, including our choices; and the choices we make are responsible choices that bring their own consequences. This tension should come as no surprise by now. Every previous chapter has contained truths that are in tension, truths that are difficult for us to put together. We have seen that these tensions comprise the glorious mystery of God, and of His relationship to us, and to all of creation! The truths we are discussing here are no exception, so the "solution" to the tensions discussed in this chapter might not be surprising either.

We can begin to address some proper distinctions related to this tension when we consider God's character. Remember that God's will is both necessary *and* free. He necessarily wills Himself, which is just one way of saying that He necessarily desires to be who He is. It would not be possible for God, in Himself, to desire to be someone or something else. Also, because He is exhaustively self-sufficient, anything that is "not God" could never define who He is as God. This means that a desire or a willing for something beyond Him could not be essential to who He is as the Triune God. This is what we mean by His necessary will.

But God also has free will. He can determine to do things He does not have to do. We saw this in the previous chapter when we were discussing God's decision to take counsel with Himself and then to decree. God could have simply remained who He is. He lacks nothing; He is sufficient unto Himself. There is nothing in Him that required that He create or that He redeem. But He determined that He would decree, and that determination was a *free choice* that God made.

Because God freely (i.e., contingently) determined to create and to redeem, creation and redemption are themselves contingent. To be "contingent" means something might exist or it might not. Thus, creation and redemption are realities that are not necessary; they are what they are because God freely decided they would be. He could just as well have decided they would *not* be. Your existence is contingent; so is mine. *Everything that is*, except God, is contingent. There is nothing that *has* to be except God; everything else did not have to be at all.

Think again for a moment about how mysterious this is. How can God, who is absolutely necessary and who lacks nothing, even *do* something that is not necessary? If His character is exhaustively necessary, how can there be any freedom or contingency at all with respect to God?

The only answer that we have is that there is both necessity (what *must* be) and contingency (what *might* be) with respect to God's will. He is absolutely necessary. While He cannot change, neither is He bound by His necessity in such a way that everything He does *must be* necessary. He is bound by His necessity such that He cannot decide that He isn't necessary, just as He cannot decide that He doesn't want to be God anymore (2 Tim 2:13). But this binding of God's will is just to say that God's character is immutable. He is who He is!

But, even as there are things that *cannot be* with respect to God, we also have to agree that the personal, Triune God wills things (Himself!) that are necessary, and He also wills things (creation) that are contingent. These two aspects of God's character are not the same in every way. In terms of God's will, we could say that His necessary will has priority, because it has *Himself* as its object; His contingency follows and flows from His necessity, but its focus is always and only on things that are outside of God (in that they are *not God*). So neither necessity nor contingency can be denied of God's will, or He would not be God. Even if He had not decided to create, He would still have the ability freely to decide to do things He did not have to do. As a personal God, He eternally has the ability freely to decide or determine something that is not necessary. We know this primarily because God determined to create.

It should not surprise us that creation is analogous to God in this way. If we descend from thinking of God's character and think about God's creation, we see embedded in creation (just as we see in God's character) both necessity *and* contingency, and both coming together in a beautifully mysterious harmony. The necessity that pertains to creation is found, first, in God's eternal, exhaustive, and comprehensive decree. The fact that He freely determined, in eternity-past, whatsoever comes to pass does, indeed, mean that everything that happens, including our choices, *must* happen in exactly the way they have been ordained to happen. Everything in creation is a product of God's eternal counsel. His providence is the application of that eternal decree in creation. In providence, God applies what He has decreed; He has decreed *everything*; and what He has decreed *must* happen— it could not happen any other way (cf. Isa 46:10; Prov 16:33).

However, although God has determined that everything that happens *must* happen, the things that we choose are themselves contingent. When we choose, in other words, *what* we choose remains contingent, even as it is determined by God's decree. As in God's character, so also in God's creation; there is a "uniting" of necessity (i.e., God's decree and providence) and contingency (i.e., our choices) without either one destroying the nature of the other. This is the crux of the mystery; we must affirm two truths that don't easily connect in our minds.

We can return here to our discussion of the person of Christ to further illustrate, by analogy, this truth. We will remember that Christ is one person with two natures. The nature of His deity is something that must be. He *must* be God. There is no possibility that He would not be God; His divine nature is necessary. But His human nature is *not* necessary. It is something that the Triune God freely decided the Son would take to Himself. Even as He did take a human nature, however, that nature did not alter or change His divine nature. He is both God (necessarily) and man (contingently). His human nature does not impose on His divine nature, even as His divine nature does not impose on His human nature. Both natures remain, fully and completely, exactly what they are. And both are united in Christ, so that necessity and contingency are harmoniously united in one person.

As in Christ there are two fundamentally different natures, so also is God able to bring together, in creation, the necessary (decree and providence) and the contingent (or covenantal) choices so that they are in harmony with each other, without one of them undermining or in any way imposing on the other.

When God decrees all things, there is no possibility that those things will not be or will not take place exactly as decreed. Once freely determined, they are necessary. But even though they are what they are by virtue of God's decree, we cannot think that the decree eclipses or negates or denies the contingency of created things. Creation, though it *must be* what God has decreed it will be, will also always be contingent; it cannot be otherwise.

Perhaps a few biblical illustrations of this real contingency will help us to see it for what it is. After King Saul disobediently offers a burnt offering to the Lord, the prophet Samuel comes to rebuke him. He asks Saul what he has done, and then Samuel says to Saul:

> You have done foolishly. You have not kept the command
> of the LORD your God, with which he commanded you.
> *For then the LORD would have established your kingdom over*
> *Israel forever.* (1 Sam 13:13)

Notice what Samuel says. He says to Saul that *if* he had kept the commandment of the Lord, then the Lord would have established his kingdom over Israel forever! By that, Samuel does not mean, "If only the Lord had decreed otherwise, He would have established your kingdom forever." Instead, he means to say that if Saul had chosen to obey rather than disobey, the Lord would have established his kingdom forever. In other words, there was, and remained, a contingency to Saul's choice. If he had acted differently, his kingdom would have been established over Israel.

This does not in any way mean that, from the perspective of the eternal decree, things were in flux. Even though what Saul did was according to the necessity and foreordination of God's decree and providence, there remained a real contingency to his choice. From history's perspective (which is *our* perspective, since we are not privy to the details of God's decree), he could have chosen to obey, and Samuel makes that clear to Saul by declaring from the Lord what would have happened if Saul had obeyed. But from the perspective of the eternal decree, things happened exactly as they were decreed to happen. From Saul's perspective, and from the perspective of his choice, contingency remained. In some mysterious way, therefore, the necessity of God's eternal decree does not rule out the reality, in history, of what could have been. As a matter of fact, as we have seen in each chapter, the eternal and necessary establishes the contingent; it is the eternal decree that grounds and gives meaning to the contingency of the choices we make.

There is an even more mysterious example of this in the New Testament. At the time of Jesus' betrayal by Judas, Peter took his sword and cut off the ear of one of the guards who came to arrest Christ. The words of Christ following this incident are pregnant with mystery. He says to Peter:

> Put your sword back into its place. For all who take the sword will perish by the sword. *Do you think that I cannot appeal to my Father, and he will at once send me more than twelve legions of angels?* But how then should the Scriptures be fulfilled, *that it must be so?* (Matt 26:52–54)

Christ says to Peter that He has the ability to appeal to His Father, at that very moment, and the Father could immediately send angels to help Him. In other words, at the very moment when Christ is being betrayed, *even as events are unfolding exactly according to the eternal plan and counsel of God*, Christ is, nevertheless, *able* to call on His Father to stop the betrayal.

We might expect Christ to say, at this point, "But then how could God's decree be carried out?" But He doesn't appeal to the eternal decree. Instead, He appeals to what all could know: He appeals to Holy Scripture. If Christ asked His Father for a legion of angels to help Him, the Scriptures that say "that it must be so" would not be fulfilled. In one statement of Christ, we have the contingency of what He *could* do and the necessity of what Scripture says *must* be. Both work together in utter and magnificent mystery, and Jesus, in his statement to Peter, is not in the least troubled by this.

It is worth pausing over Jesus' response. Isn't it fascinating that Jesus does *not* say to Peter and His audience, "But because God has decreed that I must die, and has providentially controlled events accordingly"? Instead, Christ says, "But how would Scripture be fulfilled?" Even in His betrayal, as He *willingly chooses* to be obedient to His Father, He recognizes that He has come, not as a puppet who goes through the motions of what has been eternally decreed, but as one who delights in choosing to accomplish the will of His Father (Heb 10:7)! Christ—the very one in whom necessity (His deity) and contingency (His humanity) are brought together into a unity—affirms the contingency (what *might* be) of His own death, even though that death was necessary (what *must* be) according to the Scriptures and the eternal decree and providence of the Triune God (see Acts 2:23). It would be difficult to imagine, in God's covenant, a more profound mystery than this!

Perhaps we can now more clearly see the mystery of God's all-encompassing providence and our responsible choices. Remember how the confession puts it:

> Although, in relation to the foreknowledge and decree of God, the first Cause, all things come to pass immutably, and infallibly; yet, by the same providence, he ordereth them to fall out, according to the nature of second causes, either necessarily, freely, or contingently.[10]

---

10. *Westminster Confession of Faith* 5.2.

The confession magnificently includes both aspects of our discussion. Yes, God is the "first Cause." Everything that happens happens "immutably and infallibly." But, in God's providence, in the application of God's comprehensive decree, the things of this world "fall out" according to the (covenantal) contingency of creation itself. Some things fall out "necessarily"; a square, for example, is what it is necessarily. When all the conditions of a square are met, nothing but a square is possible. Some things fall out "freely, or contingently." Our choices, though ordained and caused by the first cause, are, nevertheless, naturally free and contingent.[11] In other words, the majestic mystery of God's character, as including both His necessary will and His free will, is reflected in the majestic mystery of creation itself, which includes God's decree (what *must* be) and our choices (what *might* be).

If we seek to minimize—or worse, deny—either aspect of this mystery, not only do we fail to understand creation as God has decreed and made it, but we inevitably fall prey to the rationalism that we discussed at the beginning of this book. Rationalism will either affirm God's necessity and conclude that everything is *only* necessary, which leads to fatalism or abstract determinism, or it will affirm *only* the contingency of our choices and conclude that God could not plan and control them, which leads to a very minimal and anemic god, not the Triune God of Scripture. Rationalism never leads to proper praise and worship. It can only be smugly satisfied with its own intellectual accomplishments. It is, in that sense, grotesquely self-serving, the polar opposite of praise.[12]

---

11. "Contingency" and "freedom" are distinguished in the confession in recognition that, for example, the existence of the universe is contingent and the will of man is (according to its *nature*) free to choose.

12. Note, to use one recent example, the view of one philosopher who is arguing for what he calls "Philosophical Arminianism": "Rampant and facile appeals to the mysteries of the faith when paradox threatens is just anti-intellectualism in sophist drag. In contrast, the defense of Philosophical Arminianism ... arises in the context of a full commitment to pursue understanding than to settle for appeals to mystery" (Jonathan L. Kvanvig, *Destiny and Deliberation: Essays in Philosophical Theology* [Oxford: Oxford University Press, 2013], xiv–xv).

The Slavery of Sin

Readers aware of the Reformed view of sin and its consequences might feel a little uneasy at this point in our discussion. Reformed theology has consistently affirmed that we are all "dead in [our] trespasses and sins" (Eph 2:1); that "the natural person does not accept the things of the Spirit of God, for they are folly to him, and *he is not able to understand them* because they are spiritually discerned" (1 Cor 2:14, my emphasis); that "the mind that is set on the flesh is hostile to God, for it does not submit to God's law; indeed, *it cannot*" (Rom 8:7, my emphasis). Scripture is clear that sin has caused spiritual *death* (not simply sickness) in us; it has rendered us *unable* to understand the "things of the Spirit"; it has enslaved our thinking so that we *cannot* submit to God. How, then, dare we speak of a "freedom" of the will, when Scripture is clear that the fallen will *cannot* choose for Christ?

As we might expect by this point, we meet our friend mystery again in this question. But it might help to recognize another distinction that is important to make in this context. In the first section of the *Westminster Confession*, chapter 9, we highlighted (above) the affirmation that there is no "absolute necessity of nature" when it comes to the will of man. So the will is *naturally* free. "Natural" freedom refers to the image of God. Since we are image of God, we always have the ability to choose. Just as being the image of God means we retain the ability to think, so also with the will. It is the will's "job," as it were, to choose; if there is a *will*, there must be *choice*. Since we have a will, even after the fall, it must retain its natural ability to choose.

But just because we have the *natural* ability to choose, that does not mean we have, as Adam and Eve did, the ability to choose either good or evil. Since the fall into sin, since we are dead in our sins apart from Christ, we have lost the ability to choose for Christ. But we still choose, because sin did not destroy the image of God that we are as God's human creatures. The will always chooses, but it chooses according to the *nature* of the person choosing. In the garden, Adam's will could choose to obey or disobey. After the fall, we still choose, but we always choose what we want, and we always want sin. Our depravity does not mean that we do not choose; it means that, in our sin, we always choose sin. When we're converted to Christ, there is a change of our nature, so that we can choose either to obey or disobey, just as Adam could. In the new heaven and new earth, since we—our nature—will be glorified, we will still choose, but we will always and only choose the good. In none of these cases do we lose our wills; the will remains in its natural state. But the will, like the mind, follows the nature of the person, and those natures are subject to change.

Recall again the occasion when Jesus was lamenting over Jerusalem because they rejected the prophets, even as they had rejected Him. He wanted, repeatedly, to gather them together as a hen gathers her chicks. But what was the problem? Jesus was clear about their problem: "You were *not willing*" (Matt 23:37; Luke 13:34). That is what moral slavery is. That is the problem that sin brings. We still have a will naturally able to choose, but, in our sins, we always *want only* to choose sin.

BIBLICAL DOXOLOGY

As we have emphasized in every chapter, the mystery of God and of God's relationship to creation is a cause for praise and worship. The more we delve into the nature of God's character, given to us in Scripture, and the more we reflect on God's relationship to creation, the more mysteriously and majestically complex things become. That complexity points us to "the depth of the riches and wisdom and knowledge of God" (Rom 11:33). Each of these mysteries presents to us new and unfathomable aspects of God and His work. All of these mysteries are meant to point us to God and to evoke in us the need to laud and honor His holy name.

This is no less true as we consider God's providence in relation to our choices. Again, this is the point of that one, long sentence that we have already looked at in Ephesians 1:3–14. It begins with doxology:

> Blessed be the God and Father of our Lord Jesus Christ, who has blessed us in Christ with every spiritual blessing in the heavenly places, even as he chose us in him before the foundation of the world, that we should be holy and blameless before him. In love he predestined us for adoption as sons through Jesus Christ, according to the purpose of his will, to the praise of his glorious grace, with which he has blessed us in the Beloved. In him we have redemption through his blood, the forgiveness of our trespasses, according to the riches of his grace, which

> he lavished upon us, in all wisdom and insight making
> known to us the mystery of his will, according to his pur-
> pose, which he set forth in Christ as a plan for the fullness
> of time, to unite all things in him, things in heaven and
> things on earth. In him we have obtained an inheritance,
> having been predestined according to the purpose of him
> who works all things according to the counsel of his will,
> so that we who were the first to hope in Christ might be to
> the praise of his glory (Eph 1:3–12).

We refer to this passage again because to read this section slowly, in light of our discussion thus far, is to catch a glimpse of the glory of God as He "works all things according to the counsel of His will." As He does so, however, we also see that there are many choices that we must make, as God's providence is always at work. God chose us in Christ; from that point, there is no possibility that we could not be found in Him in the end. But that fact does not negate the contingency of our choice to be "holy and blameless"; we are predestined that we might be adopted as sons. And Scripture commands us to be holy (1 Pet 1:15–16). So, we are chosen and predestined to salvation and holiness, and we are commanded to be saved and to be holy.

All of this—the tensions that exist in light of God's providence and our real, contingent choices—is meant to move us to praise. As Ephesians 1:3 begins, it begins with "blessing" to God because of the unfathomable blessings with which He has blessed the church.

Scrooge was correct. From our (historical) perspective, if he were to depart from his courses, the ends would indeed change. But they won't change simply *because* they were departed from. Whatever the ends, they were all eternally decreed and ordained by God in eterni-ty-past. Both truths work together.

There is no hint that these tensions and mysteries have to be resolved in our own minds; attempts at resolution always blur the truth of the matter in contexts like this. The biblical view is to affirm both together and to keep them in biblical balance. They are designed by God to be a catalyst for our worship. As we think of God's prov-idence, as we are confronted with choices that we must make, we are to recognize God at work. We should see His unbreakable and impenetrable plan, and we should choose to be holy, to be obedient.

We should praise Him for the majestic mystery that His providence, and our responsible choices, reveal to us.

> While all our hearts and all our songs
> Join to admire the feast,
> Each of us cry, with thankful tongue,
> "Lord, why was I a guest?
> Why was I made to hear your voice,
> And enter while there's room,
> When thousands make a wretched choice,
> And rather starve than come?"

—Isaac Watts, "How Sweet and Awful Is the Place"

CHAPTER 8

The Majesty of the Mystery of Prayer

The God of the Bible, who has revealed Himself as the hearer of prayer, is not mere intelligence and power. He is love. He feels as well as thinks. Like as a father pitieth his children, so the Lord pitieth them that fear Him. He is full of tenderness, compassion, long-suffering, and benevolence. This is not anthropomorphism. These declarations of Scripture are not mere "regulative truths." They reveal what God really is.

—Charles Hodge

Systematic Theology

T here is, perhaps, nothing so obvious in our Christian experience, and nothing so neglected, as the reality of prayer. We know we are meant to "pray without ceasing" (1 Thess 5:17), to "pray earnestly" (Matt 9:38), to devote ourselves to prayer (Acts 1:14), to "be constant in prayer" (Rom 12:12). So much of Scripture assumes that we pray, and then regulates how our prayers ought to be offered (see, for example, Matt 6:5-15).

The concern of this chapter, however, will not be with the practice of prayer *per se*. That practice is monumentally important for our Christian growth, so the neglect of it here is not meant to undermine its sanctifying significance for us. Instead, we want to discuss prayer in light of the mystery of God and His relationship to us. There is much, much more of substance that could be said about prayer, but our focus will remain intentionally narrow as we highlight the tension that might be present when we consider the reality of prayer for the Christian.

The quote above from Charles Hodge is found in the section in his *Systematic Theology* entitled "Prayer." As Hodge is concerned to highlight, the fact that Christians pray to God assumes that He is a personal God who loves, feels, and thinks; He is full of tenderness and compassion. He loves to hear from His children. Hodge affirms what we have been at pains to elaborate in this book: The same Triune God who is infinite, eternal, and unchangeable also is "full of tenderness, compassion, long-suffering, and benevolence." As Hodge affirms, *this is not mere anthropomorphism*. That is, Scripture does not present these truths as simple metaphor. Instead, says Hodge, the truths of God's compassion, tenderness, and so forth, "reveal what God really is." As we have seen already, this truth is a mystery, and we have tried to show a proper way to think about these mysteries in previous chapters.

However, as we consider the biblical truth of God's comprehensive decree and providence, perhaps nothing brings to light the tension of God's decree and providence in light of the contingency of creation more than the biblical emphasis on prayer. The tension can be expressed like this: Since God has decreed and providentially controls "whatsoever comes to pass," what meaning can prayer have? Why should we petition God about *anything*, since *everything* has already been determined by Him in eternity-past? What significance can such petitions have if they're all settled in eternity?

This tension may not be, for most of us, the primary reason that we are prone, at least at times, to neglect to pray. But anyone who has thought about prayer in light of God's sovereignty has likely struggled with this tension. By this point, it might be obvious how we will want to discuss this tension. If so, then the book has been a success. It has instilled in the reader the practice of seeing some of these majestic mysteries of Scripture in light of a "both/and" equation rather than an "either/or." Because the earlier formula has been applied throughout our previous discussions, we should be able to apply it here a bit more briefly.

BIBLICAL DOCTRINE

We should have firmly in place the model of majestic mystery that is God's covenantal condescension, and we will now recognize the "both/and" of combining God's providence with the "what might be" (contingency) of creation. In that "both/and," we recognize that prayer, like everything else that comes to pass, is decreed by God. That has to be our starting point. But we also see that our prayers are more than a necessary component of God's decree. It is a contingent choice of obedience that, in some mysterious way, contributes to the plan of God.

Our discussion of prayer is simply a more specific example of our discussion in the last chapter. Prayer is an example of *choices* we make, even as we recognize that such choices are themselves included in God's immutable decree and His meticulous providence. Because this chapter continues our discussion from the last chapter, we can focus our discussion of prayer more narrowly. In that focus, we will consider a couple of the key prayers of Jesus Christ.

For example, in Luke 22, we learn that the disciples were aware of their place of privilege. They knew that they were chosen to be close companions of Jesus Christ. But the great blessing that they had received from their Master turned into an occasion for dissension. We don't know exactly how the topic came up, but they began to argue about which of them would be the greatest in the kingdom. Matthew tells us that the dispute began with the two sons of Zebedee (James and John), and that the rest of them became indignant about it (Matt 20:20–28). Jesus responds to their dispute, first, by comparing it to what the Gentiles do:

> The kings of the Gentiles exercise lordship over them, and those in authority over them are called benefactors (Luke 22:25).

He then explains something to them that might have sounded initially enigmatic to them:

> Let the greatest among you become as the youngest, and the leader as one who serves. For who is the greater, one who reclines at table or one who serves? Is it not the one who reclines at table? But I am among you as the one who serves (Luke 22:26–27).

This is gospel logic that Jesus is teaching his disciples. It is logic that is patterned after the life of the Messiah Himself. Those who are great in the kingdom of God are those who serve. This is the pattern of their Savior, as the Son of Man came not to be served, but to serve. Jesus is telling them, in effect, that His kingdom will not be a kingdom where those who think themselves to be the greatest lord it over the rest. Rather, the kingdom will be like the King, who humiliated Himself and came to serve, not counting His own greatness and status as something to be exploited (see Phil 2:7–11).

It was in this context that Scripture recounts a brief and fascinating interchange between Jesus and Peter. Jesus says to Peter:

> Simon, Simon, behold, Satan demanded to have you, that he might sift you like wheat, but I have prayed for you that your faith may not fail (Luke 22:31–32).

Jesus immediately addresses Simon Peter. One of the reasons the Lord singles out Peter here is because He has in view Peter's soon-to-come threefold denial (see Luke 22:34). Though Christ is speaking directly to Peter, He tells him that Satan has set his sights on *all* of the disciples—the "you" in "sift *you* like wheat" is plural. It is particularly about Peter, however, that Christ is here concerned. He knows that Peter will deny Him; but Christ also knows that Peter's denial, unlike Judas' betrayal, will not destroy him.

The cross of Christ and all the events surrounding it were saturated with satanic subversion. Satan had deceived himself into thinking that if he could somehow thwart the ministry and message of Christ *and His followers*, his victory would be assured. (As we know all too well, Satan's deception continues, as does his onslaught). So Satan makes a request of God; he asks God if he can shake up and destroy the faith of Christ's closest companions.

This heavenly scene, to which Christ is privy, is similar to the one we see at the beginning of the book of Job. There, Satan comes before God and is given permission to curse Job (see Job 1:7–12). In Luke 22, we learn that a similar scene has transpired, and Jesus has knowledge of it. Satan has come before God and has asked to shake the disciples' faith to the core.

Of all of Jesus' true disciples who were in danger of a failing faith, Peter was one of the most susceptible. Though all of Jesus' companions left Him when the trial of the cross came, Peter was the one, Jesus recognized, whom Satan would tempt in a special and focused way. He would tempt him to deny his Master, not once, or twice, but three times. Such an intense and repeated denial could easily lead Peter to an ultimate and final rejection of his Savior. But Peter would not reject Christ in the end. And why not? Because, says Jesus, "I *have prayed for you* that your faith may not fail."

Here, then, is a picture of the heavenly battle that is raging around Peter's faith. Christ is moving inexorably toward the cross. Satan foolishly thinks he has a chance to thwart what Christ will accomplish. One way to make the cross irrelevant is to make sure that Jesus' disciples, in the end, reject Him and refuse His message. That message, Satan fears, is one that will be propagated, promoted, and passed down in the church.

It is upon Peter's confession ("You are the Christ, the Son of the living God," Matt 16:16) that the Church will be built. Not only so, but as the Church marches on in history, Jesus promises that "the gates of hell shall not prevail against it" (Matt 16:18). Satan is well aware of this promise, and of the "rock" of Peter's confession, on which the Church will be built. He hates this promise. He wants the gates of hell to confine and constrain everyone, including those who claim allegiance to Christ!

So Satan asks God for the Twelve; he wants their souls. Could this request of Satan's be the reason they began disputing over who was the greatest? Could it be that Satan, as he had done with Eve ("You will be like God," Gen 3:5), was attempting to convince the Twelve that their own fellowship with Christ was not enough for them, and that they needed *more*, they needed to be *greatest* in God's kingdom? Perhaps. But what is clear from this passage is that Satan had convinced the Twelve that the way of greatness could not be the way of suffering. They were more committed to their own preservation than they were to following in the footsteps of their Master, the "Suffering Servant."

Jesus knows that Satan will tempt Peter, and the temptation will be a success, because Peter will deny Him. Jesus predicts it. His prediction is based on His certain knowledge of the future. There is no possibility, once predicted, that Peter will not deny his Master (though, as we have already seen, it is *Peter* who is responsible for his denial). Given this knowledge, what does Jesus do? He doesn't resign Himself to a certain and decreed future. Instead, *He prays*! He prays that the denial will not lead to utter rejection.

There can be no question that Peter was one of God's elect. He was, with the rest of the Lord's people, chosen before the foundation of the world. He begins his first epistle writing to those who, like him, are chosen "according to the foreknowledge of God the Father, in the sanctification of the Spirit, for obedience to Jesus Christ and for sprinkling with his blood" (1 Pet 1:2).

Jesus, of course, knew this as well. Even so, His reaction to the demand of Satan before the throne of God was to pray. His reaction was not to try to deduce from the truth of election to the conclusion of the impossibility of Peter's faith failing. Instead, He beseeched His heavenly Father so that Peter's faith would remain intact, even amidst the onslaught of Satan's schemes.

But if Peter is one of God's elect, why did Jesus think it necessary to pray for Peter's faith? Because, as we saw in our previous chapter, when we train our minds to think biblically, the guarantee of the salvation of the elect—even if we were to know who the elect are—does not allow us to ignore, undermine, or disregard "what might be." The truth of God's certain election must be seen in light of the real contingency of our day-to-day choices.

Was it possible that Peter's faith would fail under Satan's sway? From eternity's perspective, certainly not! Nothing in God's decree—and God's decree encompasses everything—can ultimately fail. But Jesus' prayer surely assumes that possibility. The possibility, however, was not from the perspective of eternity; it was from the perspective of history. From the perspective of our daily, contingent lives, Peter's faith might fail.[1] Jesus' prayer assumes that contingency. We have no knowledge of the details of the eternal decree. So Christ recognizes the centrality (and the effects) of prayer in light of His, and our, daily experiences.

As we have seen from the beginning of our discussion in this book, the model of majestic mystery requires us to see things that look to be opposites as working in unity and harmony as God interacts with His creatures. God's electing purposes are not opposed to the possibility of Peter's faith failing; Christ's prayer (itself decreed) is needed so that Peter would persevere. Somehow, mysteriously and majestically, the two work perfectly together. As a matter of fact, the truth of God's decree requires the reality of prayer, since prayer itself is a part of what God decrees.

There is another passage that shows us the attitude of the Savior as He moves inexorably toward His dreadful destiny:

> And he came out and went, as was his custom, to the Mount of Olives, and the disciples followed him. And when he came to the place, he said to them, "Pray that you may not enter into temptation." And he withdrew from them

---

1. In other words, we must train our minds to think of "possibility" from both the perspective of eternity and the perspective of history. What is not possible according to the eternal decree is not possible, period. But since we are not privy to the details of the decree, possibility has to be calibrated by us within the context of our daily decisions.

about a stone's throw, and knelt down and prayed, say-ing, "Father, if you are willing, remove this cup from me. Nevertheless, not my will, but yours, be done." And there appeared to him an angel from heaven, strengthening him. (Luke 22:39-43)

We have already seen in our previous chapters that the cross of Christ was determined and arranged and thus was certain, even before the foundation of the world. To be chosen *in Christ* includes the fact of Christ accomplishing redemption by way of the cross (see Eph 1:4-6). The cross was a central and integral element of the covenant of redemption between the Father, the Son, and the Holy Spirit. Once planned in eternity, it must take place, exactly as planned, in history.

But now we see Christ nearing the event of the cross, recognizing all that it would entail. We might think Christ's attitude toward the cross would be one of holy resignation. He knew He had to die; He was clear about that (see, for example, Matt 20:18; Mark 10:33, 45; Luke 22:14-20; John 16:4-7). There is no indication anywhere in the Gospels that Jesus thought His death was in any way uncertain or doubtful.

Even so, before He was to die, Scripture gives us the actual con-tent of Jesus' prayer to His Father. He is entreating His Father to find another way. He prays to His Father according to His own will, even as He submits His will to the will of His Father. In that moment of anguish, Jesus acknowledges that His desire is for another way. Surely, as He is contemplating the reality of being rejected by His Father, whose love for His Son is as strong and close as any love could be, Jesus is constrained to request that such a rejection not become a reality.

There are two important things to note about this prayer. First, the request that Jesus made of His heavenly Father was in no way sinful. It could not be sinful because Jesus obeyed His Father perfectly. It is not sinful, therefore, to request something of our heavenly Father that might go against the way things appear to be. We are not meant simply to accept everything that comes our way, as if we had no recourse to our Father. The Christian life is not characterized by a stoic attitude that just takes everything that comes. Much that comes our way is a result of sin and evil in the world, and it is not sinful to ask our Father to override those sinful effects. In one sense, that's what Jesus was doing. The cross itself was a result of sin; it was the epitome of evil. The death that it would bring would be the only underserved death in all of history. And Jesus didn't want it, if there was any other way.

Second, when what we ask for in our prayers is not granted, we should never think that our prayers are not heard or answered. We often speak of "answered" prayer, and by that we mean that the Lord has granted our request. But even if He does not grant the request, He has still heard, and He has answered.

This can be seen explicitly in Jesus' request in the garden. Notice how the book of Hebrews explains this event in Jesus' life:

> In the days of his flesh, Jesus offered up prayers and sup-
> plications, with loud cries and tears, to him who was able
> to save him from death, and he was heard because of his
> reverence. (Heb 5:7)

This is Scripture's own interpretation of Jesus' prayer in the garden of Gethsemane. He offered up his prayers "with loud cries and tears" because He knew that His Father "was able to save him from death." And, Scripture says, Jesus "*was heard* because of his reverence." In other words, Jesus received an answer to His prayer. That answer, as Hebrews goes on to say, shows us what the Father was concerned to do with His Son:

> Although he was a son, he learned obedience through
> what he suffered. And being made perfect, he became
> the source of eternal salvation to all who obey him.
> (Heb 5:8–9)

The reason the Father answered "no" to His Son was because His Son had to continue to learn obedience through what He was about to suffer (see Phil 2:8). The reason the Son had to learn obedience was so that He could be the source of our eternal salvation.

This, then, is the sobering and humbling truth about the Son's prayer to His Father: The Father heard His Son, and He said "no" to His Son *for our sakes*, not for His. There was nothing that Jesus had done that required that He suffer. His suffering was necessary only *for us*, not for Him. If the Father had said "yes" to His Son on that day, then there would not have been, and would never be, the possibility of salvation for anyone, ever!

The more we think about this, the more we see majestic mystery on top of majestic mystery. Here we have the eternal Son, in the flesh, according to His human will, beseeching His Father to grant something that would subvert what the Father, Son, and Spirit had already decreed from eternity.

But gospel logic requires that we see all of this as God's mysterious harmony in creation. Christ saw no conflict in His distressful request; His human will was that His course to the cross be changed. But His Father's will was different. He said "no"; He heard, but He denied the request. In all of this, there can be no question that, in the mind of Christ Himself, the possibility of avoiding the cross was very real, and was worthy of a passionate request to His Father.

We can picture it, perhaps, like this: As the Triune God condescends to covenant with creation, and with His people, all that He did in His eternal decree lays the foundation for everything that would happen in history. Nothing that happens could happen unless it was first decreed. But that decree does not take away from the real contingencies of creation. As a matter of fact, the decree must be understood in light of those contingencies.

In God's covenantal condescension, what *must* be (the decree) is in perfect harmony with what *might* be (in history)—just as what *must* be in the Son (His divine nature) is in perfect harmony with what *might* be (His human nature). The same God who unifies the two natures of Christ in history also unifies His own providence and our prayers in history. How this can be remains mysterious to us. As we get an all-too-frail glimpse into the incomprehensible ocean of God's ways, mystery on mystery should bring forth worship on worship in us.

BIBLICAL DOXOLOGY

Speaking of worship, one of the passages that we discussed earlier is particularly important here as well for a proper understanding of this "both/and" relationship of God's plan and our prayers.

After the apostle John is transported to the throne room of heaven, he sees God on the throne (Rev 4:2–11). Following this vision of God, John is treated to the heavenly image of Christ's redemption accomplished:

> Then I saw in the right hand of him who was seated on
> the throne a scroll written within and on the back, sealed

with seven seals. And I saw a mighty angel proclaiming with a loud voice, "Who is worthy to open the scroll and break its seals?" And no one in heaven or on earth or under the earth was able to open the scroll or to look into it, and I began to weep loudly because no one was found worthy to open the scroll or to look into it. And one of the elders said to me, "Weep no more; behold, the Lion of the tribe of Judah, the Root of David, has conquered, so that he can open the scroll and its seven seals."

And between the throne and the four living creatures and among the elders I saw a Lamb standing, as though it had been slain, with seven horns and with seven eyes, which are the seven spirits of God sent out into all the earth. And he went and took the scroll from the right hand of him who was seated on the throne. And when he had taken the scroll, the four living creatures and the twenty-four elders fell down before the Lamb, each holding a harp, and golden bowls full of incense, which are the prayers of the saints. And they sang a new song, saying,

"Worthy are you to take the scroll
    and to open its seals,
for you were slain, and by your blood you ransomed people for
    God
    from every tribe and language and people and nation,
and you have made them a kingdom and priests to our God,
    and they shall reign on the earth." (Rev 5:1–11)

We find out in this chapter that the One sitting on the throne has a scroll in His hand, which is sealed with seven seals. This scroll is the redemptive plan of God, and there is no one worthy to open it—*until* the Lamb comes and is pronounced worthy to break the seals and to open the scroll.

The image we have in this chapter is of the redemptive plan of God, written on a scroll. It is a *complete* plan, which is why it is written "within and on the back." Only one who is worthy to carry out such a complete plan may open the scroll. To carry out God's plan one would have to be perfect. He would have to be one who is pleasing to God and who has the ability perfectly to execute the plan. Only the Lamb is worthy. He takes the scroll, which is in the right hand of God, and He carries out the plan from the place (the right hand of God) where the scroll used to be (see, for example, Psa 110:1; Heb 1:1–3).

We should recognize here that what the apostle John sees in this vision is something that has already happened at the time that he sees it. We might think that the book of Revelation shows us only what is going to happen in the future, but that is not the case. Here, John sees what the Lamb has accomplished, and what His accomplishments mean for the rest of history.

There are two aspects to this revelation from the apostle John that bear directly on our discussion of prayer in this chapter. First, we see that the scroll contains a complete and comprehensive plan. It is full of writing, and there is no room left to write anything else. It is, in other words, God's redemptive decree, encompassing everything, and it is in need of someone who has the authority to carry out that decree (see Matt 28:18ff.).

But notice, secondly, what is included in the worship of the Lamb: "And when he had taken the scroll, the four living creatures and the twenty-four elders fell down before the Lamb, each holding a harp, and golden bowls full of incense, *which are the prayers of the saints*" (Rev 5:8).

As the Lamb enacts the redemptive decree of God, worship is offered to Him. Included in that worship is the incense, which are the prayers of the saints! In other words, what we have in the throne room of heaven is the worthy Lamb commencing the complete and comprehensive redemptive plan of God, but doing so in the context of the prayers of the saints that are offered to Him in worship.

This heavenly altar combines the redemptive plan of God, which itself needs no addition and from which nothing can be subtracted, with the prayers of the saints, and the result of this combination is redemption itself! That redemption, as the "new song" in this chapter shows, has its central focus in the Lamb (who is the Lion—Rev 5:5) and His perfectly accomplished work. Mingled with that work, however, are the prayers of the saints.

This is simply one more example that pictures for us the "both/ and" of God's decree/providence and the efficacy of our prayers. In this heavenly scene, the Lord brings together the truth of both. The Lamb's work on earth is finished. He alone is worthy to carry out the redemption that God had planned from eternity-past. But included in the worship of the Lamb and His perfect work are all the pleas of the saints. Those pleas rise up as sweet incense to God Himself, as they constitute a necessary aspect of the plan and worship of the Lamb in heaven.

But there is one more glorious and mysterious truth about prayer that must be the conclusion to our discussion. When we recognize, as we saw above, that Jesus prays for Peter, we may think to ourselves, "Wouldn't it be incredible to have Jesus pray for me?" As a matter of fact, it is incredible, and *He does* (see, for example, John 17:20, 23-24)!

In Hebrews 7:25, the author tells us something significant about Christ's ongoing ministry in heaven:

> Consequently, he is able to save to the uttermost those who draw near to God through him, since he always lives to make intercession for them.

In the ongoing ministry of the Lamb who was slain, even as He now sits on the throne to rule as King of kings (Heb 1:3), He lives there to make intercession for us. The One who is the true and final prophet (Heb 1:2) is also our Great High Priest. As our High Priest, He always lives, and He stands in heaven before the throne of His—and our—Father, and He pleads our case. His earthly work is finished, but He continues His work in heaven in order to save us "to the uttermost."

It would be difficult to imagine or construe something that is so utterly and majestically mysterious as this. Think of our discussion thus far in these pages, and now see how they all merge together in Christ's ministry of intercession. Here is the Son of God, the Second Person of the Trinity, who Himself is truly and fully God. As this Triune God relates to finite and temporal people such as us, this Son has permanently assumed to Himself a human nature, which has been united in His one person. This Son, together with the Father and the Spirit in His triune counsel in eternity-past, chose a people for Himself. In order to save those who were chosen, there would have to be forged a way back to the Father, which only the Son could do. He prepares that way by His obedient life and obedient death. He calls many to repent and believe, and He sincerely desires that they follow Him.

And now here He is, exalted in heaven, at the right hand of the Father, praying to the Father in our behalf. *Even in heaven,* as the prayers of the saints are mingled together with the sovereign plan of God, the Son, Jesus Christ, is interceding for us. That intercession, without a doubt, makes a difference in our status before God. It makes a difference in our perseverance, in our holiness. We live in Him now, because He is interceding for us now. His earthly work in our behalf— His life, His death, His resurrection—were all necessary for our salvation. But they were not the end of His work.

There was and is more that our Savior has to do. He has to be our High Priest *forever* (see Heb 5:6; 6:20; 7:3, 17, 21, 24, 28; 13:8). And the priestly work that He continues to do for us is to intercede. He stands in the gap between the Father and us, and it is only because He stands there that we can be saved "to the uttermost." In fact, it is Christ's intercession that is the necessary background to our own prayers. He prays so that we might pray.

We can conclude our discussion here with John Owen's trenchant comments on this verse in Hebrews:

> What is the glory of the throne of God, what the order and ministry of his saints and holy ones, what is the manner of the worship that is given unto Him that sits on the throne, and to the Lamb, the Scripture doth sparingly deliver, as knowing our disability, whilst we are clothed with flesh and inhabit tabernacles of clay, to comprehend aright such transcendent glories. The best and most steady view we can have of these things, is in the account which is given us of the intercession of Christ. For herein we see him by faith yet vested with the office of the priesthood, and continuing in the discharge of it. This makes heaven a temple, as was said, and the seat of instituted worship. ... Upon all these grounds, unto all these purposes, hath he appointed the continual intercession of the Lord Christ in the most holy place. This he saw needful and expedient, unto the salvation of the church and his own glory. So will he exert his own almighty power unto those ends. The good Lord help me to believe and adore the mystery of it.[2]

---

2. John Owen, "An Exposition of the Epistle to the Hebrews," ed. W. H. Goold. The Works of John Owen 5 (Edinburgh: Johnstone and Hunter, 1855), 544.

Arise, my soul, arise; shake off thy guilty fears;
The bleeding sacrifice in my behalf appears:
Before the throne my surety stands,
My name is written on His hands.

He ever lives above, for me to intercede;
His all-redeeming love, His precious blood, to plead:
His blood atoned for every race,
And sprinkles now the throne of grace.

My God is reconciled; His pardoning voice I hear;
He owns me for His child; I can no longer fear:
With confidence I now draw nigh,
And "Father, Abba, Father," cry.

—Charles Wesley, "Arise, My Soul, Arise"

CHAPTER 9

The Majesty of the Mystery of Our Eternal Joy

Is Christ so glorious? What will heaven be, but the seeing of the glory of Christ? If God had created worlds of glorious creatures, they could have never expressed his glory as his Son; therefore heaven is thus expressed, John 17, "I will that they be with me, to behold my glory." Wherein lies therefore that great communion of glory that shall be in heaven? It is in seeing the glory of Christ, who is the image of the invisible God that is worshipped.

—Thomas Goodwin

Sermon on Hebrews

S ince we have been focusing all along on the majesty of mystery that Scripture gives us, we want to continue and conclude that focus in this chapter. This chapter is not meant to be a thorough, biblical exposition of our eternal existence with Christ. There are resources available that can provide a helpful way to think about our eternal future.[1] What we hope to do instead is provide a way of looking forward to the glorious mysteries that will occupy us as we worship and praise our Triune God in the new heaven and the new earth.

When it comes to the mode and manner of our existence after death and before Christ comes back, the Scriptures give us only hints. This is the case, we should recognize, because our existence after death and before Christ comes back *is a result of the entrance of sin in the world*. In other words, the so-called "intermediate state"—which means our existence between physical death and our bodily resurrection at the second coming of Christ—is an *un*natural existence; it is what it is because sin has come into the world, and death through sin (Rom 5:12). The unnatural reality of the intermediate state has two significant implications.

First, it means that the intermediate state is *temporary*. We sometimes forget that when our loved ones die they go to a place that is *not* their (and our) final home. Instead, they go to a place that is a transition toward, in that it looks forward to, that final destination. So, even after death, there is still a "waiting" that characterizes our existence there.

Second, because the reality of the intermediate state is unnatural, the mode of our existence there is unnatural as well. The fact that, after death, we are separated from our bodies is a product of sin. It is not the way we were intended originally to function as human beings.

---

1. One of the most helpful resources available is Anthony A. Hoekema, *The Bible and the Future* (Grand Rapids: Eerdmans, 1994).

To be separated from our bodies is unnatural, and not the way we will function for eternity (see 1 Cor 15:50–54).

So, the mystery that surrounds our unnatural, intermediate existence has to do with the paucity of information that Scripture gives to us about that existence. It is not that the Lord failed to give us all the information we *need*. Rather, the information given still leaves unanswered a number of questions that we might want to ask. But since Scripture is sufficient to give us all that we need to live as Christians in this world, it is our duty to be content with what the Lord has given us in His Word, even when questions might remain.

BIBLICAL DEVELOPMENT

The Hebrew word "Sheol" is used some 67 times in the Old Testament (the Greek word used to translate "Sheol" is "Hades"). In the Old Testament, the place where the dead exist is called "Sheol," or sometimes also "Abaddon." "Sheol" can mean a pit or ravine; it can also mean a place for the dead. When used in conjunction with "Abaddon" (which means "destruction"), it typically means a place reserved for punishment. What seems clear in the Old Testament is that Sheol is a less-than-desirable place to be (see, for example, Gen 37:35; Num 16:30; Deut 32:22; 2 Sam 22:6; Job 7:9; Psa 6:5; Prov 7:27; Isa 14:11; Hos 13:14).

Some have speculated that Sheol is the place where *all* who die must wait until the second coming. In this scenario, Sheol is seen to have two different "spaces" within it, one for the wicked and one for the righteous. This interpretation is consistent with the parable that Jesus told about the rich man and Lazarus (Luke 16:19–31). In that parable, both the righteous Lazarus and the wicked rich man are in a place of waiting. Lazarus is at Abraham's side, far away from the rich man, and the rich man is in torment (16:23), but both are waiting for the end.

In the Old Testament, the place of Sheol was not clearly defined. In Hosea, for example, the Lord asks, "O Death, where are your plagues? O Sheol, where is your sting?" (Hos 13:14). These questions will be familiar to us, as Paul repeats them in 1 Corinthians 15:55. However, as Paul quotes Hosea and translates these questions into Greek, he does not use the word "Hades," the typical Greek substitute for "Sheol." Instead, he uses *thanatos*, the Greek word for "death."

This understanding is consistent with the general theme of Sheol in the Old Testament. Sheol, then, is a product of the reality of death; in that sense, it is not a "reward," but a place looking forward to our final destiny. Whatever or wherever it is, there can be no question that its existence is due to that "last enemy," death. In that sense, it can refer simply to "the grave," or it can indicate the place where those who have died continue to exist until Christ comes to judge.

Whatever and wherever Sheol (Hades) is, two things are clear about it. First, like death itself, its existence is a result of sin, and it is, therefore, temporary. This is the primary reason that the emphasis in Scripture is that Sheol is a less-than-desirable place; it is what it is because *death* came into the world.

The Bible looks at sin as unnatural. Even though, to us, it is the "normal" way things are in our world, it is *not* the way things were originally created. Sin is an ugly and destructive intruder into God's good creation. Because of sin, we want to distort and mangle the goodness of God's creation according to our own selfish desires. So much of what we see in the world is a result of those sinful desires.

But sin is not normal. As it imposes itself on what God has made—both internally, as we seek to distort the image of God, and externally, as creation groans because of sin—it (we) wants to destroy the original intent of creation.

It is in this sense that Sheol (Hades) and Abaddon are *abnormal* places that are only necessary, and temporarily so, because of the entrance of sin and disobedience in the world. Just as sin came into the world and interrupted God's perfect work of creation, so also Sheol is an interruption in the final destiny of the Lord's people. As an interruption, therefore, Sheol is the result of sin and death, both of which will meet their final and complete end when the Lord returns.

The second thing that is clear in Scripture—clearer, of course, in the New Testament than in the Old—is this: Whatever and wherever Sheol is, there is no question in Scripture that those who die *in Christ* go to be with Him, as they wait for their final consummation.

The parable referred to earlier indicates as much. While the rich man is waiting in torment, Lazarus waits at Abraham's side. Because this parable is told before Christ's work is finished, the "natural" place for the Lord's true people to be is at the side of their Old Testament "father." This place of waiting was a place for the *living*, as Jesus made clear (Matt 22:30-33); both the rich man and Lazarus are conscious and alive after death. The Lord identifies Himself as the God of the living. Those who are His are those who live, because He lives. Jesus indicates that those who rightly knew their Old Testaments would have recognized this truth.

In the New Testament, there is movement from the Lord's people waiting at Abraham's side, as they continue to live after death, to the Lord's people waiting with Christ, as they continue to live after death (2 Cor 5:6-8; Phil 1:23; Rev 6:9; 7:9; 15:2).

What is clear from Scripture is that, once the Lord breathed into man the breath of life so that he became a living soul (Gen 2:7), and once He created Eve from Adam, the life that was given to each of them would never be extinguished. Changes would occur, due to the radical effects of sin. We will, for a time, be separated from our bodies until Christ comes back. Even so, each and every one of us will continue to exist somewhere, consciously, after death.

Physical death is, therefore, for one and all, a *transition*, not an *end*. It is a movement from our familiar surroundings to a place that is unfamiliar to us. For those who die in their sins, in Adam, that place continues to be a place characterized by God's wrath (even as their existence on earth was so characterized). For those who die in Christ, they continue to be with Him at death, and they are with Him in such a way that it is "far better" (Phil 1:23) than life here with Him. So, even though the death of a Christian does not signal our final destiny in the new heaven and the new earth, it does move us to a place that is better than what we currently experience. In that way, it is a welcome transition place, as we await the new heaven and the new earth.

In our existence after death, therefore, whether we are in Adam or in Christ, the covenantal relationship that God established with His human creatures continues. It is a relationship that will never end. When Christ comes back, that relationship will reach its consummate end, as those who are in Adam are forever under His wrath, in hell, and those who are in Christ are forever partakers of His unmerited grace, in the new heaven and the new earth. The reality is that once God establishes a relationship with us, initially in and through Adam, that relationship will never cease. He breathes His breath into us, and that signals for us the guarantee of continued existence, into eternity.

It is impossible for us, given what God has told us in Scripture, to know the details of what our intermediate state, as well as our existence in the new heaven and new earth, will look like. We are not given a specific picture of those places or of our existence in those places. What we do know is that God will continue to be present with all of His human creatures, and their existence in His presence will either be one of eternal torment, or it will be one of eternal fulfillment, in Him. This, too, is an unfathomable mystery for us on "this side." For the Christian, it is a glorious mystery as we look forward to a "far better" life with Christ, even in a state that exists because of sin! After that, our existence is nothing but consummate bliss, as we are and do, for eternity, exactly what we were created to be and to do, in Christ.

BIBLICAL DESTINY

There is a fascinating passage in the first letter to the Corinthians that is often overshadowed by its context. First Corinthians 13 is famously known as "the love chapter." It is indeed an exposition of the biblical view of love; that is the main point of the chapter. It is important to recognize, however, the reason why such an exposition was needed.

The Corinthians wrote a letter to the apostle Paul. In that letter, they asked him a number of questions. Paul set out to answer their questions, beginning in chapter 7. Notice: "Now concerning the matters about which you wrote" (1 Cor 7:1). As Paul moves through the questions in their letter to him, he typically begins by addressing them in the same way: "Now concerning ..." (see 1 Cor 7:25; 8:1; 12:1). Beginning in chapter 12, he addresses their questions about spiritual gifts.

It is not clear exactly what the Corinthians had asked Paul about spiritual gifts. What is clear is that Paul knew, perhaps from their questions, how they were viewing and using their gifts in the church in Corinth. The Corinthians were taking the good gifts that the Lord had established in and given to the church and were making those gifts the focus of dissension and pride. As with the disciples who argued about who was the greatest in Christ's kingdom, the Corinthians were arguing about whose gifts were the greatest. They were ranking their spiritual gifts, from the least to the greatest. Those who had the "greatest" gifts thought themselves to be in no need of those who had "lesser" gifts. Thus, many in the church, because of the gifts God had graciously given to them, determined that they were not in need of the church at all. They had the "greater" gifts, or so they thought, and that was all that they needed.

Paul rebukes them for their self-centered pride and for thinking that the church is, like the military, simply a collection of "ranked" individuals. He uses the analogy of a body to show that all parts of the church are equally important and equally needed, if a body is to function properly. No part of a body would say to another, "I don't need you," because then it would cease to function as it should. So also the individuals of a church are meant to function as the body of Christ, not working as greater or lesser individuals, but working together properly to show forth the unity-in-diversity of God Himself.

It is in this context of the Corinthians' questions about spiritual gifts that Paul pens "the love chapter." The point of that chapter is, ultimately, to show the supremacy of the gift of love: "So now faith, hope, and love abide, these three; but the greatest of these is love" (1 Cor 13:13). If it is a ranking of gifts that is important to the Corinthians, then Paul's instruction is that love must be seen to be the greatest gift, even over the gifts of prophecy, tongues, and teaching. Surely, no matter what other gifts people in the Church might have, the gift of love is the great equalizer. All in the Church are meant to have it and to exercise it toward each other (cf. Matt 22:36–40).

One of the ways that Paul argues in 1 Corinthians 13 is to remind his readers of the temporary character of so much that is now integral and necessary for our Christian walk. It will be helpful to have the passage in front of us as we consider it in light of our discussions of mystery:

> Love never ends. As for prophecies, they will pass away;
> as for tongues, they will cease; as for knowledge, it will
> pass away. For we know in part and we prophesy in part,
> but when the perfect comes, the partial will pass away.
> When I was a child, I spoke like a child, I thought like a
> child, I reasoned like a child. When I became a man, I gave
> up childish ways. For now we see in a mirror dimly, but
> then face to face. Now I know in part; then I shall know
> fully, even as I have been fully known. So now faith, hope,

and love abide, these three; but the greatest of these is love (1 Cor 13:8–13).

Paul invokes two analogies to explain the supremacy of love as our greatest spiritual gift. The first is the analogy of childhood to adulthood; the second is the analogy of a reflection in a mirror to its reality.

The two analogies are not identical in their scope but are meant to provide two important, distinct but related, truths concerning the relationship of this life to the next. The first analogy teaches us that this life is analogous to childhood. Children speak differently than adults; their thinking is partial, even while it grows. The first analogy shows us that this life, especially our Christian life, is a process of *growth* and of moving forward to adulthood and to completion in glory.

The second analogy tells us more about that "childhood to adulthood" stage, in which we all reside this side of heaven. To "speak like a child" and to "think like a child" means, says Paul, that, for now "we see in a mirror dimly." The term Paul uses here, translated "dimly," is the Greek word *ainigma*, from which we get the English word "enigma." An enigma is something mysterious or puzzling. Paul's point is that, in this life, what we see with the eyes of faith we see "enigmatically." We do see, but our mode of seeing is as through a mirror. It is not the fullness of the actual thing that we see, but a reflection of the actual, and that reflection remains an enigma to us. Charles Hodge, in his commentary on the word "dimly," puts it this way:

> The idea may be that we see divine things as it were wrapped up in enigmas. We do not see the things themselves, but those things as set forth in symbols and words which imperfectly express them.[2]

It is important at this stage to recognize what Paul is *not* saying in these analogies. It might be tempting to conclude that the truth that we now have from the Lord, as it is given in His Word, is therefore imperfect and insufficient to reveal what it purports to reveal. But this is no part of Paul's teaching here.

---

2. Charles Hodge, *An Exposition of the First Epistle to the Corinthians* (New York: Robert Carter & Brothers, 1857), 274.

Paul's analogy of childhood to adulthood, for example, is meant to communicate the *process* of *true* speaking and *true* knowledge, not a *contrast* of false knowledge and true knowledge. So also, a mirror *adequately* reflects, even if "dimly," the reality of which it is a reflection. A mirror does the job it is meant to do. But the image in a mirror, even when adequate, is an indirect reflection of reality. Paul's point here is *not* that childhood and mirrors are distortions or denials of the way things are, or of our knowledge of them. His main point is that there is more, much more, to come.

We can see that the way Paul brings up these analogies explains their use. He uses the analogies of "childhood/adulthood" and "mirror images/face to face" in order to illustrate what he means when he further says, "But when the perfect comes, the partial will pass away." The word "perfect" (*teleion*) here is not referring to a moral quality. It refers to "completion" or "fullness." So, adulthood is analogous to the "perfect" and childhood is compared to the "partial." "Face to face" provides the completion of reality, whereas a mirror image is only partial. In both cases, however, there is continuity, and not discontinuity, between the "partial" and the "perfect." Childhood *leads to* adulthood; a mirror image *points to* the reality it reflects.

The point of our discussion of this passage thus far, in relation to our overall discussion of mystery, is found in what Paul says at the end of verse 12: "Now I know in part; then I shall know fully, even as I have been fully known." This verse can sound confusing if taken on its own and out of context. On its own, it might be thought that Scripture is telling us that there will be a point at which we will know everything; we will know "fully." There will be no more mystery, as we will know all that there is to know. As a matter of fact, this is not Paul's point. Now that we have looked at the context, what Scripture says here will be more obvious to us. Paul is explaining the fact that, as history advances toward its final goal, the Church is in process. That process includes good and necessary gifts, gifts that the Church is given for encouragement and for spiritual growth in this life. But, as with childhood, some of those gifts are only for a time; they are partial and will not be needed when time is no more and when the perfect comes. The gifts are given because the full reality is not yet present to us; they are given to those who must see that reality in a mirror dimly in this life.

So, to paraphrase our passage, it is not as though we don't know at all. Rather, it is that we know, but in part. It is not as if we are unable to see; we *do* see, but we see as in a mirror. We see "enigmatically." But, there will come a day when we will no longer see in a mirror dimly; we will no longer walk by faith. The faith that is necessary for us now in this life will give way to sight then, in the new heaven and new earth. The enigmatic images that we see now will give way to our face-to-face knowledge of Jesus Christ. The love that will remain in and for us, as faith and hope no longer remain, is a direct consequence of God's eternal love for us. B.B. Warfield masterfully sums up these aspects of our eternal joy. The quotation is full, and worth every word:

> Surely, we shall not wish to measure the saving work of God by what has been already accomplished in these unripe days in which our lot is cast. The sands of time have not yet run out. And before us stretch, not merely the reaches of the ages, but the infinitely resourceful reaches of the promise of God. Are not the saints to inherit the earth? Is not the recreated earth theirs? Are not the kingdoms of the world to become the Kingdom of God? Is not the knowledge of the glory of God to cover the earth as the waters cover the sea? Shall not the day dawn when no man need say to his neighbour, "Know the Lord," for all shall know Him from the least unto the greatest? O raise your eyes, raise your eyes, I beseech you, to the far horizon: let them rest nowhere short of the extreme limit of the divine purpose of grace. And tell me what you see there. Is it not the supreme, the glorious, issue of that love of God which loved, not one here and there only in the world, but the world in its organic completeness; and gave His Son, not to judge the world, but that the world through Him should be saved? And He said unto me, "Come hither, I will shew thee the bride, the wife of the Lamb. And he ... shewed me the holy city Jerusalem, coming down out of heaven from God, having the glory of God. ... And the city hath no need of the sun, neither of the moon, to shine upon it: for the glory of God did lighten it, and the Lamb, the lamp thereof. And the nations shall walk amidst the

light thereof; and the kings of the earth do bring their glory into it. And the gates thereof shall in no wise be shut by day (for there shall be no night there): and they shall bring the glory and the honour of the nations into it: and there shall in no wise enter into it anything unclean, or he that maketh an abomination and a lie; but only they which are written in the Lamb's book of life." Only those written in the Lamb's book of life, and yet all the nations! It is the vision of the saved world. "For God so loved the world, that He gave His only begotten Son, that whosoever believeth in Him should not perish, but have eternal life." It is the vision of the consummated purpose of the immeasurable love of God.[3]

Isn't this why love is the greatest gift? Isn't this why it is love that remains in us when faith and hope are no longer needed? Knowing "fully," as Paul puts it, means knowing according to the culmination of the love of God, which is demonstrated on that final day, when we will walk, for eternity, by sight. On that day, the mysteries that have occupied us in this book will all be visible as we peer into the revelation of the Triune God in His glorified Son. Then only will we know as we have been known.

ETERNAL MYSTERY

This is the glorious truth of our eternal destiny. Our entrance into eternity, in the new heaven and the new earth, is what everyone in Christ is destined for. *But that entrance into the fullness and completion of eternity-future will not diminish—but rather will enhance—the majestic mysteries of the Christian faith.* To know "fully" is to be face to face ("by sight") with the mysteries that have occupied our attention throughout this study.

Speaking of our "perfection" on that last day, Charles Hodge puts it this way: "We may be perfect in our narrow sphere, as God is perfect

---

3. B. B. Warfield, *The Saviour of the World* (1916; repr., Carlisle PA: Banner of Truth, 1991), 129–30.

in his; and yet the distance between him and us remains infinite."[4] In other words, we should never expect, nor should we desire, that the majesty of mystery will cease with our full and complete, face to face, walk with the living, Triune God in eternity.

Let's see what this means in light of our discussion up to this point. We recognize the truth that God is, and will always be, triune. As three persons, He will always be one God. We should not expect that we can ever, not even in eternity-future, plumb the depths of God's ontological triunity. To exhaust the character of God would be to *be* God. The Spirit of God knows the deep things of God (1 Cor 2:10–11), but man can never know in the way that God knows. We can and do know *truly*, if we have the Spirit of God (1 Cor 2:12), but we cannot know exhaustively, not now, and not ever. The character of God as altogether holy and utterly independent will remain for us a majestic mystery and will be our motivation for worshiping Him for eternity.

As triune, we also saw that God condescends in order to decree and establish a relationship with His creation, especially His human creatures. His condescension includes the "new" expression of characteristics that initiate, maintain, and define His relationship to us. So, for example, the God who alone is self-sufficient is also the God of Abraham, Isaac, and Jacob (see Exod 3:1–14). He is a God who is gracious to those who do not deserve it. But He also is a God who is angry toward sinners and who will not clear the guilty (Exod 34:6; Num 14:18).

When the end of time comes and we are ushered into the new heaven and the new earth, the relationship that the Triune God decreed and established in eternity-past will reach its climax in eternity-future. The focus of our eternal relationship to God is His covenantal condescension to us. Notice:

> And I heard a loud voice from the throne saying, "Behold, the dwelling place of God is with man. He will dwell with them, and they will be his people, and God himself will be with them as their God" (Rev 21:3).

---

4. Charles Hodge, *First Epistle to the Corinthians* (New York: Robert Carter & Brothers, 1857), 274.

The Apostle John tells us here that the dwelling of man will be with God, doesn't he? No, he doesn't. It might be easy to read it that way. But what he says is that the *dwelling place of God is with man*. This is covenantal condescension in all its glorious, perfect, and eternal fullness! What began in eternity-past reaches its completion in eternity-future. The infinite, Triune God condescends to dwell eternally with His people.

What does that dwelling look like? It looks like the perfection and completion of the temple, which, throughout Scripture, is the place of God's special presence.

> And I saw no temple in the city, for its temple is the Lord
> God the Almighty and the Lamb (Rev 21:22).

The temple, which played such a central and seminal role in God's relationship to His people in the Old Testament (see, for example, Ezek 40–43), is not, in the end, a building, but the building was a partial, mirror-image representation of the dwelling place of God in eternity. So closely are these ideas allied in Scripture that John says that the temple *is* the Lord God Almighty and the Lamb. As we live in the city built not by man but by God (Heb 11:10), it is *in* the Lord God and the Lamb that we actually dwell. So intensive is His presence with us, that there will be no need for the created lights, installed in the sky on the fourth day of creation. Instead, as it was on the first three days of creation, *God Himself* will be the light and lamp.

We should mention here, as it is more implicit than explicit in the description, that the Spirit Himself will be present with us as well. The temple, in Scripture, is described as the dwelling of the Holy Spirit (see John 14:16–17; 1 Cor 2:16). It is the presence of the *Holy* Spirit that makes the temple a *holy* place.

So also in the new heaven and the new earth, as the final and complete temple of God. The Spirit dwells there. He is "the river of the water of life, bright as crystal, flowing from the throne of God and of the Lamb" (Rev 22:1; see also John 7:37–39). As the One whom Jesus said would glorify Him (John 16:14), He is the one who glorifies the Lord God and the Lamb. As Jesus said He would do, the Spirit takes what belongs to Christ and declares it to His people. So much is the Spirit's work defined by the completed work of Christ that Scripture identifies the two (2 Cor 3:17; 1 Cor 15:45).

What we have, therefore, in the majestic mystery of our eternal and heavenly city is the mystery of the economic Trinity—the three Persons who are the one God—dwelling with the Church, the Lord's people, for eternity.

As we would expect, that eternal dwelling has a particular (though not exclusive!) focus in the Second Person of the Trinity. It is the Lord God *and the Lamb* who will be the light and lamp in the new heavenly temple, which is the city of God. In other words, when the Son of God took to Himself a human nature, He will always, into eternity-future, remain fully God and fully man. One of the reasons that the book of Revelation refers to Him in a few places as "the Lamb" is to highlight the fact that He will always be our sacrifice, the One who ransomed a people for God (Rev 5:9).

This truth only magnifies and extends the majesty of the mystery of the incarnation. When the Triune God determined, before the foundation of the world, to save a people *in Christ* (Eph 1:4-6), it was not as though the Son agreed, for a short time on earth, to take a human nature, only afterward to resume His "non-incarnational" status when He ascended. He did not simply take a human nature, accomplish salvation for us, then shed that nature in order to return to His pre-incarnate state. The glorious mystery of God's eternal grace is that the Son agreed that His human nature, once taken, would remain for eternity! The One who committed to *be* our Mediator committed to be our Mediator *for eternity*.

It should go without saying that we will never exhaust the riches of this mystery, not even in eternity. Even as we see Christ face to face, so that we know as we are known, we will still not be able to get to the bottom of the Triune God's eternal grace and condescension for the likes of us.

One of the biblical pictures of our consummate relationship to Christ is marriage. Even though once we come into the family of God we are found to be "in Christ" (see Eph 1:3-14, for example), that union is, to use Paul's language from 1 Corinthians 13, "partial"; we know it indirectly, as in a mirror. But when history is complete, the "marriage of the Lamb" has come, and the bride of Christ, His Church, will have made herself ready. On that day, we will be—fully, perfectly, completely, and consummately—united to our faithful and glorified Savior, the Lamb of God (see Rev 19:6-9).

This means, we should recognize, that the mystery-upon-mystery we have seen all along in our study reaches its ultimate climax in the mystery-upon-mystery that will occupy us for eternity in the new heaven and the new earth. The mysteries of the Christian faith that we have been discussing are seen only partially, for now, "in a mirror dimly." When we see the Lamb and participate in the marriage feast, we will know these mysteries perfectly, which means we will be face to face with their majesty. We will worship, for eternity, because we will perfectly and fully recognize just how majestic and incomprehensible our Triune God is. To "solve" the mystery, were that even possible, would be to undermine and deny the majesty. The two, both now and in eternity, must go together.

We will conclude with a couple of quotes from John Owen, one of which we introduced earlier. Given all that we have discussed up to this point, and as we consider the eternal character of the mysteries of our faith, these truths expressed by Owen should point us to the majesty of mystery in our eternal destiny:

> There are some doctrines of the Scripture, some revelations in it, so sublimely glorious, of so profound and mysterious an excellency, that at the first proposal of them, nature startles, shrinks, and is taken with horror, meeting with that which is above it, too great and too excellent for it, which it could desirously avoid and decline; but yet, gathering itself up to them, it yields, and finds that unless they are accepted and submitted unto, though unsearchable, not only all that hath been received must be rejected, but also the whole dependence of the creature on God be dissolved, or rendered only dreadful, terrible, and destructive to nature itself. Such are the doctrines of the Trinity, of the incarnation of the Son of God, of the resurrection of the dead, of the new birth, and the like.[5]

> I shall only say, that those who are inconversant with these objects of faith—whose minds are not delighted in the admiration of, and acquiescency in, things incomprehensible ... who would reduce all things to the measure

---

5. John Owen, *The Works of John Owen*, ed. William H. Goold (Edinburgh: T&T Clark, 1862), 16:339–40.

of their own understandings, or else wilfully live in the neglect of what they cannot comprehend—*do not much prepare themselves for that vision of these things in glory, wherein our blessedness doth consist.*[6]

The majesty of mystery will be ours into eternity. Our eternal existence will be gloriously enshrouded in these mysteries, and all to the praise and glory of our Triune God. Not only do we acknowledge that, but it is and will be our eternal joy always to acknowledge it. In and for eternity, as in this life, we will say again and again:

Oh, the depth of the riches and wisdom and knowledge of God! How unsearchable are his judgments and how inscrutable his ways!

"For who has known the mind of the Lord,
    or who has been his counselor?"
"Or who has given a gift to him
    that he might be repaid?"

For from him and through him and to him are all things. To him be glory forever. Amen (Rom 11:33–36).

By the sea of crystal, saints in glory stand,
Myriads in number, drawn from every land,
Robed in white apparel, washed in Jesus' blood,
They now reign in heaven with the Lamb of God.

Out of tribulation, death and Satan's hand,
They have been translated at the Lord's command.
In their hands they're holding palms of victory;
Hark! the jubilant chorus shouts triumphantly:

"Unto God Almighty, sitting on the throne,
And the Lamb, victorious, be the praise alone,
God has wrought salvation, He did wondrous things,
Who shall not extol Thee, holy King of kings?"

—William Kuipers, "By the Sea of Crystal"

---

6. John Owen, *The Works of John Owen*, ed. William H. Goold (Edinburgh: T&T Clark, 1862), 1:152; my emphasis.

Conclusion

· · · ·

We began our look into the majestic mystery of Christianity by looking at God's unfathomable depth. We highlighted the privilege we have as His people to worship Him for His character, even for the fact that His character cannot be comprehended. We worship Him, in other words, because *as God* He can be known according to what He has said, but He cannot be exhausted by the human mind.

We moved from there to consider what it means that this incomprehensible God is triune. We recognize, again, that our confession of one God in three distinct persons is beyond our ability to grasp. We confess it because it is, literally, gospel truth. When we confess it we are able to describe what it is we are confessing. But even then we recognize that our descriptions move us more and more beyond our intellectual limits. And for this, we worship God as utterly inexhaustible.

Tacking unfathomable mystery onto unfathomable mystery, we peered into the depth of the incarnation. There we saw that the One who is the Second Person of the Trinity, while remaining who He is as fully God, also, at a particular point in history, took on a human nature. We know from what His Word has told us that the Holy Spirit united this human nature in the One person, so that even as each nature retained its own distinctive characteristics, the two were not opposed but brought into personal harmony, in the person of the Son. We have no way of knowing how such truths can be, but we know that they *are* the truth, because *the* Truth Himself has told us who He is.

To this point, the glorious perplexities that we considered referred to God Himself—as incomprehensible to us, as triune, as incarnate in the Son. After these considerations, we turned to the "model of majestic mystery," which just is the magnificent covenantal condescension of this Triune God. The incarnation, of course, is the substance and climax of that condescension. Not only so, but *everything* that we have discussed can only be known by us because the Triune God has condescended to reveal Himself to us. In that way, the model of majestic mystery encompasses everything that we have affirmed. Even those truths—such as God's ontological triunity—that are not, in themselves, a product of His condescension, nevertheless can only be known *because* He condescended to speak and to reveal Himself to us.

So, it is covenantal condescension that envelops all that we have said, because it is the only way we can know and affirm anything with respect to God. In His condescension, the Triune God established, permanently, a relationship with His human creatures. Because it is the incomprehensible, Triune God who relates Himself to a finite and sinful creation, we can expect that there will be mystery at every point of that relationship. Once the infinite God determines to "come down" to the finite, mystery must underline every part and process of that coming down.

So, as we saw, the model of majestic mystery includes the "both/and" reality and truth of God's eternal decree, together with His desire that all would come to repentance. To affirm one without the other is to do an injustice, biblically, to both. The one who chose a people before the foundation of the world nevertheless takes no delight in the death of the wicked. He calls all men to repentance, and that call is well-meant. To be understood properly (i.e., biblically), the one truth has to be affirmed in light of the other.

So also for God's providence, which includes both "whatsoever comes to pass" and our responsible choices. Here there is a *concursus* of God's work and ours. God has decreed each and every choice. In His providence, He controls those choices. But the choices themselves are *our* choices, not His, and it is we who are responsible for them. To affirm God's providence and deny our responsibility is to misunderstand that providence. Likewise, to affirm our choices as responsible and then to conclude for a denial of God controlling "whatsoever comes to pass" is to misconstrue our choices. Both have to be included if we are properly (biblically) to understand each of them.

The same is true with the reality of prayer. We pray not *only* because God has commanded it. That much is certainly true. But we pray because, in God's decree and providence, our prayers truly make a difference. Those prayers are the incense in the throne room of heaven; they combine with God's exhaustive plan, so that together they move history forward toward its climax in Christ.

In all of these "both/and," covenantal relationships, we have to reiterate an all-important point. In each and every case, it is the *ontological* that takes priority over the *historical*. In other words, just because we have to see these dual aspects of the various mysteries together does not mean that each is on a par with, or in every way equal to, the other. In all cases, it is the divine aspect that must take precedence over the historical one. So, God's decree is not *simply* to be seen in light of His well-meant offer of the gospel, but it is the decree which *grounds and founds* that well-meant offer, and *not* vice versa. Similarly, as we see God's providence in light of our responsible choices, it is that providence that orchestrates and initiates those responsible choices. Seeing each in light of the other does not mean that they operate on the same level.

The model of majestic mystery is a model that must motivate our worship. None of this, of course, fully explains exactly *how* these mysteries work, or even how they can *be*! But *that* they are is the sum and substance of our Christian lives and experience. Affirming these mysteries means affirming that the Triune God is intimately and exhaustively involved in each and every aspect of His creation and of our lives. And it means that His exhaustive involvement demands our devotion to Him. That devotion is not bent toward the resolution of these mysteries. Instead, we revel in them. In each and every mystery, as they constitute the lifeblood of Christian thinking and living, we are further motivated to worship and praise Him until, on that great day, the mysteries we affirm by faith become the eternal mysteries we will affirm by sight—as we begin, in His glory, to worship Him for eternity.

> *Holy Father, Holy Son*
> *Holy Spirit, Three we name thee;*
> *while in essence only One,*
> *undivided God we claim thee;*
> *and adoring bend the knee,*
> *while we own the mystery.*
>
> —Ignaz Franz, "Holy God, We Praise Thy Name"

APPENDIX

Selections from the *Westminster Confession of Faith*

. . . .

The *Westminster Confession of Faith* was written in 1643–1648 by a number of pastors and theologians, convened by order of England's Parliament to advise Protestant churches on matters of theology, worship, and Christian conduct. The full confession contains thirty-three chapters, the first nine of which are printed below as they appear on the website of the Orthodox Presbyterian Church (www.opc.org/wcf.html). For further study, see B.B. Warfield, *The Westminster Assembly and Its Work* (New York: Oxford University Press, 1931).

CHAPTER 1

OF THE HOLY SCRIPTURE

1. Although the light of nature, and the works of creation and providence do so far manifest the goodness, wisdom, and power of God, as to leave men unexcusable; yet are they not sufficient to give that knowledge of God, and of his will, which is necessary unto salvation. Therefore it pleased the Lord, at sundry times, and in divers manners, to reveal himself, and to declare that his will unto his church; and afterwards, for the better preserving and propagating of the truth, and for the more sure establishment and comfort of the church against the corruption of the flesh, and the malice of Satan and of the world, to commit the same wholly unto writing: which maketh the Holy Scripture to be most necessary; those former ways of God's revealing his will unto his people being now ceased.

2. Under the name of Holy Scripture, or the Word of God written, are now contained all the books of the Old and New Testaments, which are these:

OF THE OLD TESTAMENT:

Genesis	II Chronicles	Daniel
Exodus	Ezra	Hosea
Leviticus	Nehemiah	Joel
Numbers	Esther	Amos
Deuteronomy	Job	Obadiah
Joshua	Psalms	Jonah
Judges	Proverbs	Micah
Ruth	Ecclesiastes	Nahum
I Samuel	The Song of Songs	Habakkuk
II Samuel	Isaiah	Zephaniah
I Kings	Jeremiah	Haggai
II Kings	Lamentations	Zechariah
I Chronicles	Ezekiel	Malachi

OF THE NEW TESTAMENT:

The Gospels	Galatians	The Epistle
according to	Ephesians	of James
Matthew	Philippians	The first and
Mark	Colossians	second Epistles
Luke	Thessalonians I	of Peter
John	Thessalonians II	The first, second,
The Acts of the	to Timothy I	and third Epistles
Apostles	to Timothy II	of John
Paul's Epistles	to Titus	The Epistle
to the Romans	to Philemon	of Jude
Corinthians I	The Epistle to	The Revelation
Corinthians II	the Hebrews	of John

All which are given by inspiration of God to be the rule of faith and life.

3. The books commonly called Apocrypha, not being of divine inspiration, are no part of the canon of the Scripture, and therefore are of no authority in the church of God, nor to be any otherwise approved, or made use of, than other human writings.

4. The authority of the Holy Scripture, for which it ought to be believed, and obeyed, dependeth not upon the testimony of any man, or church; but wholly upon God (who is truth itself) the author thereof: and therefore it is to be received, because it is the Word of God.

5. We may be moved and induced by the testimony of the church to an high and reverent esteem of the Holy Scripture. And the heavenliness of the matter, the efficacy of the doctrine, the majesty of the style, the consent of all the parts, the scope of the whole (which is, to give all glory to God), the full discovery it makes of the only way of man's salvation, the many other incomparable excellencies, and the entire perfection thereof, are arguments whereby it doth abundantly evidence itself to be the Word of God: yet notwithstanding, our full persuasion and assurance of the infallible truth and divine authority thereof, is from the inward work of the Holy Spirit bearing witness by and with the Word in our hearts.

6. The whole counsel of God concerning all things necessary for his own glory, man's salvation, faith and life, is either expressly set down in Scripture, or by good and necessary consequence may be deduced from Scripture: unto which nothing at any time is to be added, whether by new revelations of the Spirit, or traditions of men. Nevertheless, we acknowledge the inward illumination of the Spirit of God to be necessary for the saving understanding of such things as are revealed in the Word: and that there are some circumstances concerning the worship of God, and government of the church, common to human actions and societies, which are to be ordered by the light of nature, and Christian prudence, according to the general rules of the Word, which are always to be observed.

7. All things in Scripture are not alike plain in themselves, nor alike clear unto all: yet those things which are necessary to be known, believed, and observed for salvation, are so clearly propounded, and opened in some place of Scripture or other, that not only the learned,

but the unlearned, in a due use of the ordinary means, may attain unto a sufficient understanding of them.

8. The Old Testament in Hebrew (which was the native language of the people of God of old), and the New Testament in Greek (which, at the time of the writing of it, was most generally known to the nations), being immediately inspired by God, and, by his singular care and providence, kept pure in all ages, are therefore authentical; so as, in all controversies of religion, the church is finally to appeal unto them. But, because these original tongues are not known to all the people of God, who have right unto, and interest in the Scriptures, and are commanded, in the fear of God, to read and search them, therefore they are to be translated into the vulgar language of every nation unto which they come, that, the Word of God dwelling plentifully in all, they may worship him in an acceptable manner; and, through patience and comfort of the Scriptures, may have hope.

9. The infallible rule of interpretation of Scripture is the Scripture itself: and therefore, when there is a question about the true and full sense of any Scripture (which is not manifold, but one), it must be searched and known by other places that speak more clearly.

10. The supreme judge by which all controversies of religion are to be determined, and all decrees of councils, opinions of ancient writers, doctrines of men, and private spirits, are to be examined, and in whose sentence we are to rest, can be no other but the Holy Spirit speaking in the Scripture.

CHAPTER 2

OF GOD, AND OF THE HOLY TRINITY

1. There is but one only, living, and true God, who is infinite in being and perfection, a most pure spirit, invisible, without body, parts, or passions; immutable, immense, eternal, incomprehensible, almighty, most wise, most holy, most free, most absolute; working all things according to the counsel of his own immutable and most righteous will, for his own glory; most loving, gracious, merciful, long-suffering, abundant in goodness and truth, forgiving iniquity, transgression, and sin; the rewarder of them that diligently seek him; and withal,

most just, and terrible in his judgments, hating all sin, and who will by no means clear the guilty.

2. God hath all life, glory, goodness, blessedness, in and of himself; and is alone in and unto himself all-sufficient, not standing in need of any creatures which he hath made, nor deriving any glory from them, but only manifesting his own glory in, by, unto, and upon them. He is the alone fountain of all being, of whom, through whom, and to whom are all things; and hath most sovereign dominion over them, to do by them, for them, or upon them whatsoever himself pleaseth. In his sight all things are open and manifest, his knowledge is infinite, infallible, and independent upon the creature, so as nothing is to him contingent, or uncertain. He is most holy in all his counsels, in all his works, and in all his commands. To him is due from angels and men, and every other creature, whatsoever worship, service, or obedience he is pleased to require of them.

3. In the unity of the Godhead there be three persons, of one substance, power, and eternity: God the Father, God the Son, and God the Holy Ghost: the Father is of none, neither begotten, nor proceeding; the Son is eternally begotten of the Father; the Holy Ghost eternally proceeding from the Father and the Son.

CHAPTER 3
OF GOD'S ETERNAL DECREE

1. God, from all eternity, did, by the most wise and holy counsel of his own will, freely, and unchangeably ordain whatsoever comes to pass: yet so, as thereby neither is God the author of sin, nor is violence offered to the will of the creatures; nor is the liberty or contingency of second causes taken away, but rather established.

2. Although God knows whatsoever may or can come to pass upon all supposed conditions, yet hath he not decreed anything because he foresaw it as future, or as that which would come to pass upon such conditions.

3. By the decree of God, for the manifestation of his glory, some men and angels are predestinated unto everlasting life; and others foreordained to everlasting death.

4. These angels and men, thus predestinated, and foreordained, are particularly and unchangeably designed, and their number so certain and definite, that it cannot be either increased or diminished.

5. Those of mankind that are predestinated unto life, God, before the foundation of the world was laid, according to his eternal and immutable purpose, and the secret counsel and good pleasure of his will, hath chosen, in Christ, unto everlasting glory, out of his mere free grace and love, without any foresight of faith, or good works, or perseverance in either of them, or any other thing in the creature, as conditions, or causes moving him thereunto; and all to the praise of his glorious grace.

6. As God hath appointed the elect unto glory, so hath he, by the eternal and most free purpose of his will, foreordained all the means thereunto. Wherefore, they who are elected, being fallen in Adam, are redeemed by Christ, are effectually called unto faith in Christ by his Spirit working in due season, are justified, adopted, sanctified, and kept by his power, through faith, unto salvation. Neither are any other redeemed by Christ, effectually called, justified, adopted, sanctified, and saved, but the elect only.

7. The rest of mankind God was pleased, according to the unsearchable counsel of his own will, whereby he extendeth or withholdeth mercy, as he pleaseth, for the glory of his sovereign power over his creatures, to pass by; and to ordain them to dishonor and wrath for their sin, to the praise of his glorious justice.

8. The doctrine of this high mystery of predestination is to be handled with special prudence and care, that men, attending the will of God revealed in his Word, and yielding obedience thereunto, may, from the certainty of their effectual vocation, be assured of their eternal election. So shall this doctrine afford matter of praise, reverence, and admiration of God; and of humility, diligence, and abundant consolation to all that sincerely obey the gospel.

CHAPTER 4

OF CREATION

1. It pleased God the Father, Son, and Holy Ghost, for the manifestation of the glory of his eternal power, wisdom, and goodness, in the beginning, to create, or make of nothing, the world, and all things therein whether visible or invisible, in the space of six days; and all very good.

2. After God had made all other creatures, he created man, male and female, with reasonable and immortal souls, endued with knowledge, righteousness, and true holiness, after his own image; having the law of God written in their hearts, and power to fulfill it: and yet under a possibility of transgressing, being left to the liberty of their own will, which was subject unto change. Beside this law written in their hearts, they received a command, not to eat of the tree of the knowledge of good and evil; which while they kept, they were happy in their communion with God, and had dominion over the creatures.

CHAPTER 5

OF PROVIDENCE

1. God the great Creator of all things doth uphold, direct, dispose, and govern all creatures, actions, and things, from the greatest even to the least, by his most wise and holy providence, according to his infallible foreknowledge, and the free and immutable counsel of his own will, to the praise of the glory of his wisdom, power, justice, goodness, and mercy.

2. Although, in relation to the foreknowledge and decree of God, the first Cause, all things come to pass immutably, and infallibly; yet, by the same providence, he ordereth them to fall out, according to the nature of second causes, either necessarily, freely, or contingently.

3. God, in his ordinary providence, maketh use of means, yet is free to work without, above, and against them, at his pleasure.

4. The almighty power, unsearchable wisdom, and infinite goodness of God so far manifest themselves in his providence, that it extendeth itself even to the first fall, and all other sins of angels and men; and that not by a bare permission, but such as hath joined with it a most

wise and powerful bounding, and otherwise ordering, and governing of them, in a manifold dispensation, to his own holy ends; yet so, as the sinfulness thereof proceedeth only from the creature, and not from God, who, being most holy and righteous, neither is nor can be the author or approver of sin.

5. The most wise, righteous, and gracious God doth oftentimes leave, for a season, his own children to manifold temptations, and the corruption of their own hearts, to chastise them for their former sins, or to discover unto them the hidden strength of corruption and deceitfulness of their hearts, that they may be humbled; and, to raise them to a more close and constant dependence for their support upon himself, and to make them more watchful against all future occasions of sin, and for sundry other just and holy ends.

6. As for those wicked and ungodly men whom God, as a righteous Judge, for former sins, doth blind and harden, from them he not only withholdeth his grace whereby they might have been enlightened in their understandings, and wrought upon in their hearts; but sometimes also withdraweth the gifts which they had, and exposeth them to such objects as their corruption makes occasions of sin; and, withal, gives them over to their own lusts, the temptations of the world, and the power of Satan, whereby it comes to pass that they harden themselves, even under those means which God useth for the softening of others.

7. As the providence of God doth, in general, reach to all creatures; so, after a most special manner, it taketh care of his church, and disposeth all things to the good thereof.

CHAPTER 6

OF THE FALL OF MAN, OF SIN, AND OF THE PUNISHMENT THEREOF

1. Our first parents, being seduced by the subtlety and temptation of Satan, sinned, in eating the forbidden fruit. This their sin, God was pleased, according to his wise and holy counsel, to permit, having purposed to order it to his own glory.

2. By this sin they fell from their original righteousness and communion with God, and so became dead in sin, and wholly defiled in all the parts and faculties of soul and body.

3. They being the root of all mankind, the guilt of this sin was imputed; and the same death in sin, and corrupted nature, conveyed to all their posterity descending from them by ordinary generation.

4. From this original corruption, whereby we are utterly indisposed, disabled, and made opposite to all good, and wholly inclined to all evil, do proceed all actual transgressions.

5. This corruption of nature, during this life, doth remain in those that are regenerated; and although it be, through Christ, pardoned, and mortified; yet both itself, and all the motions thereof, are truly and properly sin.

6. Every sin, both original and actual, being a transgression of the righteous law of God, and contrary thereunto, doth, in its own nature, bring guilt upon the sinner, whereby he is bound over to the wrath of God, and curse of the law, and so made subject to death, with all miseries spiritual, temporal, and eternal.

CHAPTER 7
OF GOD'S COVENANT WITH MAN

1. The distance between God and the creature is so great, that although reasonable creatures do owe obedience unto him as their Creator, yet they could never have any fruition of him as their blessedness and reward, but by some voluntary condescension on God's part, which he hath been pleased to express by way of covenant.

2. The first covenant made with man was a covenant of works, wherein life was promised to Adam; and in him to his posterity, upon condition of perfect and personal obedience.

3. Man, by his fall, having made himself incapable of life by that covenant, the Lord was pleased to make a second, commonly called the covenant of grace; wherein he freely offereth unto sinners life and salvation by Jesus Christ; requiring of them faith in him, that they may

be saved, and promising to give unto all those that are ordained unto eternal life his Holy Spirit, to make them willing, and able to believe.

4. This covenant of grace is frequently set forth in Scripture by the name of a testament, in reference to the death of Jesus Christ the Testator, and to the everlasting inheritance, with all things belonging to it, therein bequeathed.

5. This covenant was differently administered in the time of the law, and in the time of the gospel: under the law, it was administered by promises, prophecies, sacrifices, circumcision, the paschal lamb, and other types and ordinances delivered to the people of the Jews, all foresignifying Christ to come; which were, for that time, sufficient and efficacious, through the operation of the Spirit, to instruct and build up the elect in faith in the promised Messiah, by whom they had full remission of sins, and eternal salvation; and is called the old testament.

6. Under the gospel, when Christ, the substance, was exhibited, the ordinances in which this covenant is dispensed are the preaching of the Word, and the administration of the sacraments of baptism and the Lord's Supper: which, though fewer in number, and administered with more simplicity, and less outward glory, yet, in them, it is held forth in more fullness, evidence and spiritual efficacy, to all nations, both Jews and Gentiles; and is called the new testament. There are not therefore two covenants of grace, differing in substance, but one and the same, under various dispensations.

CHAPTER 8

OF CHRIST THE MEDIATOR

1. It pleased God, in his eternal purpose, to choose and ordain the Lord Jesus, his only begotten Son, to be the Mediator between God and man, the Prophet, Priest, and King, the Head and Savior of his church, the Heir of all things, and Judge of the world: unto whom he did from all eternity give a people, to be his seed, and to be by him in time redeemed, called, justified, sanctified, and glorified.

2. The Son of God, the second person in the Trinity, being very and eternal God, of one substance and equal with the Father, did, when the fullness of time was come, take upon him man's nature, with all the essential properties, and common infirmities thereof, yet without sin; being conceived by the power of the Holy Ghost, in the womb of the virgin Mary, of her substance. So that two whole, perfect, and distinct natures, the Godhead and the manhood, were inseparably joined together in one person, without conversion, composition, or confusion. Which person is very God, and very man, yet one Christ, the only Mediator between God and man.

3. The Lord Jesus, in his human nature thus united to the divine, was sanctified, and anointed with the Holy Spirit, above measure, having in him all the treasures of wisdom and knowledge; in whom it pleased the Father that all fullness should dwell; to the end that, being holy, harmless, undefiled, and full of grace and truth, he might be thoroughly furnished to execute the office of a mediator, and surety. Which office he took not unto himself, but was thereunto called by his Father, who put all power and judgment into his hand, and gave him commandment to execute the same.

4. This office the Lord Jesus did most willingly undertake; which that he might discharge, he was made under the law, and did perfectly fulfill it; endured most grievous torments immediately in his soul, and most painful sufferings in his body; was crucified, and died, was buried, and remained under the power of death, yet saw no corruption. On the third day he arose from the dead, with the same body in which he suffered, with which also he ascended into heaven, and there sitteth at the right hand of his Father, making intercession, and shall return, to judge men and angels, at the end of the world.

5. The Lord Jesus, by his perfect obedience, and sacrifice of himself, which he, through the eternal Spirit, once offered up unto God, hath fully satisfied the justice of his Father; and purchased, not only reconciliation, but an everlasting inheritance in the kingdom of heaven, for all those whom the Father hath given unto him.

6. Although the work of redemption was not actually wrought by Christ till after his incarnation, yet the virtue, efficacy, and benefits thereof were communicated unto the elect, in all ages successively

from the beginning of the world, in and by those promises, types, and sacrifices, wherein he was revealed, and signified to be the seed of the woman which should bruise the serpent's head; and the Lamb slain from the beginning of the world; being yesterday and today the same, and forever.

7. Christ, in the work of mediation, acts according to both natures, by each nature doing that which is proper to itself; yet, by reason of the unity of the person, that which is proper to one nature is sometimes in Scripture attributed to the person denominated by the other nature.

8. To all those for whom Christ hath purchased redemption, he doth certainly and effectually apply and communicate the same; making intercession for them, and revealing unto them, in and by the Word, the mysteries of salvation; effectually persuading them by his Spirit to believe and obey, and governing their hearts by his Word and Spirit; overcoming all their enemies by his almighty power and wisdom, in such manner, and ways, as are most consonant to his wonderful and unsearchable dispensation.

CHAPTER 9

OF FREE WILL

1. God hath endued the will of man with that natural liberty, that it is neither forced, nor, by any absolute necessity of nature, determined to good, or evil.

2. Man, in his state of innocency, had freedom, and power to will and to do that which was good and well pleasing to God; but yet, mutably, so that he might fall from it.

3. Man, by his fall into a state of sin, hath wholly lost all ability of will to any spiritual good accompanying salvation: so as, a natural man, being altogether averse from that good, and dead in sin, is not able, by his own strength, to convert himself, or to prepare himself thereunto.

4. When God converts a sinner, and translates him into the state of grace, he freeth him from his natural bondage under sin; and, by his grace alone, enables him freely to will and to do that which is spiritually good; yet so, as that by reason of his remaining corruption, he

doth not perfectly, nor only, will that which is good, but doth also will that which is evil.

5. The will of man is made perfectly and immutably free to good alone, in the state of glory only.

Bibliography

Augustine. *On the Trinity*. Translated by Arthur West Haddon. New York: Christian Literature Publishing Co., 1887).

———. *The Confessions of St. Augustine*. Translated by Edward Bouverie Pusey. Oak Harbor, WA: Logos Research Systems, 1996.

Barry, W. "Arianism." In *The Catholic Encyclopedia*. New York: Robert Appleton Company, 1907. http://www.newadvent.org/cathen/01707c.htm.

Bavinck, Herman. *Reformed Dogmatics*. Edited by John Bolt. Translated by John Vriend. 4 vols. Grand Rapids: Baker Academic, 2003-08.

Baxter, Richard. *The Practical Works of the Rev. Richard Baxter*. Edited by William Orme. Vol. 16. London: James Duncan, 1830.

Beck, Andreas J. "Gisbertus Voetius (1589-1676): Basic Features of His Doctrine of God." In *Reformation and Scholasticism*, edited by Willem van Asselt and Eef Dekker, 205-26. Grand Rapids: Baker Academic, 2001.

Calvin, John. *Acts*. Crossway Classic Commentaries. Wheaton, IL: Crossway, 1995.

———. *Commentaries on the Epistles of Paul the Apostle to the Philippians, Colossians, and Thessalonians*. Translated by John Pringle. Edinburgh: Calvin Translation Society, 1851.

———. *Commentaries on the Four Last Books of Moses Arranged in the Form of a Harmony*. Translated and edited by Charles William Bingham. Vol. 1. Edinburgh: Calvin Translation Society, 1852.

———. *Commentary on the Epistle of Paul the Apostle to the Hebrews*. Translated by John Owen. Edinburgh: Calvin Translation Society, 1853.

———. *Commentary on the Epistle of Paul the Apostle to the Romans*. Edited and translated by John Owen. Edinburgh: Calvin Translation Society, 1849.

———. *Commentary on the First Book of Moses Called Genesis*. Translated by John King. Vol. 2. Edinburgh: Calvin Translation Society, 1850.

————. *Commentary on the Gospel according to John*. Translated by William Pringle. Vol. 1. Edinburgh: Calvin Translation Society, 1847.

————. *Institutes of the Christian Religion*. Edited by John T. McNeill. Translated by Ford Lewis Battles. Library of Christian Classics 1. Philadelphia: Westminster, 1960.

————. *Institutes of the Christian Religion*. Translated and edited by Henry Beveridge. Edinburgh: Calvin Translation Society, 1845. Repr., Grand Rapids: Eerdmans, 1957.

Charnock, Stephen. *The Existence and Attributes of God*. 2 vols. Grand Rapids: Baker, 1979.

Dickens, Charles. *A Christmas Carol*. London: Blackie and Son, 1908.

Eckhart, Meister. *Meister Eckhart*. Translated by C. de B. Evans. London: John M. Watkins, 1924.

Goodwin, Thomas. *The Works of Thomas Goodwin*. Vol. 5. Edinburgh: James Nichol, 1863.

Hefele, Charles Joseph. *A History of the Councils of the Church*. Translated by William R. Clark. Vol. 1. Edinburgh: T&T Clark, 1871.

Hodge, A. A., and J. A. Hodge. *The System of Theology Contained in the Westminster Shorter Catechism: Opened and Explained*. New York: A. C. Armstrong and Son, 1888.

Hodge, Charles. *An Exposition of the First Epistle to the Corinthians*. New York: Robert Carter & Brothers, 1857.

————. *Systematic Theology*. Vol. 3. New York: Charles Scribner, 1873.

Hoekema, Anthony A. *The Bible and the Future*. Grand Rapids: Eerdmans, 1994.

Keil, C. F., and F. Delitzsch. *The Pentateuch*. Translated by James Martin. Commentary on the Old Testament in Ten Volumes 1. Grand Rapids: Eerdmans, 1980.

Keller, James M. *Handel's Messiah: Notes on the Program*. New York: New York Philharmonic, 2014. Concert program.

Kvanvig, Jonathan L. *Destiny and Deliberation: Essays in Philosophical Theology*. Repr. ed. Oxford University Press, 2013.

Lewis, C. S. Introduction to *The Incarnation of the Word, Being the Treatise of St. Athanasius, De Incarnatione Verbi Dei*, by Saint Athanasius, 5–12. New York: Macmillan, 1946.

————. *The Lion, the Witch and the Wardrobe*. New York: Scholastic, 1995.

Muller, Richard A. *Post-Reformation Reformed Dogmatics: The Rise and Development of Reformed Orthodoxy*. Vol. 3. *The Divine Essence and Attributes*. Grand Rapids: Baker Academic, 2003.

Murray, John. "The Free Offer of the Gospel." In *Collected Writings of John Murray*. Vol. 4, *Studies in Theology*. Edinburgh: Banner of Truth, 1977.

———. *The Epistle to the Romans*. Vol. 1. New International Commentary on the Old and New Testament. Grand Rapids: Eerdmans, 1959.

Oliphint, K. Scott. *Covenantal Apologetics: Principles and Practice in Defense of Our Faith*. Wheaton, IL: Crossway, 2013.

Orthodox Presbyterian Church. "Confession of Faith." http://www.opc.org/wcf.html.

Owen, John. *The Works of John Owen*. Edited by William H. Goold. 16 vols. Edinburgh: T&T Clark, 1862.

Schaff, Philip. "On the Trinity: Introductory Essay." In *St Augustine: On the Holy Trinity, Doctrinal Treatises, Moral Treatises*. Vol. 3 of *A Select Library of the Nicene and Post-Nicene Fathers of the Christian Church*, First Series. Edited by Philip Schaff. Buffalo, NY: Christian Literature Company, 1887.

———, ed. *The Creeds of Christendom, with a History and Critical Notes: The Greek and Latin Creeds, with Translations*. Vol. 2. New York: Harper & Brothers, 1890.

Turretin, Francis. *Institutes of Elenctic Theology*. Translated by George Musgrave Giger. Edited by James T. Dennison, Jr. Phillipsburg, NJ: P&R, 1992–1997.

Vos, Geerhardus. *Biblical Theology, Old and New Testaments*. Grand Rapids: Eerdmans, 1948.

———. *Reformed Dogmatics*. Vol. 1, *Theology Proper*. Translated and edited by Richard B. Gaffin with Kim Batteau, Annemie Godbehere, and Roelof van Ijken. Bellingham, WA: Lexham Press, 2012–2014.

Warfield, B. B. "The Emotional Life of Our Lord." In *The Person and Work of Christ*, 93–148. Phillipsburg, NJ: Presbyterian and Reformed, 1950.

———. *The Lord of Glory: A Study of the Designations of Our Lord in the New Testament with Especial Reference to His Deity*. New York: American Tract Society, 1907.

————. *The Westminster Assembly and Its Work*. New York: Oxford University Press, 1931.

————. *The Works of Benjamin B. Warfield: Biblical Doctrines*. Vol. 2. 1921. Repr., Grand Rapids: Baker, 2000.

Subject/Author Index

Scripture Index

Old Testament

Genesis

Exodus

Leviticus

Numbers

Deuteronomy

Joshua

1 Samuel

New Testament